"This is travel writing at its glorious best."

— *Chicago Tribune*

"The Travelers' Tales series is altogether remarkable."
—Jan Morris, author of *The World: Travels 1950–2000*

"For the thoughtful traveler, these books are invaluable."
—Pico Iyer, author of *The Global Soul*

"Nightstand reading of the first order."

—*Los Angeles Times*

"…the popular Travelers' Tales collections offer a perfect fit for just about anyone, with themes of geography, women's travel and a passel of special-interest titles on topics including shopping, pets, diners and toilets around the world."

—*Chicago Sun-Times*

"These well-edited anthologies of first-person travel narratives are like mosaics: Each piece may add only a single note of color, but combine them and step back, and a rich and multifaceted portrait emerges."
—*San Francisco Chronicle*

"The Travelers' Tales series should become required reading for anyone visiting a foreign country who wants to truly step off the tourist track and experience anther culture, another place, firsthand."
—*St. Petersburg Times*

"This is the stuff that memories can be duplicated from."
—*Foreign Service Journal*

Travelers' Tale

AUSTRALIA

TRUE STORIES

T R A V E L E R S ' T A L E S

AUSTRALIA

TRUE STORIES

Edited by

LARRY HABEGGER

Research Editor

AMY GREIMANN CARLSON

Series Editors
JAMES O'REILLY AND LARRY HABEGGER

TRAVELERS' TALES
SAN FRANCISCO

Cover and interior design by Diana Howard, Judy Anderson, Susan Bailey,
  and Kathryn Heflin
Cover photograph: Copyright © Frans Lanting/Minden Pictures. Emu Dreaming,
  Aboriginal Artwork. Central Desert, Australia.
Map by Keith Granger
Page layout by Cynthia Lamb using the fonts Bembo and Boulevard

Library of Congress Cataloging-in-Publication Data

Australia: true stories / edited by Larry Habegger. — 1st ed.
        p.   cm.
    Includes index.
    ISBN 1-932361-13-8 (pbk.)
    1. Australia—Description and travel. 2. Travelers—Australia. 3. Travelers' writings.
I. Title: Australia. II. Habegger, Larry..
    DU105.2.T73   2004
    919.404—dc22   2004018773

First Edition
Printed in the United States of America
10 9 8 7 6 5 4 3

The land is here, sky high and blue and new as if you'd never taken a breath out of it. And the air is new, strong, fresh as silver.... The country has a fourth dimension and the white people float like shadows on the surface.

—D. H. LAWRENCE (1922)

Table of Contents

Part Two
SOME THINGS TO DO

Part Three
GOING YOUR OWN WAY

Part Four
IN THE SHADOWS

Part Five
THE LAST WORD

Australia: An Introduction

Australia is too big to comprehend. It's too barren, too rich, too foreign, too far away—which of course is also why it's so appealing. The island-country-continent baffles the imagination through its mere presence—its age, aridity, the searing red of its deserts, the luminescent green of its rainforests, the deep blues of its tropical seas, the crisp clarity of its ethereal light. Australia entices, seduces, and seeps into the bloodstream until there's no choice but to go see for yourself.

When Australia first entered the Western consciousness, it was a remote land full of unknown creatures, inhabited by a people whose traditions were as far removed from the Western norm as any on the planet. Today, while Australia is in the firm grip of Western traditions, it remains a place apart, a land still distant even in this age of easy air travel, with regions that are the very definition of "remote and forbidding."

But Australia is also a country of cosmopolitan cities made all the more appealing by immigration from Asia and southern Europe over the last several decades. Because the interior is so intimidating, most of the human settlement is clustered around the perimeter or in smaller cities and towns that prosper on the edge of frontier. Sheep and cattle stations, what North Americans would call ranches, range for thousands of square miles, as big as some American states. And across that vast landscape which has been baked and scoured for millions of years by intense sun and geologic forces, often there is little sign of life beyond the low-lying spinifex or ghostly gum trees.

This deep isolation gave rise to a culture of rugged individualism and "we're all in this together" philosophy that dates to the country's founding as a dumping ground for convicts from England. It has also helped nurture stereotypes that present Australians at once as racist, sexist, beer-swilling boors and rugged, egalitarian, hospitable "mates." There's a bit of truth in these broad brushstrokes, but without question Australians who are descended from European settlers take pride in living on the edge of the familiar world, self-reliant and independent. The Aboriginals likewise know they live in a special world, one created by their ancestors through song and honored and respected in their culture for thousands of years.

These two cultures couldn't be more different, and their coexistence has been one of the country's greatest challenges—some would say greatest failures. Much as the European settlers of North America slaughtered, imprisoned, and marginalized the native inhabitants, the European Australians pushed the Aboriginals off their ancestral lands, oppressed them mercilessly, and in the case of Tasmania, simply killed them all. But in recent decades much has been done to right these wrongs. Vast tracks of land have been returned to the traditional owners, and Aboriginal culture has maintained its vitality.

The world of the Aboriginals is also the world of the Outback, which has given us some of Australia's most familiar icons— kangaroos and dingoes, Uluru or Ayers Rock, songlines and the Dreamtime—but who could go to Australia without wanting also to see a koala in the wild, or a platypus?

There are too many choices in Australia for easy decisions, and this book will help unveil what the country has to offer. Explore with James G. Cowan the Aboriginal spirit world of the *rai*; cruise with Roff Martin Smith down the Murray River through Australia's wine country; find ancient climbing routes with Greg Child that suggest the Aboriginals were expert rock climbers; hunt with Tim Cahill for the elusive platypus and discover secrets of the cosmos; wander with Jan Morris through the historic lanes of Sydney; travel with Jill Ker Conway to shearing time on a sheep station; learn with Robyn Davidson how the vast desert spaces can alter your reality; face an unforgettable crocodile attack with Val

Plumwood; dive with Stephen Harrigan along the Great Barrier Reef; and then pack your bags for your own travels to this extra-ordinary land. It's just there, on the far reaches of the imagination, an air ticket away from reality.

—LARRY HABEGGER

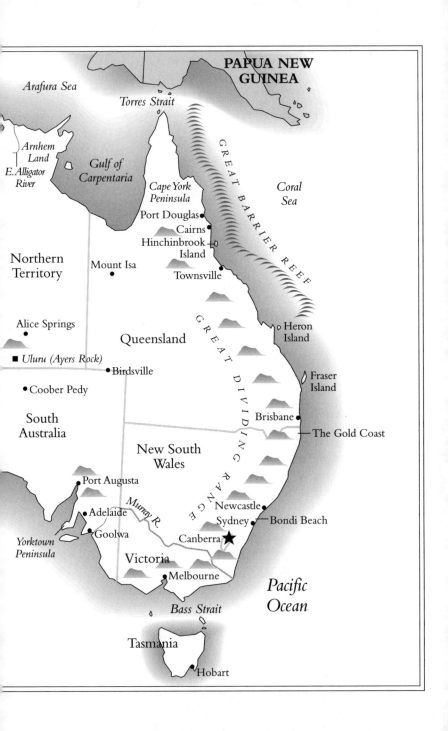

PART ONE

ESSENCE OF AUSTRALIA

A Rock and a Hard Place

Australia the ancient reveals time like no other place.

I GREW UP IN BRITAIN, BUT PART OF ME HAD ALWAYS BEEN Australian. Australia was Britain's frontier. It was where you went if you fell out with your parents, lost your job, left your wife, or simply got suffocated by the stale proprieties of little England. The only time I got good marks in geography was when I had to do an "Australia Project." My twelve-year-old hand-stencilled GOLD, URANIUM, OPALS on a country thirty times bigger than my own. I cut out pictures of a golden land beneath a hard, clear light. I imagined the smell of gum trees and the spoor of strange marsupials. Then I turned to the louring sky outside the classroom window and smelled the boiled cabbage we would have, again, for lunch; and I knew that Australia was where I'd go when I failed my exams.

The Australia I imagined had no schools or towns. It was invoked by one word: *Outback.* Perhaps I knew, even then, that the Outback is a country of the mind. It waits at the fringe of civilization, where the surveyed web spun by the coastal cities runs out of thread. Its border depends on your definition of the wild. To Sydneysiders it might be somewhere beyond the Blue Mountains that bulge under the western sky. To an Adelaider it starts up the railway line, near Port Augusta, where the irrigated wheatland gives way to bush country and salt pans shown disingenuously on maps as Lake Torrens and Lake Eyre. The Woomera Prohibited Area near these "lakes" is most certainly Outback, even though it bears the stamp of Aussie humour and twentieth-century madness: a lavatory bowl stands at ground zero of a British nuclear test, and radioactive dust still drifts across the saltbush and the spinifex.

Thirty years later I was there, heading north by train from Adelaide to Alice Springs. I'm not fond of trains, but I'd imagined this one to be a romantic affair of iron, mahogany, and brass. It was called the Ghan, after Afghani camel drivers who plied this route a century ago; it turned out to be a pale cigar tube of aluminium, stainless steel, and bleached-oak formica. You couldn't control the air-conditioning and you couldn't open a window. My cabin measured about six feet by three. The wall opposite my seat was dominated by a foldaway steel toilet as daunting in appearance and operation as the zero-gravity contraption in Stanley Kubrick's *2001*.

I fled to watch the dawn from the bar car, where I found one occupant stranded from the night before. Bruce MacIntyre had eyebrows like two fuzzy white caterpillars. His strawberry nose had been marinated for a good many years in bourbon, which he had been drinking with Coke until the small hours. The caterpillars buckled as he squinted at the sunrise.

Yesterday's dusk had fallen on a landscape like the prairies—great wheatfields in grim, logical squares—except that roads and creeks were lined with gums instead of poplars. But the sun rose on red earth and gaunt vegetation mirrored in pools of floodwater. I'd seen deserts elsewhere but nothing like this. It didn't seem to belong to planet Earth. Not a single plant species was familiar, and the vibrant brick-red soil looked exactly like those pictures sent back from the surface of Mars.

"The Territory," MacIntyre said, nodding at the window.

"Outback?" I said. "Would you call this part the Outback?"

"The whole bloody thing is Outback, mate. 'Cept Darwin City, I spose."

I'd asked a stupid question. I turned to the window and for once saw something I could recognize: a windmill, idling.

"What kind of stock would they have here? Sheep?"

"No, not sheep 'ere, mate. Cattle more like. Sheep's dahn sahth."

MacIntyre was surprisingly bright for a man who had been drinking bourbon and Coke.

"How can they live? There's no soil."

"Course there's soil! All it wants is water." He pronounced it in the Cockney way, with a glottal stop in the middle. "Give it wau'er— grow like a bastard. Look at them trees—buggers are lush now 'cause they've 'ad rine."

As the sun climbed, it woke the desert colours: every green from reseda to jade to avocado; crimson flowers like Indian paintbrush; patches of raw soil so bright I mistook them for blooms.

> *A*ustralia's coastline varies in height, substance, and character; it is unique in being breached by no large, navigable rivers [except, perhaps, the Murray]—a circumstance that led to the most persistent theories of inland seas. Captain Charles Sturt commenced his inland explorations of 1844–1846 with the strong conviction "that the interior was occupied by a sea of greater or lesser extent...." After his return he wrote: "I am still of the opinion that there is more than one sea in the interior of the Australian continent, but such may not be the case."
>
> ◆
>
> —John Mayston Béchervaise,
> *Australia: World of Difference*

MacIntyre took out a pipe, tapped it on the door, and started to fill it.

"Them Asians could live here. Grow their own food. Work 'ard. They'd live 'igh." He meant boat people and Hong Kong Chinese. It seemed a generous thought, given that Australians of his generation once feared the yellow peril. In this empty continent, not far from the world's most crowded nations, it wasn't hard to understand that old fear, and to see that it was really guilt: Asia's millions overrunning the whites as thoroughly as the whites had overrun the Aboriginals. I looked again at the desert. The country had been the same for hours. I'd seen no people, no vehicles, no cattle, no more windmills, not a single kangaroo. The only human presence was the railway itself. Put someone from Hong Kong here, I thought, and he'd go mad in a day.

In Alice Springs every bookshop and newsstand sells Nevil Shute's *A Town Like Alice*, less than ten pages of which are actually about Alice. His title is a bit like the town's River Todd, which can go years without a drop. It was winter here, south of the equator, and central Australia felt like a prairie fall. You could live like a lizard on the dazzling light, but the dry air held no warmth. When darkness came the mercury sank to zero and I shivered in my cotton sweater. The Ghan had arrived at noon. Alice, I'd observed, was a prim town of 26,000 people, three traffic lights, and a pedestrian mall. Bungaloid growth stretched off into the bush. Alice ran on government jobs and tourism. Alice was a town like Whitehorse.

I went to a steakhouse and washed down dinner with Red Back, a beer named after a venomous spider dreaded for its habit of lurking under backyard "dunny" seats. Afterwards I sat at the bar, trying to numb myself sufficiently before walking back to my hotel.

"G'day."

"G'day."

"You the new journo in town? They told me to look out for ya. Denham's the nime." Denham held out a relaxed hand. He said he was from a place called Bendigo, in the state of Victoria. His passion for Australian Rules football had cost him two front teeth. But his face, which seemed always in repose, was a natural smile. It showed the contentment of a man who has found a place and a life that suit him perfectly.

"Media coordinator and professional drunk," he added, patting pockets forgetfully. "Know what I done? Just left me wallet behind, that's what. And me propaganda."

"No worries. Have a drink."

Denham's smile lit up: "A man's not a camel!"

"Camels I've seen. But I've been in Australia a week now, and I've yet to see a kangaroo."

"You drivin'?"

"Picking up a car tomorrow."

"Usually the first 'roo you see is the one that comes through yer windscreen. Take it easy after dark, mate. That's when they come out."

He asked me how long I had and ran his finger over my map. "Don't waste yer time in The Alice, get out and see the country— that's what yer 'ere for." His finger stabbed at a place in the middle of nowhere called Wallara Ranch, on the back route to Ayers Rock. "Wallara's a great pub. It's been known to roar." The finger circled and his tone grew wistful: "Ah, the brine demmage. The brine demmage you can suffer there."

By this time a certain amount of brain damage seemed likely at the steakhouse. If I was going to get out of "The Alice" tomorrow, I had to leave. Stars filled a sky that seemed much closer than usual, and the air smelt of eucalyptus smoke. I went back to my room, flipped on the TV, and watched a young Aboriginal woman read the news. Aboriginals run Imparja, the Territory's television network. It's a measure of how things have changed since the federal government recognized their title to large tracts of land in the 1970s. This was something new in Australia. The British had never acknowledged that the world's biggest penal colony had any prior inhabitants. Australia was *terra nullius*, empty land. There were no treaties, not even broken ones, with the "Blackfellow," because officially he did not exist. But there were massacres and smallpox and poisoned waterholes.

I'd seen Aboriginals in town, wandering uncertainly on prim sidewalks, as if expecting to be chased away, their skin a carbon-paper black that absorbs all light, and what you notice are large soft eyes beneath heavy brows, eyes that seem sad and yet forgiving. Down in the dry bed of the Todd, they slept off their drinking and despair—small knots of ragged cowboy clothes, print dresses, woollen "beanies" and felt hats among the chalky trunks of the ghost gums.

The stink of air freshener in my car was so powerful I suspected it concealed something nasty, but then I'd smelled this same air-spray in most of the rooms I'd stayed in. It was another of those quaint relics of the 1950s that survive in Australia, like lace curtains and Vegemite, a spread that looks and tastes like a mixture of soy sauce and putty. I opened all the windows, turned the heater on full blast, and headed north up the Stuart Highway, named after John Stuart, who crossed the continent from south to north in 1861–1862. Until then central Australia was thought to hold an inland sea, but Stuart found that the rivers ended in salt pans, and there had been no sea here for millions of years. "Yew'd love Australia," an Australian told me years ago in an Earls Court pub. "There's nothing better than drahvin' out in the desert on a Saturday, drinkin' beer, and throwin' the cans out the window. Man! What a sense of freedom!" I was on open highway and I knew what he meant. Primeval trees and bushes stretched away to infinity. There was no other traffic and, best of all, no speed limit. I was riding a black asphalt gunbarrel aimed at a tiny notch on the horizon. The white line seemed to pull me along. I peeled open a Fosters and grew a heavy foot.

At times like this, years of conditioning slip away and you begin running movies in your head. The needle hits 160 kph (100 miles an hour: the magic ton), 170, 180, and suddenly this isn't a de-odorized Toyota sedan—it's a V-8 Holden with a drum of nitro in the trunk, and you're the Road Warrior.

I don't know how long this reverie lasted, but eventually I saw something big and blue coming straight for me in the middle of the road. The space between us vanished in a second. I ran my wheels onto the dirt. Sixty-two wheels of road train went by like a Tokyo express. Ah yes, Denham had warned me about those: a big Mack, three trailers, and a Rasputin-bearded "truckie" living on lager and little white pills. My foot came off the pedal and the desert slowed down. I began to notice hazards. Every few miles there were dead cattle, some bloated like sex dolls, others as flat as bearskin rugs; the older ones were just a few bones and a brown stain on the dirt.

I was about to turn back to Alice when my eye was caught by what looked like a gypsy camp near the road. A limp brown flag hung above an old bus covered in Aboriginal motifs; there were shanties and lean-tos made of branches and corrugated iron. A sign said *Take Your Stock Route, Give Us Back Our Country*. Another amounted to a succinct history of Australia: *Station Owners 3 Generations, Us Mob 40,000 Years*.

I drove up to the first shack and met a white man with a socket wrench in his hand. He had a thin beard, blue eyes, and dusty glasses; he wore jeans, an old grey sweater, and suspicion. I told him I was a journo and he put the wrench down. Des

> $\mathcal{W}$hen meeting a road train on a narrow bitumen road you have two options—(i) retain your 50 percent of the bitumen (which the law provides for) or (ii) pull off the bitumen and leave it for the larger vehicles. Once you have made your choice, act immediately. If you chose (i), slow down and move over, keeping your nearside wheel on the bitumen. (Prepare for flying stones and dusty conditions!) If you chose (ii) slow down, pull right off the bitumen and allow the large vehicles to pass. THIS IS THE BETTER OPTION.
>
> ◆
>
> —David Yeadon, *Lost Worlds: Exploring the Earth's Remote Places*

Carne was from Sydney—he'd come up to the Territory a few years ago and got involved in Aboriginal land rights. "I've made this me home," he said, squinting at the desert where the afternoon light spilled through a gap between the horizon and the overcast. He said he was an adviser, with the Department of Aboriginal Affairs. He also had a personal connection: he'd married an elder's daughter. "You want to know what we're doing? It's a long story. Got an hour?"

Carne talked of land claims and conflicting interests. About 30 percent of the Northern Territory's population is Aboriginal—the highest proportion in Australia—and a comparable area of land was returned by the federal government to "traditional owners" shortly before the Territory became self-governing in 1976. Of course there were problems. Crown land was given back, but cattle stations—ranches that own or lease thousands of square miles of the best land—were scarcely touched. The Aboriginals are highly diverse, speaking many languages and belonging to different kin groups. Some did well; others were left out.

"Our protest here," Carne said, "directly concerns about 120 adults—the people in this camp—who are trying to get a few square kilometres that they can call home excised from a cattle station. But it also concerns thousands of others in the same boat."

It was five o'clock by now. The sun gathered itself like a teardrop and slipped from behind the cloud. The desert changed from sombre greys and greens to gold. "Come on," Carne said. "I'll show you around." Under an iron "humpie" (a lean-to) sat an old man with rheumy eyes and a bandaged hand. He was warming his face in the sun and a tin of meat in his fire. Carne introduced him as Henry Turner; we shook hands. I felt the texture of the bandages and noticed he was very shy. Beyond was a small clearing with some children playing beneath an acacia tree. They were laughing and speaking their own language, Arrernte. Carne pointed to the bus with the cheerful paint job. "How do you like that? That's our school." The designs looked abstract to me, dots and squiggles arranged in swirling patterns, but to an Aboriginal each shape symbolizes plants and animals and things we have no words for: a complete iconography of the world. In Sydney I'd seen a photograph of a BMW painted like this by Michael Jagamara Nelson—a surreal image of Australia's two solitudes. As art, the painting on the bus was less impressive, but it was an eloquent attempt to humanize the inhuman.

Silas Turner, Carne's father-in-law, was standing beside a larger shack near the bus. He stood tall and very straight in a navy felt jacket and dark stetson with an orange hatband. He looked like a black sergeant from the American Civil War. The two spoke in Arrernte for a while, and then Carne told me more. Their strategy was to occupy this stock route (a mile-wide right-of-way for cattle drives) which could in theory be returned to Aboriginals. They did not want this particular stretch of land, but they were hoping to swap it with the rancher for the piece they did want.

Like all Aboriginal clans, these people belong to a certain "country"—an area where every rock, tree, and waterhole has deep religious meaning going back to the primordial Dreamtime. At such sacred sites throughout Australia the heroes of the Dreamtime—be they kangaroos, lizards, or honey ants—sang themselves and the world into existence. The Dreamtime heroes are totemic ancestors of woman and man. An Aboriginal's country is thus her Eden, her Mecca, her family tree, her cathedral, and her tomb.

Unfortunately, it isn't always easy for today's Aboriginals to prove such things in white courts which, according to Carne, are seldom sympathetic: "The Territorial government is still a colonial one. They defend the landed gentry, the pastoralists. They think the federal government went too far. They'd like to keep the Blackfellow in his place. And that usually means keeping him in town."

Aboriginals and ranchers had for years lived in a kind of symbiosis—unequal but interdependent on the same land. Aboriginal stockmen drove the cattle across vast reaches of Outback which only they knew. The ranchers drilled wells and supplied water and other essentials in a changing world. Then, about thirty years ago, it got out that Aboriginal workers were being paid far less than white ones. An outcry was raised and a well-meaning law was passed. If there had been no alternative, ranchers might have kept their stockmen and paid them more. But mechanization was cheaper. The motorbike and aeroplane replaced the black cowboy; thousands were forced off the land and into towns like Alice.

I don't know how many times I've heard that old Australian song, "Tie Me Kangaroo Down, Sport." For the first time a verse of it made sense:

Let me Abos go loose, Bruce,
Let me Abos go loose.
They're of no further use, Bruce,
Let me Abos go loose.

I wanted to see that great red monolith, Ayers Rock, Australia's petrified heart. I drove south from Alice for an hour or so, then left the pavement and turned west along a road that was merely a strip of red sand kept free of vegetation by a grader. I saw no other vehicles. I felt marooned by the laconic signs: Wallara 99; Kings Canyon 199. Those who think the prairies are empty should come here. One grain elevator every half hour is a suburb compared to this. In days of driving I saw: no Aboriginals, no ranchers, no kangaroos, no camels, one dingo, one wedge-tailed eagle, two emus (a pair), and maybe six cows—not counting dead ones. But this emptiness was an illusion. Feral camels are so numerous that Australia exports meat and breeding stock to Arabia, kangaroos have to be culled, dingos have been known to snatch babies from campgrounds, and Aboriginals still follow their "dreaming tracks," the unseen web of history, myth, and genealogy that exists in their minds and souls (and which Bruce Chatwin popularized in *The Songlines*). The desert does not give up its secrets easily to strangers. The emptiness was not real; it was my ignorance. And most of what I did see I could not describe. I had entered another creation, to which I did not belong and for which I had no words. I was out of place and time. English has no good names for these trees and bushes that were old when the dinosaurs were young. The desert oaks are not oaks; the corkwoods are not corks; the desert poplar is not a poplar. Australia is flat, but the flatness is not the work of glaciers (which were still scraping over Europe and America a mere 12,000 years ago). This flatness is the work of nothing but wind, sun, rain, and frost. And time. Aeons of time. The oldest rocks in the world are here, and they are almost as old as the earth itself—more than four billion years. Australia is a great fragment of the old supercontinent, Gondwanaland; and while other fragments became new continents with new lives—new mountains, new volcanoes—nothing much happened here but time. So much time that Australia's mountains turned to dust.

I drove on, past Wallara Ranch, to Kings Canyon; past verges lined with ruby dock and paddy melon, past silver grasslands heaving in the wind. Of course, Australia's climate changed over the ages—the inland seas evaporated, the topsoil blew away, the eucalypt forests crept to the fringes of the continent—but all this happened so gradually that life could adapt. At the bottom of Kings Canyon, beside deep crevices where pools of dark water survive throughout the dry season, I saw cycads and palms whose ancestors grew in jungles and on vanished shores. There are burrowing frogs that hold water in their bodies for years; there are aquatic scorpions that fly when their pools disappear; there's a lizard, called the thorny devil, with catchment areas for dew all over its back. And the birds—the emerald-green lorikeets and red-and-

*I*ts knobbly bark looks like a chocolatey breakfast cereal. Its trunk grows up to one meter in diameter and up to forty meters high. Its leaves, even the mature ones, are light green, with a complex, unusual structure. Its upper branches carry bright green female cones and brown, cylindrical male ones. Until 1994 nobody had the least notion it existed— except perhaps in fossil form.

Botanists studying this "new" tree believe it may be more closely related to certain fossils than to any living species. They even think it may be not only a new species, but also a new genus.

It was found 200 kilometers from Sydney.

◆

—Christopher Andreae, "Australian Botanists Unveil 'New-Old' Tree," *The Christian Science Monitor*

grey galahs, the white corellas and the green-and-yellow Port Lincoln parrots—these too are jungle dwellers who stayed on in the central desert because it dried up so slowly that they failed to notice.

Wallara Ranch is a watering hole for less-adapted life forms. I got back there at dusk and checked into one of the best rooms—a clean but Spartan Atco trailer. After a camel T-bone, I repaired to the bar, where I hoped to witness, if not experience, some of the "brine demmage" so fondly recalled by Denham. You cannot enjoy Australia without enjoying pubs. Australia drinks more alcohol per capita than any other English-speaking nation. In Sydney I'd drunk at the Hero of Waterloo, which claims to be the oldest pub in the land. I was persuaded when I saw the cellar: a dungeon, complete with iron shackles, where sturdy lads who got too pissed were held for sale to navy press gangs. To sit in the Hero's nineteenth-century drinking chairs—like pews with arms—was to understand the sacramental role of alcohol in Australia. It would be a formidable task to work out how many gallons of beer and rum, on that very spot, have been poured down the gizzard of Oz.

Wallara makes no claim to antiquity, though it is mentioned in *A Town Like Alice*. The bar was already full and the plywood floor awash with beer. GONDWANALAND was painted on a door. Young men in singlets and shorts were milling round a billiard table, jabbing their cues in the air like tribesmen at a spear dance. Hanging above their heads was an array of underpants—forfeited by heavy losers.

"See that bloke there?" Jane the barmaid handed me a Fourex (XXXX) and nodded at a player with a leonine head and a gut like a deck chair in a wind. "He was propping up the bar in nothing but his shirt and a smile last time. Bloody oath!" The walls were covered in postcards and droll stickers like this: *I hate this bloody job. Who do you have to sleep with to get the sack?* A bulldozer driver from New Zealand—a Maori whom everyone called Kiwi—was strumming a guitar and singing dubious songs at the top of his voice: "Two pist… Two pist… Two pistols in yer 'and…." Underpants came over and belched. "Scuse. Shout you a beer? Whatcher 'avin?" I drained my Fourex and decided to try VB (Victoria Bitter).

Underpants was with the telephone company, stringing lines through the Outback, a job that gave him "a thirst you could take a picture of." His mate was wearing mirror sunglasses and a gimme cap that said *Share Your Banana with Me*. More introductions and where-are-you-froms; I shouted a round. Underpants stood back and said: "So yore 'riginally a Pom, are yer?" I thought: that does it, Australians don't like Poms.

"My ancestors…" He was stabbing my chest with a finger. "My ancestors were chosen to come out here by some of the *finest* judges in England."

At this point I thought it a good idea to include two elderly ladies sitting at a corner table in the conversation. They were from Adelaide, Emmeline and Vale. Vale had lost her husband not long before this trip and she was pining. Even the wildlife made her think of him.

"You get possums round 'ere?" she asked Underpants. She drank a VB straight down. "I can't bear to see a possum. We had one on our station. Me and Bert had a thousand square miles, you know." She took out a hanky and dabbed at her rouged cheeks. "There was this possum lived in a tree we called the possum tree. How my Bert loved that possum! When Bert was goin' —he knew it, see—he said to me, 'Vile. That's where you can scatter me ashes. Under the possum tree.'"

"Nuther round, Jane love!" Underpants called.

"Comin' up."

"Beauty!"

"Well, the time came—cheers everyone!—and I went down to the possum tree with Bert in the urn. And there was that little face, up on a branch, looking down at me, and I thought, *he knows. He knows*, that possum does." Vale was sobbing again; Underpants stepped into the breach.

"When I go, mate," he said with a wink at Jane, "I want 'em to take me ashes and scatter 'em dahn on the beach. That way the crabs can get a dose of me for a change, instead of me gettin' a dose of the crabs."

Next morning I had that brittle, eidetic clarity that sometimes follows a rough night. The oaks, mulgas, and coolibahs stood out from sand like powdered blood. The desert seemed to glow, and it wasn't as empty as before. I saw flocks of crested pigeons—odd little birds with punky black tufts on their heads—and when I stopped to look at them they took flight with a metallic whistling from their wings. I drove south on dirt for a while, then turned west on the paved highway to Ayers Rock. I passed about two or three vehicles per hour—heavy traffic—usually a Toyota 4WD with jerry cans on the roof and New South Wales plates. Every so often there was a rest area with a picnic table, a rubbish barrel, and a water tank. SAVED WATER SAVES LIVES: TAKE ONLY WHAT YOU NEED.

Grasslands and desert oaks gave way to a rippled country of dunes sparsely covered with dryland bushes. (Australia has no cacti, which are native only to the Americas.) It had rained recently, and nearly all were in bloom—brilliant umbelliferous white flowers like baby's breath, yellow lupinelike grevillea blossoms, scarlets, purples, and mauves among blackened skeletons from bushfires— all embroidered on the magenta sand.

A dingo, huge, loped across the road. Then I saw something more astonishing, a mountain: Mount Conner, a mesa surrounded by talus slopes. Half an hour later Ayers Rock rose like a moon on the horizon.

Uluru, the Aboriginals call it. It is a mountain all of a piece, one stone five miles in circumference, a thousand feet high, and who knows how deep. Oddest of all is the lack of erosional debris at its base. Uluru's walls drop straight into the ground, as if it were float- ing in the sand.

As the rock comes closer, a third eminence rises beyond it: the Olgas, a huddle of domes like the stone helmets of a war memor- ial. This is the extraordinary thing: here in the very centre of the continent are these three small mountains, all that is left of a range worn away to dust. And yet they are not in the least alike. Mount Conner would fit in the American Southwest. The Olgas might have bubbled from the earth. And Uluru, the world's largest monolith, seems to have fallen from the sky.

I climbed a dune and sat to watch cloud shadows drifting across

Uluru's surface. The stone blushed, frowned darkly, blushed again, and smiled in pink.

I waited until evening for the climb. It's about an hour's walk, far steeper and more strenuous than one imagines from the ground. But the greatest surprise is the texture and form of the rock. The smooth contours seen from a distance resolve into a complex and baffling sculpture: ridges, valleys, caves, and hollows, folded and sinuous as if the surface were petrified skin. Set here and there like cabochons are hollows filled with water—cobalt pools of sky. And when it rains, the rock erupts in waterfalls.

From the top I could just make out Mount Conner, on the horizon fifty miles away and fading quickly. To the west and nearer, the Olgas were swallowing the sun. People came in twos and threes and sat by the small cairn that marks the summit. Nobody spoke above the wind.

Ronald Wright was born in England and now lives in Canada. His books include Time Among the Maya, Stolen Continents: The 'New World' through Indian Eyes, Henderson's Spear, *and* Home and Away, *from which this story was excerpted. His novel,* A Scientific Romance, *won Britain's David Higham Prize for Fiction and was a* New York Times *notable book.*

Sing

The world was created with song.

My reason for coming to Australia was to try to learn for myself, and not from other men's books, what a Songline was—and how it worked. Obviously, I was not going to get to the heart of the matter, nor would I want to. I had asked a friend in Adelaide if she knew of an expert. She gave me Arkady's phone number.

"Do you mind if I use my notebook?" I asked.

"Go ahead."

I pulled from my pocket a black, oilcloth-covered notebook, its pages held in place with an elastic band.

"Nice notebook," he said.

"I used to get them in Paris," I said. "But now they don't make them any more."

"Paris?" he repeated, raising an eyebrow as if he'd never heard anything so pretentious.

Then he winked and went on talking.

To get to grips with the concept of the Dreamtime, he said, you had to understand it as an Aboriginal equivalent of the first two chapters of Genesis—with one significant difference.

In Genesis, God first created the "living things" and then fash-

ioned Father Adam from clay. Here in Australia, the Ancestors created themselves from clay, hundreds and thousands of them, one
for each totemic species.

"So when an Aboriginal tells you, 'I have a Wallaby Dreaming,'
he means, 'My totem is Wallaby. I am a member of the Wallaby
Clan.'"

"So a Dreaming is a clan emblem? A badge to distinguish 'us'
from 'them'? 'Our country' from 'their country'?"

"Much more than that," he said.

Every Wallaby Man believed he was descended from a universal Wallaby Father, who was the ancestor of all other Wallaby Men
and of all living wallabies. Wallabies, therefore, were his brothers.
To kill one for food was both fratricide and cannibalism.

"Yet," I persisted, "the man was no more wallaby than the
British are lions, the Russians bears, or the Americans bald eagles?"

"Any species," he said, "can be a Dreaming. A virus can be a
Dreaming. You can have a chickenpox Dreaming, a rain Dreaming,
a desert-orange Dreaming, a lice Dreaming. In the Kimberleys
they've now got a money Dreaming."

"And the Welsh have leeks, the Scots thistles and Daphne was
changed into a laurel."

"Same old story," he said.

He went on to explain how each totemic ancestor, while travelling through the country, was thought to have scattered a trail of
words and musical notes along the line of his footprints, and how
these Dreaming-tracks lay over the land as "ways" of communication between the most far-flung tribes.

"A song," he said, "was both map and direction-finder.
Providing you knew the song, you could always find your way
across country."

"And would a man on 'Walkabout' always be travelling down
one of the Songlines?"

"In the old days, yes," he agreed. "Nowadays, they go by train
or car."

"Suppose the man strayed from his Songline?"

"He was trespassing. He might get speared for it."

*N*ow, this is some-
thing I've told no
one. You mightn't believe me.
'Member when we first moved
there? Couple of nights, you
came out on the back verandah
and found Gladdie and me sittin' there, 'member we made
you go away? You was always in
the wrong place at the wrong
time. Well, we was listenin' to
music. It was the blackfellas
playin' their didgeridoos and
singin' and laughin' down in the
swamp. Your mother could hear
it. I said to her one night, "I'm
goin' down there and tell those
natives off. Who do they think
they are, wakin' all the white
people up." That's when
Gladdie told me. She said,
"Don't go down there, Mum,
there's no one there, only bush."
You see, we was hearin' the
people from long ago. Our people who used to live here
before the white man came.
Funny, they stopped playin' after
your father died. I think now
they was protectin' us. Fancy,
eh? Those dear, old people. You
see, the blackfella knows all
'bout spirits.

◆

—Sally Morgan, *My Place*

"But as long as he stuck to
the track, he'd always find
people who shared his
Dreaming? Who were, in
fact, his brothers?"

"Yes."

"From whom he could
expect hospitality?"

"And vice versa."

"So song is a kind of pass-
port and meal ticket?"

"Again, it's more compli-
cated."

In theory, at least, the
whole of Australia could be
read as a musical score. There
was hardly a rock or creek in
the country that could not or
had not been sung. One
should perhaps visualise the
Songlines as a spaghetti of
*Iliad*s and *Odyssey*s, writhing
this way and that, in which
every "episode" was readable
in terms of geology.

"By episode," I asked,
"you mean 'sacred site'?"

"I do."

"The kind of site you're
surveying for the railway?"

"Put it this way," he said.
"Anywhere in the bush you
can point to some feature of
the landscape and ask the
Aboriginal with you, 'What's
the story there?' or 'Who's

that?' The chances are he'll answer 'Kangaroo' or 'Budgerigar' or 'Jew Lizard,' depending on which Ancestor walked that way."

"And the distance between two such sites can be measured as a stretch of song?"

"That," said Arkady, "is the cause of all my troubles with the railway people."

It was one thing to persuade a surveyor that a heap of boulders were the eggs of the Rainbow Snake, or a lump of reddish sandstone was the liver of a speared kangaroo. It was something else to convince him that a featureless stretch of gravel was the musical equivalent of Beethoven's *Opus III*.

By singing the world into existence, he said, the Ancestors had been poets in the original sense of *poesis*, meaning "creation." No Aboriginal could conceive that the created world was in any way imperfect. His religious life had a single aim: to keep the land the way it was and should be. The man who went "Walkabout" was making a ritual journey. He trod in the footprints of his Ancestor. He sang the Ancestor's stanzas without changing a word or note— and so recreated the Creation.

"Sometimes," said Arkady, "I'll be driving my 'old men' through the desert, and we'll come to a ridge of sandhills, and suddenly they'll all start singing. 'What are you mob singing?' I'll ask, and they'll say, 'Singing up the country, boss. Makes the country come up quicker.'"

Aboriginals could not believe the country existed until they could see and sing it—just as, in the Dreamtime, the country had not existed until the Ancestors sang it.

"So the land," I said, "must first exist as a concept in the mind? Then it must be sung? Only then can it be said to exist?"

"True."

"In other words, 'to exist' is 'to be perceived'?"

"Yes."

"Sounds suspiciously like Bishop Berkeley's Refutation of Matter."

"Or Pure Mind Buddhism," said Arkady, "which also sees the world as an illusion."

"Then I suppose these 300 miles of steel, slicing through innumerable songs, are bound to upset your 'old men's' mental balance?"

"Yes and no," he said. "They're very tough, emotionally, and very pragmatic. Besides, they've seen far worse than a railway."

Aboriginals believed that all the "living things" had been made in secret beneath the earth's crust, as well as all the white man's gear—his aeroplanes, his guns, his Toyota Land Cruisers—and every invention that will ever be invented; slumbering below the surface, waiting their turn to be called.

"Perhaps," I suggested, "they could sing the railway back into the created world of God?"

"You bet," said Arkady.

Bruce Chatwin was the author of In Patagonia, The Viceroy of Ouidah, On the Black Hill, Utz, *and* The Songlines, *from which this story was excerpted.* What Am I Doing Here, *a collection of essays, travelogues, and portraits, was his last book. Chatwin died outside Nice, France, on January 17, 1989.*

ROBYN DAVIDSON

✶ ✶ ✶

Patterns in the Sand

The vast open space of the desert
alters a pilgrim's reality.

I SET OFF IN MY NEW SANDALS AND AFTER A FEW HOURS I DECIDED to cut across country rather than follow the track. There was nothing but sandhills and spinifex and interminable space. I was perhaps treading now on country where no one had ever walked before, there was so much room—pure, virgin desert, not even cattle to mar it and nowhere in that vastness even an atom of anything human. The sandhills here were not the parallel waves that I had been through before, but jumbled, crashing together like chop against the wind, or breakers against a riptide. They had not been burnt so were different in character from the ones I had experienced. Not as clean, or as deceptively lush with green. The drab, inedible spinifex covered them and kept them stationary.

Throughout the trip I had been gaining an awareness and an understanding of the earth as I learnt how to depend upon it. The openness and emptiness which had at first threatened me were now a comfort which allowed my sense of freedom and joyful aimlessness to grow. This sense of space works deep in the Australian collective consciousness. It is frightening and most of the people huddle around the eastern seaboard where life is easy and space a graspable concept, but it produces a sense of potential and possibility nevertheless that may not exist now in any European country. It will not be long, however, before the land is conquered, fenced up and beaten into submission. But here, here it was free, unspoilt and seemingly indestructible.

> *T*he "dry heart" of Australia, she said, was a jigsaw of microclimates, of different minerals in the soil and different plants and animals. A man raised in one part of the desert would know its flora and fauna backwards. He knew which plant attracted game. He knew his water. He knew where there were tubers underground. In other words, by *naming* all the "things" in his territory, he could always count on survival.
>
> ◆
>
> —Bruce Chatwin, *The Songlines*

And as I walked through that country, I was becoming involved with it in a most intense and yet not fully conscious way. The motions and patterns and connections of things became apparent on a gut level. I didn't just see the animal tracks, I knew them. I didn't just see the bird, I knew it in relationship to its actions and effects. My environment began to teach me about itself without my full awareness of the process. It became an animate being of which I was a part. The only way I can describe how the process occurred is to give an example: I would see a beetle's tracks in the sand. What once would have been merely a pretty visual design with few associations attached, now became a sign which produced in me instantaneous association—the type of beetle, which direction it was going in and why, when it made the tracks, who its predators were. Having been taught some rudimentary knowledge of the pattern of things at the beginning of the trip, I now had enough to provide a structure in which I could learn to learn. A new plant would appear and I would recognize it immediately because I could perceive its association with other plants and animals in the overall pattern, its place. I would recognize and know the plant without naming it or studying it away from its environment. What was once a thing that merely existed became something that everything else acted upon and had a relationship with and vice versa. In picking up a rock I could no longer simply say, "This is a rock," I could now say, "This is part of a net," or closer, "This, which everything acts upon, acts." When this way of thinking became ordinary for me, I too became lost in the net and the boundaries of myself stretched out for ever. In the beginning I had known at some level that this could happen. It had frightened me then. I had seen it as a chaotic principle, and I fought it tooth and nail. I had given myself the structures of habit and routine with which to fortify myself and these were very necessary at the time. Because if you are fragmented and uncertain it is terrifying to find the boundaries of yourself melt. Survival in a desert, then, requires that you lose this fragmentation, and fast. It is not a mystical experience, or rather, it is dangerous to attach these sorts of words to it. They are too hackneyed and prone to misinterpretation. It is something that happens, that's all. Cause and effect. In different places, survival requires different things, based on the environment. Capacity for survival may be the ability to be changed by environment.

Changing to this view of reality had been a long hard struggle against the old conditioning. Not that it was a conscious battle, rather it was being forced on me and I could either accept it or reject it. In rejecting it I had almost gone over the edge. The person inside whom I had previously relied on for survival had, out here and in a different circumstance, become the enemy. This internal warring had almost sent me around the bend. The intellectual and critical faculties did everything they could think of to keep the boundaries there. They dredged up memory. They became obsessed with time and measurement. But they were having to take second place, because they simply were no longer necessary. The subconscious mind became much more active and important. And this is the form of dreams, feelings. A growing awareness of the character of a particular place, whether it was a good place to be with a calming influence, or whether it gave me the creeps. And this all linked up with Aboriginal reality, their vision of the world as being something they could never be separate from, which showed in their language. In Pitjantjara and, I suspect, all other Aboriginal languages, there is no word for "exist." Everything in the universe is in constant interaction with everything else. You cannot say, this is a rock. You can only say, there sits, leans, stands, falls over, lies down, a rock.

The self did not seem to be an entity living somewhere inside the skull, but a reaction between mind and stimulus. And when the stimulus was nonsocial, the self had a hard time defining its essence and realizing its dimensions. The self in a desert becomes more and more like the desert. It has to, to survive. It becomes limitless, with its roots more in the subconscious than the conscious—it gets stripped of nonmeaningful habits and becomes more concerned with realities related to survival. But as is its nature, it desperately wants to assimilate and make sense of the information it receives, which in a desert is almost always going to be translated into the language of mysticism.

What I'm trying to say is, when you walk on, sleep on, stand on, defecate on, wallow in, get covered in, and eat the dirt around you, and when there is no one to remind you what society's rules are, and nothing to keep you linked to that society, you had better be prepared for some startling changes. And just as Aborigines seem to be in perfect rapport with themselves and their country, so the embryonic beginnings of that rapport were happening to me. I loved it.

And my fear had a different quality now too. It was direct and useful. It did not incapacitate me or interfere with my competence. It was the natural, healthy fear one needs for survival.

Although I talked constantly to myself, or Diggity or the country around me, I was not lonely—on the contrary, had I suddenly stumbled across another human being, I would have either hidden, or treated it as if it were just another bush or rock or lizard.

Robyn Davidson is an Australian adventurer and writer best known for her remarkable overland journey from Australia's Red Center at Alice Springs to the Indian Ocean at the age of twenty-seven. Her book about the experience, Tracks, *has been translated into more than ten languages, and was transformed into a CD-ROM product and photo book called* From Alice to Ocean: Alone Across the Outback. *She is also the author of* Desert Places *and* Traveling Light, *and the editor of* The Picador Book of Journeys. *This story was excerpted from her book,* Tracks.

PICO IYER

✦ ✦ ✦

Five Thousand Miles
from Anywhere

Is Australia a Lonely Place?

THE LIGHT IN AUSTRALIA IS LIKE NOTHING ELSE ON EARTH—AS
befits, perhaps, a country that feels as if it has fallen off the planet.
"Australia's like an open door with the blue beyond," wrote D. H.
Lawrence. "You just walk out of the world and into Australia." And
the startled intensity of the heavens hints at all the weird paradoxes
of this young old land of sunny ironists, a British California caught
between a world it has abandoned and one it has yet to colonize.
In the vast open blueness of Australia, the only presiding authority, it often seems, is the light.

Australia is, of course, the definitive—perhaps the ultimate—
terra incognita, its very name derived from the Latin phrase *terra aus-
tralis incognita*, or unknown land of the south. Captain Cook first
bumped into the land of anomalies while trying to observe a tran-
sit of the planet Venus. And even today the world's largest island
seems to occupy a huge open space in the mind, beyond the reach
of our sights. Australia, for one thing, borders nothing and is on the
way to nowhere. It feels, in every sense, like the last place on earth.
Colonized originally by the British as a place for posthumous

lives—a kind of Alcatraz on an epic scale—Australia has always seemed the natural setting for postapocalyptic imaginings, from Lawrence's utopian visions to Nevil Shute's nuclear wasteland to the haunted deathscape of *Mad Max*.

What little we know of this tabula rasa, moreover, has generally sounded like fiction. "In Australia alone," as Marcus Clarke wrote, "is to be found the Grotesque, the Weird, the strange scribblings of Nature learning to write." The flattest and driest of the continents defies all the laws of probability with its natural—or unnatural—wonders: not just the world's only egg-laying mammals (the echidna and the duckbill platypus) but the wombat and the wallaby, the koala, the kangaroo, the kookaburra and the quokka. A land of extremes, it is also one of inversions, an antipodean place where Christmas is celebrated in midsummer and the water goes the wrong way down the drain, a looking-glass world in which trees lose their bark but not their leaves, and crows, it is said, fly backwards (to keep the dust from their eyes). Even the country's social origins are the stuff of Restoration comedy, a down-underworld in which convicts were known as "government men" and thieves were appointed as magistrates—less the Promised than the Threatened Land.

Yet it is in the nature of Lonely Places to attract people, in large part because of their loneliness, and...the greatest reason of all for Australia's appeal is, in the end, the very thing that has outlawed it for so long: the tyranny of distance. Suddenly, people are

> *A*fter seeing the impressions of light and colour, of land and sky, that were painted by John Glover, and now driving through it, knowing that it's the same as what he saw, I like everything better. The bush and that distinctly Australian light. Those guys wandering around in their smocks with their easels and palettes, seeing the same stuff as me and being able to capture it. You have to like that.
>
> ◆
>
> —Sean Condon, *Sean & David's Long Drive*

realizing that Australia is so far from the world that it is the ideal place for people who wish to get away from the world, do nothing, and watch others do the same. The quietness, and unhurried spaciousness, of the Empty Continent can make one feel as if one has all the time in the world—indeed, as if time and the world have both been annulled: "rush hour" is not a term in common currency here. And though irreverence is an Australian article of faith, the most urbanized society on earth (70 percent of Aussies live in eight major cities) is increasingly endowed with all the gentrified accoutrements of a brunch culture: hotels so untouched they feel like resorts, towns that are drawing-board models of clean lines and open spaces, people who are devoted to life, liberty, and the pursuit of happiness. Not the least of the ironies governing a nation whose founding fathers were convicts is, in fact, that it is now most noted for its air of freedom, safety, and civic order.

Australia's achievement, in that sense, is to conflate, or overturn, the very notions of urban and pastoral: its biggest city enjoys 342 days of sunshine a year; and even drizzly, Victorian Melbourne has a hundred beaches in its vicinity. The pastel-perfect new hotels are less than a day away from barrier reefs, crocodile forests, and sere spaces: even the high-flying elegance of Sydney's Opera House is shadowed by the rooted, runic magic of Ayers Rock. Some of the popular myths about Australia may be little more than myths (a visitor can spend three weeks in the country without seeing a 'roo or meeting a Bruce), but some are undoubtedly true. They do play lagerphones here, made entirely of beer-bottle caps; the long *a* is an endangered species; and in the "Red Centre," fat flies do drop like men.

Though Australia appears on the map of *Gulliver's Travels*, nobody has determined whether it is Brobdingnag, Lilliput, or the land of the Yahoos. The overwhelming fact about the place is its size: cattle stations the size of Massachusetts, an Outback so vast that doctors make their house calls by plane; a land so outstretched that Perth, capital of a state ten times the size of Great Britain, is as close to the nearest big city, Adelaide, as London is to Leningrad. The terms themselves insist on grandeur: the Great Dividing Range, the Great Barrier Reef, the Great Artesian Basin, the Great Western Plateau, the Great Ocean Road, and the Great Victoria Desert.

Yet what strikes one most forcibly upon landing in Australia is, in a sense, how small it is, how empty; here, one feels, is a small town built on a giant scale, like Montana blown up to the size of a continent. Even the cities resound with an eerie quietness: a third of central Melbourne is parkland; in the capital of Canberra, kangaroos hop across the golf courses; and even in Sydney itself there is no sense of urgency or pressure. On a mild spring morning in the heart of the city, there is nothing but palm trees, a soft breeze, and the song of birds. Here one can hardly imagine, let alone keep up with, a world that seems more than a day away.

And though Sydney is technically larger than Los Angeles County or Greater London, it is the focus for an

*T*he taxi driver had an accent I couldn't place. "I am Croatian," he said when I inquired, and then asked in return, disparagingly, "What are you doing in this village?"

"Visiting friends."

He waved dismissively at a scattering of high-rises that would be about right for a city of a couple hundred thousand. "This is all there is. Melbourne is only ten minutes across. I mean walking. From one corner to the other it's only ten minutes. They take a radius of forty kilometers for Melbourne. That's how they get three million people. Zagreb is bigger than Melbourne. Zagreb is a city. Sydney is a city."

"Why did you leave Zagreb?"

He put an imaginary pistol to his head. "I was young. Stupid. Adventurous. In Europe you can cross countries and see so many different cultures. Here, you go all the way from Melbourne to the Northern Territory and you see nothing. Nothing."

◆

—Larry Habegger, "From Tassie to the Top End"

air of neglectedness that haunts much of Australia, its sense of having been finished (or half finished) only yesterday. The solitary skyscrapers in the city are huddled in an unprepossessing bunch beside the harbor; its Greenwich Village, Paddington, lies mostly along a single street; and its center of red-lit nightlife, Kings Cross, can be seen in a mere ten minutes. The sense of an uninhabited, an inchoate land continues through the suburbs. Drive along the Pacific Highway (a modest, two-lane road), and you pass through town after lonely town of cheerful toy-box buildings, bright against a dizzy blueness, a depleted succession of cheerful one-street, one-story townships in silent Edward Hopper rows. Here, in a sense, is Rockwell's America—or, more precisely, Reagan's: a placid, idealized small-town world of village greens and local churches, an oasis of sunlit optimism suspended in a sleepy haze of laissez-faire conservatism and lazy tolerance.

The apogee of this sense of bright tranquillity is, of course, the synthetic capital, Canberra, a leafy, landscaped monument to spotlessness that even the Duke of Edinburgh called "a city without a soul" (though in fact it feels less like a city than a work of art: a stunning sculpture garden on a giant scale, its government offices and embassies placed like so many architectural conceits amidst its huge and empty lawns). Canberra is a place where nothing plays except the fountains—it has the haunting quietness of a De Chirico landscape of long shadows and lonely colonnades, a Lonely Place institutionalized. Yet at the same time, there is no denying the beauty of this Forest Lawn of designer splendor, its clean horizons undisturbed even by TV antennae or garden fences (both of which are banned). And the sense of uncreatedness that informs much of Australia here finds its pinnacle in the spacey new Parliament House. Its seats prettily designed in the pale greens and pinks of gum trees, its chambers flooded with natural light, the new center of government looks like nothing so much as another of the country's sparkling new hotels.

This disarming sense of openness extends, not surprisingly, to the citizenry, and Australians often seem as sunny and breezy as the world around them. Taxi drivers, airline officials, and waiters go about their work in shorts. Conversations are as common as people, and just about as casual....

"Everyone is happy-go-lucky, and one couldn't fret about anything if one tried," complained the congenitally fretful D. H. Lawrence in a letter back home. Mohawked boys may chew their girlfriends' lips in the beery rockabilly bars of Melbourne, and Australia may still exalt the outcast, but generally this seems an exceptionally unaggressive place: the graffiti on Melbourne's picturesque streetcars is artistically applied at government behest. Here, remember, is a country that did not have to work or fight for independence but simply backed into it, a little halfheartedly—and then let circumstance turn the Fatal Shore into the Lucky Country.

In Australia's laid-back sense of come-as-you-are "palliness," many foreign observers have found a model of democracy in action, a natural kind of Whitmanic fraternalism free of ideological baggage. Calling a spade a spade is a national habit, after all, and nothing seems to anger the Australian but pretension. Though Lawrence may have been merely being Lawrence when he claimed that Australians were such natural democrats that they did not even like to go upstairs, it is certainly true that a visitor is more likely to be called "mate" than "sir."

Yet if Australians' customs are often as unbuttoned as those of the American West, their manners are generally a little more reserved; touched with *le vice anglais* of self-containment, theirs is still a place of semidetached men in semidetached houses. And even though its feeling of space and ease, like its gold rush past and its sense of limitless future, gives Australia a somewhat Californian air, it feels more provisional, more pressureless than the frontier states of America, less troubled by introspection or ambition. Here, in fact, is a world that makes California seem positively frantic by comparison. In his novel *Bliss*, a typically Australian compound of irony, fancy, and profanity, Peter Carey shrewdly depicts his homeland as a mythic Eden "on the outposts of American Empire...(with) business more or less done in the American style, although without quite the degree of seriousness the Americans liked."

Australia, moreover, still holds to its fondness for the piratical, a sense that distinction lies not in the flaunting but in the flouting of refinement. The country delights in the marginal, glories in its freedom from convention, is determined to be different. There is a store in Sydney (as in London) exclusively for left-handers, and the sign in the Melbourne bookshop canvasses members for a *Lost in Space* club. And Australia's traditional images of rowdy nonconformity are still in constant evidence. The larrikin lives on in the eleven-year-old busker in earrings and rattail haircut who plays drinking songs in front of Sydney harbor while his Fagin looks on from the shadows; the convict and prospector are remembered in the dark humor of the names that overbrood the landscape—Lake Disappointment, Cape Grim, Double Crossing Creek; and the ocker asserts his skeptical down-to-earthiness with the bumper sticker EVERYBODY NEEDS TO BELIEVE IN SOME-THING. I BELIEVE I'LL HAVE ANOTHER BEER. In this seriously macho culture, you see more men in earrings than anywhere else—less a statement of fashion, one senses, than a badge of defiant rebelliousness.

To some extent, too, the myths of frontier still animate the culture. Many young Australians continue to take off around the world, treating jobs as way stations and anywhere as home, while many retirement couples take to their mobile homes and circumnavigate the land. And though the country feels less restless than America, it is surely just as mobile. Everywhere there are dreams of long horizons: a concierge is studying Chinese to expand his prospects; a cabbie is working sixty hours a week in the hope of visiting South America; a waiter at an exclusive French restaurant simply picks up his camera and guitar and heads off for a new life in the Outback.

Mike, a rugged, long-breeched man who runs a riding stable outside Melbourne, recalls how he came here alone on a boat at the age of fourteen, propelled by grand dreams awakened by Zane Grey. "There was a feeling that I could do nothing in England; and no matter how well I did at school, I could never go to university. That was just something that people like me didn't do. But over here, anything is possible. No way I could start up a place like this in England."

Besides, with its reverence for unorthodoxy and its sense of being away from it all, Australia remains an ideal retreat for odd men out. At times, in fact, one has the impression that it is less a culture than an aggregation of subcultures, a society of fringes— of surfers, cowboys, boozers, and hippies. Alternative lifestyles are the norm in many places, and the prospect of starting a new life has natural appeal for those committed to Rebirthing. The lush rolling hills known as the Rainbow Region, an hour east of the Gold Coast, have become a perfect haven for back-to-the-land purists and hypnotherapists, and the local bulletin board offers all the Oriental arts, from tai chi to tae kwon do. (The Breath of Life Relaxation and Healing Centre promises "Reiki healing" and "Lazaris videos"—all of this next to Woolworth's!) Still, mellowness here takes on a decidedly Aussie twang: "Shoplifting gives you bad karma!" advises a trendy Asian boutique in Sydney. "And if I catch you, I'll make sure you get it in this life—you Rat Fink! Sincerely, Sandi."

At the same time, Australia, like many a colony, has never entirely left behind the country that abandoned it here. As the relentlessly clever Tasmanian-born critic Peter Conrad points out in his half-autobiography, *Down Home*, Australians wistfully tried to

---

*A*s we drove home, I was struck by the extraordinary mixture Australia represented. Here were two Americans, a German, a Hungarian, and a Malay girl from Brunei, and we'd been talking with an Englishman who was a Buddhist monk in a monastery in Australia, founded and funded by Thais and run by an Italian abbot. I liked it.

♦

—Barbara Marie Brewster;
Down Under All Over: A Love Affair with Australia

assuage their homesickness by reinventing the motherland here—
Tasmania alone has "a cliffless Dover, a beachless Brighton, an
unindustrial Sheffield."...

Australia still revels in the paradox of its mongrel origins, the
contradictory features of a place of English institutions and
American lifestyles (reflected even in the name Crocodile
Dundee—a Scotland in the wilderness!). And if modern Australia
is often gazing over one shoulder at the land that gave it birth, it is
looking over the other at the land it most resembles: here, after all,
is a British parliamentary system with a Senate and a House of
Representatives. The divided loyalties are everywhere apparent: in
Hobart, the Doctor Syntax guest house is just down the street from
Mister Pizza; in a Reptile World not far from Darwin, two snakes
repose the vigorously contemporary and curiously Victorian
names of Rocky and Rowena. While Melbourne high society
dresses up in top hats and tails for the local version of Ascot, the
Melbourne Cup, many others dress down—in almost nothing at
all—to spoof the solemnity.

Of all the legacies of its English, and its castaway, roots, in fact,
perhaps the strongest is the country's sardonic and seditious wit.
Australia has a sly sense of irony that gives an edge to its sunshine,
makes it something more than just a pretty face. That air of wry
mischief is apparent in the Club Foote Cabaret, or the ad for a
"Top Tourist Attraction" that features nothing but the photo of a
sage-bearded man under the title "The Opal King." The comment in a museum's visitors' book is as dry as the Outback:
"Could be worse."...

In many ways, the country seems to mainstream, and mainline,
its idiosyncrasies: the touristy stores around Sydney's refurbished
Rocks area feature adorable koalas done up in convict suits, pine-
apples sporting shades, Punk Panda t-shirts. And the roadsides of
Australia are lined with enormous absurdities: a fifteen-foot metal
cheese, a thirty-foot dairy cow, a thirty-two-foot fiberglass banana.
The little town of Mildura sells itself as the home of the most of the
biggest, a title that apparently includes having the longest deck chair
in the world, the longest bar, and—great apotheosis!—the largest

talking Humpty-Dumpty. Alice Springs hosts a regatta each year, in a dry riverbed, and Darwin responds with such inimitably Australian festivities as a Beer Can Regatta, the Froggolympics, and the World's Barefoot Mud Crab Tying championship.

Recently, the Northern Territorians have discovered that the biggest growth industry of all is in crocodilians. Arrive at Darwin Airport, and you will be greeted by Crocodile Attack Insurance policies and brochures describing Alligator Airlines, which runs float planes down to Bungle Bungle. Drive into town, and you will find Crocodile Motors, the Crocodile Lodge, croc pizza at Crocodile Corner, and stores selling nothing but croc bags, croc water pistols, huge inflatable crocs, and croc t-shirts (in forty different designs). The Sweethearts piano bar at the local casino serves—inevitably—"crocktails," and one life-size croc has been created entirely out of beer cans; on the road into Kakadu National Park, some shrewd entrepreneurs have even erected a twenty-foot-tall crocodile, cruelly equipped with boxing gloves.… When a croc decapitated a fisherman last year, in front of a transfixed group of tourists, it was rumored that a tour operator promptly demanded more of the same.

Thus Australians seem at once to play up, and play down, to tourist expectations; theirs is as much a subversive as a supplicant air. On a Qantas flight into Sydney, a cabin attendant mimes along with the safety announcement, while one of the tour guides at the Opera House is as floridly self-amusing as any

*S*weetheart was the name of a rogue crocodile that terrorized the Top End of the Northern Territory in the 1970s, attacking more than fifteen boats and finally meeting his demise in September 1980 when he died during capture. He was estimated to be as old as eighty years and came in at an astonishing 1,720 pounds and almost seventeen feet in length. He achieved worldwide fame and his stuffed remains can be viewed at the Museum of Arts and Sciences in Darwin.

◆

—LH

guide this side of Key West. The Jolly Swagman show of Australiana
in the quaintly renovated 150-year-old Argyle Tavern in Sydney
suddenly causes its laughing visitors to blanch when it stages an actual sheep-shearing on stage, followed by an impromptu lecture
from a bearded Bushman over his bald, still bleeding victim. And as
a shuttle bus pulls out of Alice Springs train station, its passengers
dazed from twenty-four hours in tiny compartments, the beefy driver unexpectedly bursts into tour-guide patter: "Directly in front of
us," he begins, "we have the Kmart."

This fondness for drollery, and its attendant suspicion of all
stuffiness, breathes constant life and surprise into the country's culture. Folksingers stroll with guitars around the lovely main reading
room of Adelaide's old Mortlock Library, and the country's muse-
ums are scarcely cathedrals of orthodoxy. The Hyde Park Barracks
Museum in Sydney devotes an entire floor to plastic bags, embell-
ished with videos of people banging bags together and a guide denoting "Points in Plastic History." The National Gallery in
Melbourne fills one display case, rather surprisingly, with a pig's
head and offers, in alarming proximity, specimens designated as
"Lamb Brains," "Calves Livers," and "Spring Lamb Chops." (The
stained-glass ceiling that is the museum's centerpiece can be appreciated only by visitors supine on the floor.) When the Opera
House, financed largely by lotteries and partly by kissing contests,
staged its first performance, koalas and kangaroos bounded across
the stage in front of the visiting Queen.

It is common, of course, to hear people claim that Australian
culture is a contradiction in terms: Bronte is a beach here, they say,
and the country's unofficial national anthem, "Waltzing Matilda,"
was written by a man named Banjo. Certainly the feeling that the
world lies outside the country's borders has propelled many rare
minds to find themselves in exile: Germaine Greer, Clive James,
and Robert Hughes all evince a uniquely Australian mix of erudi-
tion and iconoclasm, yet all are features now of the Anglo-
American scene; and the brief wave of tasteful Masterpiece Movies
that put Australia on the world's screens at the beginning of the
eighties subsides when the directors of '*Breaker*' *Morant, Gallipoli,*

and *The Devil's Playground* transported their Australian myths to America. Australians have so flexible a sense of home, perhaps, that they can make themselves at home anywhere.

Nonetheless, the culture still has a native vigor constantly quickened by its unforced sense of free speech. The Old Parliament House in Adelaide reserves an entire room that any group can take over for a month, and a bulletin board on which visitors respond to the displays set up by euthanasiasts, conservationists, or just plain Liberals. And the excellent Migration Museum around the corner likewise maintains a "Community Access Gallery." Far from sanitizing the country's rocky history of migration, moreover, the museum delivers some unpretty home truths ("Racist attitudes towards Asians have a very long history in Australia") and does not shy away from asserting that the Aboriginals were "hunted and herded like animals." Provocative and hard-hitting, this is a fresh kind of art form: the museum as radical documentary.

The first-time visitor, indeed, may well be surprised at how conspicuous is the Aboriginal presence. Though their numbers once sank to almost 60,000, the original guardians of the continent now constitute a subculture of more than 228,000, and many non-Aboriginal Australians are aware that the usurpation of a people who regarded the land itself as their sacred text and mythology represents, in a very particular sense, a kind of desecration....

The other most striking feature of Australia today is the prominence of the "New Australians," the latest wave of immigrants, who have turned cities like Melbourne into a clash of alien tongues as piquant and polyglot as New York, where nothing seems outlandish except standard English. The signs for public toilets in Melbourne are written in Greek (as well as English and Italian), churches solicit worshipers in Korean script, and when the Prostitutes Collective recently put out a multilingual pamphlet urging customers to use condoms, one of the tongues they employed was Macedonian. Though Australian voices still sound blond, their heads are increasingly dark: at the stately old Windsor Hotel in Melbourne, one of the last great relics of Victorian elegance, the maître d' is Vietnamese, the waiters are Sri Lankan, the

———— ✳ ————

*A*ustralians are outrageously sexist by any American standard, and things happened to me every day that would be not only politically incorrect but also illegal here.

My cultural introduction occurred at my first client presentation. After I presented the work and the client approved it, he said, "Well done, see you next week," and then proceeded to kiss me on the mouth and slap me on the butt, all to the general hilarity of the team.

It was a disarming effort to "take the piss out of me," to make sure I wouldn't put on airs. It never happened again, but many other things did, both internally and with clients.

Feeling like a corporate Joan of Arc, I did a lot of mentoring, telling young women in advertising I'd come from the future—regarding sexism, Australia resembles America in 1970—and did what I could to help them get further faster than we did.

◆

—Bernadette Doran, "Old Blokes' Network," *Brandweek*

owners are Indian, and the courtly man serving drinks comes from Bangladesh.

Inevitably, such developments have been somewhat tumultuous in a country whose leading magazine, as recently as 1960, ran with the slogan "Australia for the White Man." For decades isolation bred ignorance, and ignorance intolerance.... "Australia is a very racist country," says a conservative English immigrant. "If you just scratch the surface, you come upon it. England's bad too, of course, but at least they've had to face up to the problem. Here it's still simmering."

The unease felt by some Australians as Vietnamese and Chinese have streamed down the golden brick road to Oz has only deepened as the new "Austr-aliens" have flourished through such imported virtues as seriousness and unrelenting hard work. For decades, as Donald Horne argued in *The Lucky Country*, his scathing attack on Aussie complacency, the country languished in a kind of lottery consciousness, content to believe that success was more the result of luck than of industry (in a single year, the estimated turnover from betting was three times the defense budget). Now, however, the determination of the immigrants, bolstered by the entrepreneurial energy of such controversial types as Rupert Murdoch and Alan Bond, has begun to invest Australia with a new sense of dynamism and to raise fresh questions about its identity as an Asian power....

Today, in many ways, Australia seems to reflect the eccentric ways of a Western European society set down in the middle of a Lonely Place; hotels as imaginatively designed as pavilions in some world's fair; cities that offer Balkan, Burmese, Mauritian, Uruguayan, and Seychellian cuisine; casinos that are typically down-home affairs where neither solemnity nor discretion is held in high regard ("Not a Poker Face in Sight," promises the Adelaide casino). Nearly all the heads in Australian bars are frothy, and tattooed bikers down 3.3-pint "stubbies" of Foster's in dusty outposts like the Humpty Doo Bar, where a bulletin board advertises pigs and a sign warns customers tersely, "Don't Ask for Credit as Refusal Often Offends." Australian entertainment, in fact, is nothing if not straightforward: a slim tourist brochure in Melbourne includes twenty-two full ads for escort agencies.

For the historically minded traveler, the main lure of the place may well be Tasmania, the oldest convict settlement after Sydney, and one of those out-of-the-way places that many people want to visit because of their vague sense that no one has visited them before. With its blustery skies and lowering, snowcapped Mount Wellington, Tasmania is in some respects an inversion of the mainland, itself an inversion of England, and so ends up a little like the mother country. But its green and pleasant land is scarred with the remnants of its gloomy penal past: the gutted gray buildings at Port Arthur, the graves on the Isle of the Dead, and all the other grisly mementos of a place once known as "Hell on Earth."

By contrast, the social history of modern Australia—and of many places like it—is summarized most tidily in the main shopping street in Adelaide, the wondrously compact little town laid out in a square by a man named Light. The thoroughfare begins life as Hindley Street, a rough-and-tumble desolation row of sailors' haunts—video arcades, take-away joints, and tawdry souvenir shops.... Then, downtown, it turns into Rundle Mall, a gleaming, pedestrian-only monument to civic order, the sort of middling Middle Australian area you expect to find in any suburban center: Florsheim Shoes, Thomas Cook Travel, Standard Books, Woolworth's, and—on both sides of the central intersection—the Golden Arches.

Finally, on its eastern edge, Rundle Mall opens up into Rundle Street, a SoHoian anthology of today: the Appar-allel boutique, Known Space books, the Campari bistro, Al Fresco gelateria, the Australian School of Meditation, Bryan's Hairdressers, the Bangkok restaurant, Kelly's Grains and Seeds—one long neon-and-mannequin line of vintage clothes and veggie restaurants, culminating (as it must culminate) in the New Age Emporium. This street alone, it seems, tells the story of how the twenties became the fifties became the eighties, or how raffishness turned

The English invasion of Van Diemen's Land [Tasmania] was by higher imperial standards a muddled and squalid affair. It produced no setpiece battles, no benevolent occupation, no heroes, profits or cultural loot. It merely opened another pit within the antipodean darkness, a small hole in the world about the size of Ireland, which would in due time swallow more than 65,000 men and women convicts—4 out of every 10 people transported to Australia. How many Tasmanian Aborigines died while the invading whites readied this cavity is not known, because no one knew how many there were to begin with.

But die they did—shot like kangaroos and poisoned like dogs.... It took less than 75 years of white settlement to wipe out most of the people who had occupied Tasmania for some 30,000 years.

◆

—Robert Hughes,
The Fatal Shore: The Epic of Australia's Founding

into Standard Shopping Center and then was reborn as Authentic Renovated and Redecorated Raffishdom.

As for the booming present tense, it is best inspected in the one area that contradicts the quiet and unpeopled air of the continent—and also, not coincidentally, the one area expressly designed for foreigners: the twenty-one-mile Floridian motel-and-minigolf seaside strip known as the Gold Coast, an hour south of Brisbane. Centered on the town of Surfers Paradise, a place as self-effacing as its name, the Coast has become a furious riot of development, Porsches cruising along its jungle of high-rises, a seemingly unending stretch of traffic-choked boulevards littered with ice cream parlors, Spanish-style motels, and Pizza Huts. There is a wax museum here, and Kenny Koala's Dream-world. Ripley's Believe It or Not! is scheduled to open any day. And in truth, Surfers Paradise—or should it be called Surface Paradise?—has all the wound-up frenzy of an amusement park writ huge, a neo-Atlantic City tricked up in Miami Vice colors and high-tech accessories. Nothing is missing here, it seems, except surfers, perhaps, and paradise.

Amidst the hustle-bustle of the Gold Coast, you can even get a glimpse into the future tense of Australia and of many other outposts of the Japanese empire. Huge toy koalas sit on sidewalks, cradling hard-sell messages in katakana script. Japanese honeymoon couples, identified by their matching outfits (or their HOMEY HONEYMOON t-shirts), crowd into pink coffee shops and "Love Buses." Neon signs flicker above prices in yen, and even male strip shows couch their ads in terms guaranteed to please wholesome visitors from Kansai—"Revealing, Naughty, but Nice." What used to be the Holiday Inn is now the All Nippon Airways Hotel, and the most-famous koala sanctuary in all Australia, Lone Pine, is now owned by Kamori Kanko Ltd. Even in the distant town of Cairns, desultory koto music drifts around the malls.

In the end, though, the greatest marvels of Australia reside simply in its land—the silence and the sky. For more than a day, you can travel through the Outback, a parched white land of ghosts, of blanched trees twisted at odd angles across a plain as vast and mysterious as Africa. Nothing breaks the vacancy but a dead cow, an upturned car, a stray eagle. Everywhere there is only emptiness and flatness. And then, rising up unanswerably against a diorama-bright landscape of shocked blue and thick red, Ayers Rock, old and mute and implacable, in powerful counterpoint to the young, pretty, somewhat uninflected society all around. The sacred rock is one of those rare places with a genuine sense of mystery: it casts a larger shadow than any postcard could suggest.

Or awaken one Edenic morning in Kakadu to see the sun gilding the swampy billabong, jackaroos hovering above the water in the golden, gauzy early light. Two hours later, on the South Alligator River, listen to a guide reciting names as if riffling through the multicolored pages of some children's picture book: pelicans and egrets and snakebirds are here; pied herons, masked plovers, and migrant warders from Siberia; lotus birds are among the mango trees, and white-breasted sea eagles (with a wingspan of six feet), glossy ibises (with sickle-shaped beaks), and whistling ducks ("not capable of quacking.") There are blue-winged kookaburras in the sky, and sulphur-crested cockatoos; frill-necked lizards along the riverbank, and even lazy crocodiles sunbathing just ten feet from the boat. At dusk, the birds honk and squawk above a huge, pink-flowering lily ponds, and flocks of black magpie geese and silver-winged corellas fly across the face of a huge full moon that sits in the middle of the darkening sky, catching the silver of their wings. In the daily enchantment of dusk, a visitor begins, at last, to catch the presence of an Australia within, a terra incognita deep inside, and a loneliness that will stay with him even when he leaves. In the twilight of Australia, the foreigner can catch an intimation of what Melville calls "the great America on the other side of the sphere," and so a sense of how everything brings him back to the natural state where he began: a lonely person in a Lonely, Lonely Place.

Pico Iyer was born in Oxford in 1957 and was educated at Eton, Oxford, and Harvard. He is an essayist for publications such as Time *magazine,*

Harper's, *and* Condé Nast Traveler, *and the author of several books, including* Video Night in Kathmandu, The Global Soul, *and* Sun After Dark. *This story was excerpted from his book,* Falling Off the Map: Some Lonely Places of the World.

JILL KER CONWAY

Shearing Time

The annual arrival of the shearers
meant hard work and good stories.

BECAUSE IT WAS CLEAR THAT I WAS EDUCATING MYSELF THROUGH reading everything within reach—a topsy-turvy mixture of children's books, my mother's books on current affairs, war correspondents' accounts of the war [World War II], my father's books on stock breeding—my parents decided not to bother with elementary school by correspondence for me the year my brothers left for boarding school. Instead, I became my father's station hand. He needed help with mustering sheep, something which needed two people on horseback to accomplish easily. I rode out with him to check the state of fences, always in need of careful attention if bloodlines were to be kept clear. We went together to clean watering troughs, carry out the maintenance of windmills, trim and dress the fly-infested spots which developed around the crutch of sheep where flies would lay eggs in the hot summer months. Dressing fly-blown sheep was hard, hot work because one had to round up the particular flock, get the sheepdogs to hold them, and then dive suddenly into the herd to tackle the one animal whose fleece needed attention. An agile child was better at doing the diving than an adult, and in time I learned to do a kind of flying tackle which would hold the animal, usually heavier than I was myself, until my father arrived with the hand shears and the disinfectant.

Most of the work with sheep involved riding slowly behind them while moving them from one paddock to another, traveling at a pace which was a comfortable walk for the animals. Often we dismounted and strolled along, horse's reins looped over an arm. Occasionally something might startle the sheep, requiring my father to shout commands to the dogs, but otherwise it was not demanding work, and it was a perfect setting for extended conversation. Why did God allow the crows to pick out the eyes of newborn lambs, I asked, as we passed a bloody carcass. My father never treated such questions as idle chatter, but tried seriously to answer. He didn't know, he replied. It was a puzzle. The world seemed set up so that the strong preyed on the weak and innocent. I would ask endless questions about the weather, the vegetation, the transmission of characteristics through several generations of sheep. How to breed to eliminate that defect, or promote this desirable characteristic. When the lambs were a year old, we would bring the sheep into the nearest sheepyards, or make a temporary one, so that we could cull the flocks, selecting the discards which would be sent for immediate sale or used for our own food.

I did reasonably well as a station hand while in sight of my father. He could shout directions, or notice that I was having trouble getting the dogs to work for me and arrive quickly to solve the problem. I didn't always do so well when we worked in the large paddocks, twelve or fifteen thousand acres in size, where we would separate, one going clockwise, one counterclockwise, turning the sheep into the middle, to be gathered into one flock and moved as a whole to a new spot. I was a long-legged seven-year-old, but not quite tall enough to remount my horse if I got off to kick some lazy sheep into motion, or to investigate a sick or lame one. Then there would be no getting back on till the next fence, or the rare occasional stump. At first I was not quite secure enough in ego to cope with the space, the silence, and the brooding sky. Occasionally I would find myself crying, half in vexation at my small size and the pigheadedness of sheep, half for the reassurance of a sound. By the family's code it was shameful to weep, and I was supposed to be too grown-up for such babyish behavior. Once the wind carried the sound to my father on the other side of the paddock. By the time we were reunited, I had reached a fence, climbed on my horse, and become secure again by seeing him in the distance. "I thought I heard someone crying," he observed to me as we met. I looked him in the eye. "I didn't," I said. There he let the matter rest.

The sheepdogs were always a trial to me. They were trained to respond to a series of calls. Their trainers were station hands and drovers whose calls were usually poetic, blasphemous, and picturesquely profane. I would try to make my voice deep, and sound as though I really meant to flay them alive when I got home if they didn't go behind or get around or whatever other command was needed, but I didn't believe it and neither did they. My father would laugh at me shouting to the black kelpie whose pink tongue and nose I loved, "You black bastard, I'll flay the hide off you if you don't go around." "You don't sound as if you mean it," he said. "Why not just try whistling, that's easier for you to do." He tried to teach me the series of whistles used to command sheepdogs. I did better at that, but they would never obey me perfectly, as they did my father.

As we did our day's work, theological questions kept cropping up. "Isn't it wrong to kill?" I would ask, as we drove home with a fat young sheep, feet tied together, who would be slaughtered when we arrived at the wooden block near the dog kennels used for such purposes. I always felt a sneaking fellow feeling for the creature as its neck was slit and its blood ebbed away to be drunk voraciously by the dogs. Skinning a sheep was a lengthy process, so there was plenty of time to explore the question. God made the creatures of the earth for man's use, my father responded. It was wrong to kill needlessly for sport, the way some people hunted kangaroos, but it was moral to kill what we needed to eat. Besides, he said, what would happen to the sheep if we never culled them. Their wool would deteriorate, their body types grow weaker, and they would all starve because we couldn't feed them all and all their natural increase. "Did you kill people during the war?" I would ask, meaning the 1914–1918 War. "Yes," he would respond. Killing in self-defense was moral also, and the war had been a generalized version of that situation. But no war was ever really just because of the pain and suffering inflicted not only on soldiers, but on civilians. We should work for a world where there were other ways of settling conflicts. It was wrong for so many generations of young men to be killed, as had happened in 1914-1918, and was happening now. He prayed the war would be over before Bob was old enough to go.

After the water supply was provided for the house, we built our own shearing shed. It was built of Oregon pine and galvanized iron, by an eccentric and talented carpenter named Obecue. Mr. Obecue, my parents said, was a secret lady-killer, who had had a series of young and wealthy wives. This information made me gaze at him with more than usual curiosity. I could not fathom his attractions, but I admired intensely the way his fingers flew about, appearing to fabricate things so fast the result seemed to be achieved by sleight of hand. I would sit on the frame of the wool-shed floor watching as he laid it, his mouth full of long nails, his hammer striking home exactly right each time, and the result a smooth floor with nails driven in an unwavering straight line. He was an excitable man, easily upset if anyone appeared to criticize his work, and equally easily made happy by praise. He was a fast worker. The shed was up before we knew it, changing our skyline permanently.

Once the shed was built, a new excitement came into life because instead of our sheep being driven overnight to the woolshed at Mossgiel Station, our neighbor to the northeast, to be shorn, the shearing team came to Coorain. There would be six or eight shearers, a "rouseabout"—the odd-job boy perpetually being set in action by the shouts for the shearers' needs: disinfectant for a cut sheep, a count-out for a full pen of shorn animals (anything that would speed the shearers at their piece work), a wool classer and his assistant, and I never tired of watching the throbbing bustle of the woolshed operating at full speed, the shearer's blades powered by an impressive black engine. Everyone's movements were so stylized that they might have been the work of a choreographer. A really good shearer knew just how to touch a sheep so that it relaxed and didn't kick. Bodies bent over the sheep, arms sweeping down the sides of the animal in long graceful strokes to the floor, the shearers looked like participants in a rite. The rouseabout would pick up each fleece as it finally lay in a pure white heap on the floor, walk with it to the classer's table, then he would fling his arms wide as if giving benediction, and let it fall. The fleece would descend to the table, laid perfectly flat, and the classer, hardly lifting his eyes from the table, would begin dividing it into sections, throwing it into bins organized by spinning classifications. Everyone's hands looked fresh and pink because of the lanolin in the wool. The shed was permeated by the smell of engine oil, from the engine which powered the sharers' blades, and by the smell of lanolin.

*R*ecords for sheep shearing are held by various people, depending on who's counting. Notable efforts include: Jack Howe at Alice Downs station, Queensland, 321 sheep in 7 hours, 40 minutes (hand sheared) on October 19, 1892; Peter Casserly in Christchurch, New Zealand, 353 lambs in 9 hours (hand sheared) on February 13, 1976; and John Fagan at Hautora Road, Pio Pio, New Zealand, 804 lambs in 9 hours (machine sheared) on December 8, 1980.

◆

—LH

Beyond the classer's bins were the wool press and the storage area, where the bales of wool would be pressed to reduce the wool's bulk, carefully weighed, numbered, branded, and then piled to await the contractor who hauled it to the nearest railroad station. Large woolsheds had mechanical presses, but ours, being small, had a hand press operated by an athletic giant of a man, naturally nicknamed Shorty. Shorty was six feet six, weighed 190 pounds, all of it muscle; there was no spare flesh on his body. He pressed the wool into bales by sheer muscle, operating the system of weights and ratchets which could compress 450 pounds of wool into the size of a small bale. Then he would take metal grappling hooks and fling the bales about the storage area as though they were weightless. I loved to watch him work, and whenever I wasn't needed in the sheepyards outside, I would come into the shed, climb to the highest point on the pile of bales, and talk to Shorty. He had a wife and family of his own, farther south, whom he missed terribly, since his team began shearing in Queensland in January and worked its way south until it got to us in June. Each year when he came back, he would exclaim over how I had grown, look purposely blank for a moment, and then with exaggerated cries of absence of mind, recall that he had brought me some candy.

In quiet moments, when he had caught up with the supply of wool and had time to sit down, we exchanged confidences. On some Mondays, he would confess to have had too much to drink over the weekend. Once, deeply troubled and exasperated with himself, he talked of going to see "the girls." I knew in a general way that this was not the best conduct for a married man, so I tut-tutted with as much wisdom as I could summon up and said once didn't matter. It seemed to offer him some relief.

Twice a day, the whistle blew for "smoko" time. The cook would bring over billies of tea and mounds of sweet pound cake and biscuits. Everyone would relax, consume vast supplies of tea from tin mugs, and roll the inevitable cigarette. Sometimes, a shearer might get what Shorty thought was too friendly with me. "The kid's a girl," he would say warningly. That would end the matter. It was easy to see how people might be mistaken, because I wore my brother's cast-off clothes for work outdoors and had my hair tucked away under the usual Australian felt hat.

Each year I waited eagerly for Shorty and the rest of the team to return. Yet I also knew that there were class boundaries to all our dealings with one another. In the evening during the two weeks of shearing, Mac, the wool classer, being an educated person, was always invited to dinner at the house. We were all eager to see Mac, a witty and ironic Scot, whose friendship my parents valued. I loved to see him because he was a great storyteller, and the hour by the fire before dinner would be filled with jokes and laughter. Because he saw the Coorain wool clip each year, he could offer valuable advice about its good and bad characteristics, and make suggestions about qualities that should be introduced into the breeding lines. Best of all for my parents, because he had been traveling from station to station year after year, he was a fount of gossip, and news about distant friends, comical happenings, marriages and divorces, signs of changes in the cycle of wet and dry years. My parents were hungry for talk with other adults, and they would stay in animated conversation till long after I had drifted off to sleep.

Jill Ker Conway is a historian specializing in the experience of women in America and was the first female president of Smith College. This story was excerpted from her book, The Road from Coorain.

RICHARD MENZIES

✳ ✳ ✳

Fear of Frying

*Typical Australian cuisine leaves
something to be desired.*

BEFORE I WENT THERE, ALL I KNEW ABOUT AUSTRALIA WAS JUST
what I'd read in the pages of *National Geographic*. So I was prepared to see kangaroos, koalas, wombats, flying foxes, crocodiles,
camels, great white sharks, and at least a dozen different kinds of
poisonous snakes. But the enduring image in my head was a
Kodachrome of an Aborigine warrior eating what appeared to be
a foot-long worm.

It was a disgusting image to be sure, and not until recently have
I been able to put it out of my mind. That's because nowadays
whenever I think of Australia, I think not of worm-eating
Aborigines, but of white men eating french fries. Not crispy
golden french fries, either—but limp, pale, greasy ones.

In my mind's eye I picture Australians gathered in groups outside a fast-food joint beside a busy highway, like clots of cholesterol
adhering to an arterial wall. One and all they're downing those
pallid half-cooked french fries, and sometimes battered calamari
rings and deep-fat-fried chicken nuggets as well.

In my sweatiest flashback the fries appear sharing a plate with a
circular sandwich any American would recognize at once as a
hamburger. But lift up the bun and you'll see it's not a hamburger

at all, but something else entirely. Instead of a dill pickle you'll find a slice of beet; where the onion is supposed to be there's a pineapple. Once, I even found a fried egg!

The so-called Aussieburger is just one of many mealtime hardships I endured during my trek across Australia, where the culinary crafts are as undeveloped as Paul Hogan's acting ability. Quick! When was the last time you saw a restaurant advertising authentic Australian cuisine? Can't think of one? That's because they've all gone out of business, is why.

Oh sure, there are high-class restaurants in Australia that serve decent food—just as there are upscale neighborhoods in Bangladesh, I suppose. If you're rich enough to stay in four-star hotels, you probably wouldn't notice that, cuisine-wise, you're traveling through a third world country.

My concerns aren't for the rich, though—but rather for those of us of the backpack set. Those of us whose budget is limited, who crave only a quick bite that won't bite back.

> *T*here are excellent restaurants in the major cities, especially Melbourne, Sydney, and Adelaide, and dining out is a very good value, even for those on a modest budget.
>
> ◆
>
> —LH

Now and then during my walkabout I would spot a column of smoke on the horizon denoting a backyard barbecue in progress. Australians are avid carnivores, consuming an average of ten kilos of meat per capita per day, by my estimate. Rump steak is a favorite, as are other leathery cuts from range cattle that evidently go directly from bush to barbie, bypassing the feedlot and all other intermediate tenderizing steps. Moo, bang, sizzle—so goes a day in the life of an Australian steer.

Once or twice I was invited to a backyard barbecue by friendly Aussies. I found Australian beer to be pretty good—but alas, not adequate enough to overcome the peculiar taste of Australian sausages. Fortunately, there's usually a hungry kookaburra kibitzing nearby, to which one can slip indigestible morsels whenever the hostess isn't looking. Another option, if the bird with the cast-iron gizzard isn't available, is to slip the rubbery gristle into your pants pocket and dispose of it later. The old marsupial carry-out strategy.

Indoor dining is more complicated; my suggestion is that you steer clear of meat dishes altogether. Either that, or ask for a table on the patio or close to an open window. Ethnic restaurants, on the increase thanks to the suspension of Australia's long-standing "whites-only" immigration policy, are a bright spot on the culinary horizon. But just remember, even foreign dishes must start out with domestic ingredients.

One good thing about dining out in Australia is that you're not expected to leave a tip. At any rate, that's the custom according to virtually every Australian I met who was not employed in a service-related industry.

"They are well paid and they don't have to depend on gratuities," I was told once. "In Australia, we feel that the price of a meal includes the service," I was told again. Such declarations were always delivered with just the slightest air of haughtiness. I was reminded of Scarlett O'Hara's explanation of how slaves were actually better off under the plantation system.

A penny-pincher by nature, I found the notion of stiffing the waiter quite attractive. No more tedious quarrels about who would leave the tip and how much, no more calculating percentages, no more mock arm wrestling or ritual drawing of toothpicks. Just get up and walk out and don't look back.

The system works best, I suspect, if you never dine at the same restaurant twice, and provided your travel plans don't include returning to Australia anytime in the near future. For in spite of what I was told, I strongly doubt any waiter, taxi driver, or bellhop would ever hold it against you if you offered him a tip.

But I could never be sure. So in order to make certain I didn't break any taboos, I stuck mostly to fast-food eateries and roadside diners, where the quality of the cuisine was such that I wouldn't feel bad about not leaving a tip even if the waiter specifically requested one.

Fast-food joints abound Down Under, the most popular franchise being Kentucky Fried Chicken. Clearly, Colonel Harlan Sanders saw that the way to an Australian's heart lay through his clogged arteries. So highly is the Colonel's original recipe revered, in fact, that the Aussies haven't even tried translating it into their own language. Had they done so, the sign on the red-and-white striped bucket would read: KENTUCKY FRIED CHOOKS.

That doesn't exactly make my mouth water, but then neither did the homemade sign I saw one day propped up alongside the Pacific Highway. "Fresh Bugs" the Day-Glo letters read.

Unfortunately, I wasn't able to stop in time to find out just what fresh bugs are. In Australia, there's no such thing as a wide spot in the road, and hardly such a thing as a shoulder. Yet there's no law says you can't pull over and set up a roadside seafood stand anytime and place the impulse strikes. Blind curves and narrow bridges are particularly attractive vending sites. Customer parking? No worries, mate. If you block the road, they will stop.

Days later and many miles down the road I discovered that "bugs" are a type of crustacean found in Moreton Bay. Quite tasty, as are the farm-raised prawns peddled from tailgates up and down the Pacific Highway.

But the ultimate aquatic delicacy Down Under is a fish they call the barramundi—so prized by sports fishermen that it's against the law in Australia for anyone to shout "The barrumundi are biting!" in a crowded theater. So popular is the succulent barrumundi as an entrée that according to some accounts, more is served up each year in Australian restaurants than is caught.

At a sidewalk eatery in the open-air Kuranda market I enjoyed a barramundi burger that stands out as the gustatory highlight of my trip. When the waitress inquired if my lunch had been satisfactory, it was a pleasure (for once!) to respond truthfully. So many other times I was obliged to prevaricate, it's a wonder my nose didn't sprout leaves.

Take the subject of Vegemite, for example. Vegemite is a dark-brown substance the approximate texture of creamy peanut butter. Australians spread it on toast like jam, but it doesn't taste anything like jam. What it tastes like is anchovy paste, only saltier. Should your face pucker up after you've taken your first bite, your Aussie host will invariably explain that you must have spread it on too thick.

Spread to a palatable degree of thinness, it's my estimate that a hundred-gram jar of Vegemite should last its purchaser nine lifetimes. Yet the label suggests an average serving size of *five* grams— a dose Kraft Food scientists estimate delivers half the minimum daily adult requirement of vitamin B1, riboflavin, and niacin. Salt? You'll never need to eat salt, ever again.

Evidently salt is the essential building block of life on the continent. At the close of World War II, I was told, scores of emaciated and malnourished Australian prisoners of war were nursed back to health by regular feedings of Vegemite—the only "food" their abused digestive systems could tolerate.

This tidbit of information only adds to the high esteem in which I hold the Aussie digger, who consistently ranks high among the world's fighting men. It also makes me wonder, if I ate more salt, would I grow strong bones and muscles like those of Australian iron man Trevor Handy? Or for that matter, were I to ingest cellulose building insulation, might I one day be able to run the field with the likes of Alfie Langer?

If what his Mum says in the television commercial is true, that's what personable Brisbane Bronco football star Langer eats for breakfast—cellulose building insulation. Only Down Under they don't call it building insulation; they market it as a cereal called Weet Bix. Weet Bix are fibrous little bricks that resemble shredded wheat, but taste like cellulose building insulation.

But if Alfie Langer advocates starting each day with a hearty bowl of insulation, then who am I to disagree? When it comes to Australian Rules football, I suppose a player can use all the insulation he can get.

Compared to the Australian version of the game, American football looks about as rough as, say, badminton. In Australia the players don't wear helmets or padding—that is, other than however many Weet Bix bricks they can stuff into their rugby shirts or down their tight shorts. There are no rest periods and precious few substitutions. Referees only call time out when a player has stopped breathing, and then only for as long as it takes to drag his body off the playing field. Minor injuries, such as broken noses and dislocated shoulders and fractured jaws—hey, no pain, no gain!

Eighty minutes of out-and-out mayhem is what it is, and the Australians love it. Some of them can even stand to watch. The only time things ever really got ugly, they tell me, was the day of the big game between arch rivals New South Wales and Queensland, when some joker in the stadium stood up and shouted, "The barramundi are biting!"

Richard Menzies went to Australia to find out how his life might have been had his great-grandfather boarded a different boat in 1898 when he fled Glasgow for America. Half the clan emigrated to New South Wales, where one relative, Richard G. Menzies, became prime minister of Australia and was later dubbed a knight. The author's work appears regularly in Nevada Magazine, *and his specialty is the American West.*

ROFF MARTIN SMITH

* * *

Down a Lazy River

*The Murray led settlers into the interior and remains
the lifeblood of three states.*

Two o'clock on a Sunday afternoon. Temperature in the low hundreds and the little South Australian village of Mannum was drowsy with heat. Barbecues were under way beneath the shade of the century-old river red gum trees along the bank of the Murray River. Kids swam in the chalky waters, a family fished for carp from the dock, and senior citizens in gleaming whites were lawn bowling on the green beside the old stone Pretoria Hotel.

Farther along, a group of boisterous, middle-aged Italians drank wine and laughed. The women shook their heads and smiled as their men danced with each other, linking arms and high kicking, while two of their mates played a tune from *Rigoletto* on squeeze boxes. The long, flat chord of a steamboat whistle sent a flock of pink-and-white galahs into the air, and the people along the riverbank paused, still as some old photograph, to watch as the *Murray Princess*, a Mississippi-style stern-wheeler, sidled up to shore.

I saw the scene unfold from the ship's bridge, feeling as if I'd just drifted into a musical. The only thing we lacked was Paul Robeson, sitting on a bale of cotton, breaking into "Ol' Man River."

A pity nobody ever wrote a musical for the Murray River. Australia's Mississippi deserves one, with its cavalcade of steamboats, prospectors, Aborigines, bush rangers, adventurers, and just plain rapscallions. The Murray is the longest and grandest river on the island continent—in this case 1,609 miles long, stretching from dusty Outback river ports, where camel trains once brought in bales of wool from remote stations, to fishing ports near the Murray's mouth, where clipper ships could take the wool to London. And with dozens of little villages and ferry landings in between, like the gum-shaded spot here in Mannum.

The first time I saw the Murray was back in the summer of 1983, when I hitch-hiked from Sydney to South Australia and found myself stranded in a little river town over on the Victoria side in the blinding white heat of a December afternoon. Fate has brought me back this way many times over the years.

For the most part, though, my experience of the river has been a vicarious one: the quirky taste of its water, which flows from most South Australian taps, or my rumbling drives across the span of iron that crosses the river near Murray Bridge.

When my children were christened in the little church in South Australia's Barossa Valley, it was tannin-rich Murray River water that stained the baptismal font (prompting their patrician Yankee grandmother to remark that the sacrament appeared to have been performed with beer).

If you love food and wine, culture and horticulture, if you support antidiscrimination reform and suffragist history, you'll find Adelaide a multifaceted jewel. But if you've already flown 10,000 miles you'd be mad not to travel up-country. Apart from Wilpena Pound and the Outback, South Australia has no celebrated natural landmarks, yet it is an unspeakably beautiful country, and the people are exceptionally friendly…and there aren't too many of them.

◆

—Rory Ross,
"Sweet Adelaide: Discovering Eden and the Outback in South Australia," *Gourmet*

Now, as I traveled along the river, I found myself marveling at its stark beauty and tenacity. All along its length the ancient river is undergoing a renaissance. Trees are being planted, fish restocked, and public bird-watching blinds built along its banks and lagoons, so travelers can stop and admire the profusion of bird life. A fleet of nineteenth-century steamboats—*Australien, Edwards, Ruby, Hero, Wanera, Success,* and *Gem*—which had lain derelict in the weeds for decades is being dredged up, lovingly restored, and put back on the water, this time to carry sight-seers rather than wool bales or sacks of grain.

The Murray starts as a few treble notes of snowmelt over mossy rocks high in the Snowy Mountains, highlands where, for thousands of years, Aborigines gathered each spring to feast on nutty-tasting *bogong* moths. The river rushes, clear and icy, through some of the prettiest wilderness in Australia—broad meadows dotted with snow gums and rioting with wildflowers and the rich native grasses that have drawn cattlemen to these heights since the 1860s. By the time the river drops to the city of Albury, less than 100 miles from its source, it has settled into the characteristic stately grace that takes it the rest of the way to the sea.

By Mississippi or Amazon standards, of course, the Murray is a trickle—a couple of hundred yards wide at most—but on this sunburned continent, it is life itself. More than half the country's fruits and vegetables, meats, grains, cotton, and wool come from the Murray's fertile basin. To the Aborigines, the river was paradise.

A Yorta Yorta elder named Des Morgan told me the story of the river that his people called Tongala: "In the beginning all this land was flat and dry. Biama, the creator of everything, sent his woman out to look for food. A giant snake came with her. As she walked along poking her stick in the ground, she made deep holes in the earth. The snake slithered behind her, leaving a deep furrow as its track. The rains came. They filled the holes and the furrows, and the river was born. Later the birds came, and the trees bloomed along the banks. Then the Yorta Yorta people were put on the land, and a man whose face shone like the sun came and walked among us, giving us the laws we should live by."

The scattered tribes of Aborigines along the river lived by those laws for 30,000 years, leaving behind rock carvings, paintings, and the smoke-stained cliff faces of ancient campsites.

The haunting evidence of this unbroken tenure came to light just four years ago, near where the Darling River adds its tea-and-milk waters to the Murray. Drought had lowered the level of a water reservoir and revealed a vast Aboriginal burial ground—thousands of skeletons all scattered over the dry lake bed. I happened to be there a couple of weeks after the graves were discovered.

"I always knew there were spirits in this lake," John Mitchell, an elder among the Barkindji people, told me as we walked among the ancient remains. "I used to hear them singing to me when I camped near here, but I never thought there was anything like this. To walk here now, amid this proof that my people lived here so peacefully for so many generations, makes me proud."

Viewing Aboriginal rock art is one of the more astounding experiences to be had in Australia, and it can be found almost everywhere indigenous people lived. Two of the best places are the Kimberley in Western Australia and Arnhem Land in the Northern Territory. The paintings on sandstone walls are at least 35,000 years old (some say even 75,000 years old), a mind-numbing record of human history.

◆

—LH

In 1824, newcomers arrived, renamed the river in honor of Colonial Secretary Sir George Murray, and with axes, plows, sheep, and steamships put the waterway and its fertile floodplain to profitable service. Within fifty years more that 200 paddle steamers were plying the river, burning 300-year-old gum trees for fuel and bringing vital supplies to settlers who were busily taming the land. A great river was going to be made even better. Goolwa, an old fishing town on the coast, near the river's sandy mouth, was going to be the Southern Hemisphere's New Orleans, while Echuca, a brawling timber town 140 miles north of Melbourne, would be its Chicago.

I rolled into Echuca late on a warmish autumn afternoon, after a long dusty drive along the river, my dashboard radio tuned to the community station, which was playing a set of crackly gramophone recordings made on the Wurlitzer organ at Blackpool, England, in the 1930s. They were just wrapping up the "Punch and Judy Polka" when I nosed my car up to the curb in front of the River Gallery Inn, a combination art gallery and bed-and-breakfast.

I took their Early Australian suite, the one with a balcony over-looking main street's row of false-front stone buildings, glowing warm in the dying sunlight. It was rush hour, and the river town was tranquil enough for me to hear kookaburras cackling in the gum trees behind the old bank building. So much for Chicago.

To get a sense of this river port in the bad old days of the 1860s, you need look no further than a photograph of the town's founder, a former convict named Henry Hopwood, who looks like an aging artful Dodger in a too-long Victorian greatcoat and oversize top hat, with a cocky grin that made me think of a rat with a gold tooth.

"I guess today he'd be what we'd call a habitual offender," the woman behind the desk at the historical society said when she noticed me looking at his poster-size photograph. "He was constantly running afoul of authorities and getting into trouble with women."

Certainly he was a shrewd and tenacious entrepreneur. He built his Hopwood's Crossing river ferry operation into a rollicking timber, cattle, and wool port, and a jumping-off place for the hordes of prospectors rushing the Victorian goldfields. By the time Hopwood died of typhoid in 1869, the town had eighty-six pubs, a thriving brothel, and a massive, forty-two-foot-high wharf that befitted its status as the nation's busiest inland port. But as happened so often along the river, bickering among jealous colonial authorities, the coming of the railways, and the fickleness of the Murray itself put an end to grandiose municipal ambitions.

Today, Echuca's population of about 10,000 isn't much bigger than in Hopwood's time. It is a holidaymakers's town now, the streets lined with art galleries, bistros, and antique shops, together with Australian versions of the old five-and-ten, with their sidewalk displays of bright plastic toys, floppy hats, sunscreen, swim fins, and crawfish nets. Bags of charcoal, tongs, fishing lures, barbecue forks. The stuff of the classic Aussie bucket-'n'-spade river holiday.

The once-bustling wharf, built of river red gum beams, has been spruced up, with restaurants and booking offices for steamboat excursions occupying century-old shop fronts. Half a dozen antique paddle steamers were tied up the morning I walked along the wharf.

Across the river, on the New South Wales side, the big gums were noisy with kookaburras. Come lunchtime, they would flock across the river to be hand-fed by diners at trendy restaurants overlooking the waterfront.

Yet for all the seeming tameness, this isn't a river under glass. Follow the riverbank for a few hundred yards, and you're in bush and have to keep a wary eye out for tiger snakes. Away from the towns, the Murray is pretty much the same rustic waterway it was at the turn of the century. One day I came upon a houseboat tied to a sapling. A middle-aged Melbourne couple had rented it for a week of Huck Finning.

"We generally travel until about noon and then look for a place to tie up," the wife explained, inviting me aboard for a cup of tea. "You can camp just about anywhere along the river. We fish, swim, and look at the stars at night. For dinner we dig a hole, build a fire, and cook a leg of lamb and some veggies in the cast-iron camp oven."

And the Murray remains a force to be reckoned with. Around Echuca's streets, signs on the buildings and trees attest to the levels of historic floods—1993, 1956, 1931, 1916, and the great gully-washer of 1870, the high-water mark, when the Murray rose nearly thirty-six feet above its banks. This river still lives.

So does the old Henry Hopwood spirit of enterprise. At dinner that night, in one of Echuca's better restaurants I was startled when my waiter murmured that if there was nothing to my liking on the surprisingly extensive wine list, he could give me a great deal on a nice Shiraz. A bit of a complicated story about its pedigree, he said, but if I didn't mind…I didn't, and he returned a moment later with a bottle—sans label—and with characteristic Australian irony, held it out for my inspection.

"Looks like the one for me," I said to him.

"Very good, sir."

He uncorked it expertly and poured. It was superb. And as I dawdled over the wine, I decided that, OK, even though Hopwood's town never got the Sears Tower, Marshall Field's, or Michael Jordan, the old rapscallion would appreciate its style.

By the time the Murray flows past Mildura, it's broad enough to accommodate six steamboats abreast, a spectacle that happens every couple of years when they hold a regatta before Australia's Greatest Paddleboat Race. The *Rothbury* finished second in the inaugural race, held on the Darling River in 1896, but has won every contest since, including the most recent in 1997. It's the hot favorite for the next competition in 2000, when paddle steamers from the length of Murray will gather in Mildura.

"That is one fast boat," laughs Greg Evans, skipper of the vintage *Melbourne*, as we steam toward Lock 11.

The lock is one of a series built along the Murray to reserve water for a century-old irrigation scheme converting a stretch of stunted eucalyptus scrub between Mildura and the South Australian town of Renmark into one of the richest fruit and vineyard regions in Australia.

"My great-great-grandparents came up here in 1891 on the paddle steamer *Gem*," Evans explains, "hoping to make their fortunes on the land. They had read all about the grand irrigation project on the Murray, sold everything they had in England, and came here believing they'd bought a developed property. Turned out to be a bit of a scam. They got a canvas tarp and a patch of scrub and had to make do living in a lean-to for two years. They weren't happy."

Understandable. I'd seen a copy of the original prospectus, which had circulated widely in Britain, in the late 1880s. Now it was faded, its binding cracked, but in its day it must have been a corker: folio-size, crimson red, a gold crest on the cover, and chock-full of sumptuous prose and sketches of orange groves luscious enough to make the gardens of Babylon look like just another realtor's dream.

Visions of endless sunshine, fruit ripe for the picking, and life as lazy as tropical sun made the lands along the Australian river a honeypot for remittance men—rich English rakes who had disgraced the family name and been sent abroad with monthly stipends—as long as they never returned.

"There were still a few of those guys around when I was growing up," a 68-year-old commercial rose grower named Dave Ruston told me, over tea and cakes on the veranda of the high-ceilinged colonial bungalow where he was born. "My father said they would live in grand style when those checks arrived. Get out their fine old clothes, which were decades out of style, then head down to the Settler's Club, buying drinks for everyone. Of course, when the money was gone, they were back to scavenging a living along the river. He remembered seeing the old gent who happened to be down on his luck sitting in a deck chair in the water around Plush's Bend. No shirt, a strawhat, and reading a classic in ancient Greek."

The development scheme's original promoters went bankrupt around the turn of the century, but irrigation was there to stay. Driving through these oasis towns now, with their manicured golf courses, bright flowers, and rows of ornamental palms, it's hard to believe the early descriptions of hissing sands and parched desert.

That is something better appreciated from the air. Up there you can see the razor line where the vineyards and orchards stop and a dusty immensity of scrub begins stretching toward the horizon. Down at street level, the riverland's endless sunshine is not a curse but a commodity, almost as precious as water.

Along this stretch of river, particularly across the border in South Australia, winemakers have been turning one of humanity's oldest arts into a New World science.

"We'll grab the best methods technology has to offer, then blend grapes from here and other regions for the flavor we're looking for," Bill Moularadellis, the proprietor of Kingston Estate

Wines, told me one morning, as we walked, forty acres of chardonnay, cabernet, and merlot just out of sight of the Murray.

"That kind of mix-and-match might be sacrilege to traditional winemakers in France, but it means we can turn out a genuinely fine bottle of reasonably priced wine better than anybody else in the world."

And the world seems to be buying. Kingston Estate alone sells almost a million cases to Europe each year. Boom times have kicked off a gold-rush-style land grab along the Murray, with Australia's biggest winemakers sinking millions of dollars into new vineyards.

Along with the scramble for land is an equally vital scramble for water. South Australia is last in line to receive the Murray's precious waters. Not surprisingly, since they have to drink it as well, the strongest voices for conservation come from this end of the river. I stopped at the Renmark Hotel Motel, a cream-and-green Art Deco building along a landscaped riverbank and, over a lunch of char-grilled kangaroo fillet, talked wetlands ecology with Mike Harper, of the Bookmark Biosphere Reserve.

*A*s wine lovers worldwide began to take note of the quality and value of Australian wines, they also recognized Adelaide's position in the middle of some of the country's—indeed, the world's—finest and most famous wine regions: the Barossa and Clare valleys to the northeast, Coonawarra and Padthaway to the southeast, all replete with wineries offering tours and tastings, and all increasingly places of pilgrimage for serious oenophiles. And recently Adelaide chefs have begun experimenting with native foods life kangaroo, emu, and the lobsterlike marron, blending them with cuisines of the recent wave of Asian and European immigrants to create a new kind of cooking that's attracted growing attention and admiration.

◆

—Mel White,
"Wine, Wildlife, and Song,"
National Geographic Traveler

"Everybody wants a piece of the Murray," he explained. "The trouble is that we're taking more than the river can give, and we've been doing it for a long time. We've changed the river's eco-system—adding locks to control its flow for irrigation, clearing trees to create farmland, introducing European carp, and letting fertilizer-rich runoff from the farms to trickle back into the river. The list goes on. The Murray can't take care of itself anymore."

The Bookmark reserve helps look after a chain of national parks along the river, as well as the holdings of companies and farms who'd volunteered for the program—about 2,700 square miles of wetlands and dwindling mallee habitat so far.

"We've been working with an offshoot of America's Ducks Unlimited, and already we're seeing results, particularly in the la-goons. Bird life is returning, the water is clearer, aquatic plants are growing again."

And as I stopped in at little pubs along the river, fishermen told me they were once again catching the occasional Murray cod, a giant freshwater fish that can grow to more than 250 pounds. And, by law, they were returning them to the river.

It is an old and majestic Murray that flows the final 400 miles through the bronzed South Australian countryside on its way to the sea. These are perhaps its finest stretches: shimmering lagoons and an incredible diversity of bird life—pelicans, white-breasted eagles, galahs, sulfur-crested cockatoos, regent parrots, magpies, kookaburras—more that 240 species in all. The citrus town of Waikerie, about 100 miles east of Adelaide, is said to get its name from the local Aboriginal word meaning "anything that flies."

I drove past the abandoned sandstone cottages of early settlers who'd tried, and failed, on forty acres of land. Past the pipeline that carries the Murray's water to small farm towns in the wheat-grow-ing country of the southern Flinders Ranges and past the old cop-per-mining hamlet of Burra, with its legacy of Cornish miners. I followed another pipeline away from the river, over a line of grassy hills burned brown by the sun, and into the appropriately bottle-shaped Barossa Valley, wall-to-wall vineyards, home of Australia's finest wines. It was harvest time, and the little towns were pungent with the aroma of the '98 vintage. The story of the Barossa Valley can be read in the phone book—with names like Henschke, Linke, Graetz, and Seppelt pointing to the German origins of the first settlers, with some of the older residents still speaking an Australianized version of German known as Barossa-Deutsch. German bakeries sell traditional pastries, butcher shops each do their own *Mettwurst*, and old bluestone Lutheran churches dominate the villages.

Back down to the river, a winding road passed the very private grounds of Lindsay Park, Australia's premier horse racing stud, then plunged almost 1,000 feet to the flat, hazy immensity of the lower Murray River floodplain. The river is barely moving here, a lazy serpentine sprawl stretching toward a desolate chain of sandbars and brackish lagoons known as the Coorong, where the river finally meets the sea.

Goolwa, the little rivermouth town that settlers hoped might one day flourish into another New Orleans, flourished instead into a cheery seaside resort, a sort of Blackpool Down

---

*A*s if in a childhood dream I was drawn to the Ferris wheel along the waterfront in Glenelg. I couldn't remember the last time I'd been on one and suddenly it seemed important to take a ride. As I rose up into the black sky the stars came out in the heavens.

Descending toward the amphitheater where the carolers held candles was like dropping into a pool of lights. Rising again I entered the constellations, dropping I fell into candlelight. Christmas carols followed me high into the sky and greeted me as I dropped toward the glowing lights with that tickle in the belly you get when the bottom falls out beneath you. Up again into the stars, down again into the candles, until the sky and the ground and the sea and the song all merged into one. No longer a child, I just rode the Ferris wheel on the edge of the sea through constellations of stars.

◆

—Larry Habegger, "Christmas Carols in Adelaide"

Under, where homesick English immigrants could play on a beach and gather cockles as they used to in the old country. It became so popular around the turn of the century that the weekend train down to Goolwa became known affectionately—then officially—as the "cockle train."

It's still a holiday town popular with Adelaide's fashionable set, cockles remain abundant, and a restored steam locomotive makes an abbreviated cockle run between Victor Harbour and Goolwa every weekend. The train was just pulling in, three carriages of sight-seers waving out the open windows, when I arrived.

It was noon on a brilliant Saturday, a taste of sea in the air and the foreshore bright with picnickers, strollers, and fishermen. Four antique paddle steamers were in town to mark the 100th birthday of the *Etona*, a missionary steamer that brought Scripture to the outlying stations and villages.

I swung around to the old Corio Hotel, a shambling limestone relic of Goolwa's earliest days, and had lunch in a dining room that used to house a tobacconist and barber shop. A fading mural for Yankee Doodle Tobacco graced the ceiling, an eye-catcher for anyone getting a barber-chair shave in the old days.

"They tell me ours is one of only two of those murals left anywhere in the world," the publican, a man named Frank, said when I paid for my meal.

Finally, I took the ferry across the river to Hindmarsh Island, a windswept bit of land that sits at the mouth of the Murray almost like a cork in a bottle. As I drove the length of the island, traffic slipped away. At last I was alone with the wind and the cries of seagulls, where the Murray finally flows into the Indian Ocean, ending as it began, more than 1,609 miles away, in seclusion.

Roff Martin Smith is the author of Australia: Journey Through a Timeless Land *and* Cold Beer and Crocodiles: A Bicycle Journey into Australia, *which chronicles his 10,000-mile solo cycling trip around the perimeter of Australia. He was a senior writer for* TIME *(South Pacific) before embarking on his cycling journey, and he has lived in Australia since 1982.*

* * *

Speak Oz

What's that you said?

MOST OF US FLAMING SEPTICS VISITING OZ EITHER SHOOT through like the Bondi tram or muck about playing silly buggers and never properly apprehend the lingo. I was pondering this phenomenon one day while demolishing several dozen stubbies in the cattle-ranching country of far North Queensland, specifically at a rubbity in the town of Coen, whose quaint motto is "Eat Beef, You Bastards." Three weeks into my trip to Australia I was aware that "bastard" is a term used to describe acceptable and pleasant members of the human race. The rubbity was located in what had been the Exchange Hotel, but the new owner—in the interest of economy and typical Aussie bullsh_—had altered the name with a single letter, so that the only sign of any size in this town of some forty houses now read, DRINK AT THE SEXCHANGE HOTEL.

One of the bastards doing just that was having a go at me: "Geez," he said, "there must have been fifty flaming 'roos out there that night." The image of fifty kangaroos leaping and lurching about in an agony of fire tugged at the mind, though I knew perfectly well that "flaming" is a universal adjective often applied to perfectly uninflammable objects, just as the word "bloody" is used to modify any noun: "I twisted me flaming ankle on a bloody rock."

Much of what is unique about Australian English derives from the flash talk of transported criminals, and rhyming slang—"I have some Gene Tunney (money) in me skyrocket (pocket), and I'm going to the rubbity (dub-pub) for a pig's ear (beer)"—is dinki-di (a dinkum Aussie term meaning genuine Oz speak.) Another ridgi-dige bit of lingo has it that Americans are "seppos" or "septics" (septic tank-Yank.)

As the only septic at the Sexchange, I had to ask directions to the snakes (rhymes with snake's hiss) so I could unbutton the mutton and wring the rattlesnake. There are dozens of phrases for this particular activity, and they range from drain the dragon to syphon the python to simply "go a snakes."

In a rubbity like the Sexchange a bastard would be a flaming galah not to demolish several dozen stubbies (small bottles of lager), and a polite bastard steps out back to have a bit of a chunder. This process of enjoying oneself in reverse may be one of Australia's most popular indoor and outdoor sports, judging by the sheer number of phrases used to describe it: "cry ruth," "hurl," "chunder," "play the whale," "do the big spit," "park the tiger," "have a nice Technicolor yawn," "laugh at the ground."

Since there were no jam tarts in evidence, a bit of the talk concerned certain Sheilas with norks like Mudgee mailbags. One potato in particular was known to root like a rattlesnake, and one of my companions expressed a desire to be "at her like a rat up a drainpipe." The preferred organ in an R.U.A.D. situation is known as "the wily old snorker," or, alternately, and more graphically, "the beef bayonet," the "port sword," or the "mutton dagger."

In all fairness I should mention that certain proper residents of Australia—wowsers of the worst ilk—object strongly to such conversation and feel that some of the words and phrases used here are "best left written on the wall in an Outback dunny." This attitude, I think, does not do justice to the distinctiveness of Australian usage. All the above words and phrases may be found in the new *Macquarie Dictionary*, a dinkum Aussie dictionary published by Macquarie University, New South Wales, after eleven years of research.

Very few of the bastards at the Sexchange were concerned with verbal propriety, however, possibly because most of us were full as a bull's bum. The English language as spoken by Aussies—toilet talk and all—seemed robust and important. Several dozen stubbies'll do that to a bastard, of course, and when someone referred to the local dentist as a "gang-ferrier," I got to laughing in an entirely hysterical manner. Someone decided, quite loudly, that "the bleeding septic is as silly as a bagful of arseholes," and I couldn't stop laughing.

"He's gone troppo," they said.

"Fair dinkum."

"Meself," one bastard opined, "I blame the climate."

Tim Cahill is the author of many books, mostly travel-related, including Lost in My Own Backyard, Hold the Enlightenment, Jaguars Ripped My Flesh, Pecked to Death by Ducks, Pass the Butterworms, *and* Dolphins, *as well as the editor of* Not So Funny When it Happened: The Best of Travel Humor and Misadventure. *Cahill is also the co-author of the Academy Award-nominated IMAX film,* The Living Sea, *as well as the films* Everest *and* Dolphins. *He lives in Montana, and shares his life with Linnea Larson, two dogs, and two cats.*

The Coral Galaxy

*The Great Barrier Reef is even
bigger than you think.*

AT LAST I HAD COME TO THE GREAT BARRIER REEF, SINCE CHILD-hood the place in the world I had most wanted to see. Now that I was finally here, I could not get my overstimulated mind to settle down. The day I arrived on Australia's Queensland coast, I made a quick tour of the Daintree Rain Forest, and that night, restlessly sleeping in a bungalow beside the Coral Sea, I dreamed that the reef and the rain forest were one phenomenon. I soared through a vast submerged woodland, rising to inspect the elkhorns and the giant basket ferns that spread out like crows' nests at the tops of the trees. Tiny kangaroos leapt out of their hiding places in the ferns, ranging ahead of me with long, fluid strides. Cassowaries, the giant flightless birds of the rain forest, floated through the dream with their thick legs paddling the air, and fruit bats and sulfur-crested cockatoos joined me in exalted flights above the tree canopy.

The next day, leaving Port Douglas on one of the Quicksilver boats that ferry tourists to the outer reef, I was still glowing with anticipation. The sea, riled by unseasonal winds, was an opaque green, and though we passed many islands and cays, each with its bright arc of clear water, the Great Barrier Reef itself remained diffuse and distant, an unreachable abstraction, like a rainbow.

I was a hostage to my own expectations. I had read that the reef was so massive it could be seen from the moon, and so I had always pictured it as a singular, looming monument, an unbroken bulwark of coral running right alongside the coast of eastern Australia.

Though it may be visible from the moon, it is not all that apparent from the Earth. The Great Barrier Reef is not one solid mass, but a 1,200-mile patchwork of reefs, islands, and coral cays extending from the Cape York Peninsula almost all the way south to Brisbane. What most people refer to as the Great Barrier Reef is an immense lagoon of 80,000 square miles sandwiched between the Queensland coast and the seaward ramparts of the outer reef. Within this lagoon are 900 islands, some of them continental islands 100 miles long, others mere specks of exposed coral.

The stretch of ocean contained within the reef is so vast that Captain James Cook, exploring the area in 1770, managed to cruise up the coast for 600 miles without ever realizing that the outer reef existed. Even today, tourists tend to be perplexed by it. You may spend a week or two snorkeling or horseback riding or playing tennis on one of the big resort islands, you may embark on a sailing expedition through the calm waters of the Whitsunday Passage. But to see the reef itself, you must head deliberately out to sea, to the distant chain of submerged coral promontories lying at the edge of the open ocean.

So, on my second morning in Port Douglas, I boarded the *Quicksilver,* a gleaming multideck catamaran "wave piercer" designed to slice through the surface turbulence on knife-edged hulls. But the waves were making themselves felt today, and the boat lurched from side to side on the hour-and-a-half trip. Morning tea was served, featuring rolls spread with Vegemite, the vile yeast extract inexplicably beloved by Australians, and afterward some of the passengers began to take on the peculiar brooding look of seasickness.

I went to the upper deck for a lecture on reef biology. As crew members stood at the ready with cool towels, we were shown slides of starfish and sea cucumbers, and coral polyps in the midst of spawning, their orange eggs floating upward from the creatures' puckering mouths like miniature beach balls. The reef had been built by such coral animals, dying in their millions and leaving behind their hardened husks.

Captain Matthew Flinders, the English explorer who charted the Great Barrier Reef in 1802, described the process nicely. "It seems to me," he wrote, "that when the animalcules which form the corals at the bottom of the ocean cease to live, their structures adhere to each other…and…a mass of rock is at length formed. Future races of these animalcules erect their habitation upon the rising bank, and die in their turn, to increase, but principally to elevate, this monument of their wonderful labor."

By the time the lecture was over, Agincourt Reef was in view, marked by a thin line of foamy surf beyond which lay limitless blue ocean. Within the reef line the water was shallow and eerily translucent, speckled with *bommies*—isolated growths of coral—and sand flats and broad coral mesas that rose to within inches of the surface. The boat docked at a midsea platform, a gleaming silver rectangle that

---

*A*t the appointed hour of 10 A.M., David and I and about 300 other people (clutching 300 video cameras) climbed aboard a titanic, brushed-steel, wave-piercing catamaran called *Quicksilver III*. It cost eight million bucks to build and looked like an airplane designed by Howard Hughes after he'd spent too much time in hotels being disinfected and reading superhero comics. We then pierced our way through 70 Ks of rough sea to Agincourt Reef. Quite a few people threw up on the way, which is always very amusing— until they throw up on you, which makes you throw up on somebody else and pretty soon you've got 300 people throwing up all over Howard Hughes's dream.

◆

—Sean Condon, *Sean & David's Long Drive*

seemed not to float but hover over a turquoise vacuum. On the platform were picnic tables, showers, bins full of masks, fins, and snorkels, and a submerged viewing tunnel from which you could see fellow passengers snorkeling awkwardly through schools of sergeant majors and quizzical-looking unicornfish.

Since I had signed up for scuba diving, I pitched my gear into a small dive boat that moved swiftly away from the *Quicksilver* and its platform. Through the metal slats of the boat's deck, I looked down at blinding stripes of sunstruck water. All around us, coral formations stippled the surface of the sea, like clouds in a mackerel sky. From above, the coral were ocher-colored blotches, no more alluring than slag heaps. But when I rolled backward into the water and descended to a floor of staghorn coral, I felt a chill of appreciation crawl up the spine of my wet suit.

The reef was a compacted landscape made up of dozens of species of coral that took the shape of brambly thickets, hypnotically patterned boulders, spreading fans, and delicate rosettes. Competing for the vital sunlight, the various types grew close together, as dense as hedgerows. The parrotfish that swarmed over this terrain were brilliantly colored, each scale like a panel on a stained-glass window, but the colors of the reef itself were as soft and subtle as the hues in a hand-tinted photograph. Studded among the coral were giant clams, three feet across, their shells open and their lurid tissues exposed to the sun. If I passed my hand over these light-sensitive mantles, the clams closed up, regarding my shadow as a threat. But I managed to steal up on one without alarming it, peering through the creature's open siphon into the milky-white interior of its body.

We roamed about underwater for an hour or so, traveling perhaps an eighth of a mile of the reef's infinitely faceted thousand-mile length. Back on board the *Quicksilver*, sipping afternoon tea as we headed back toward the coast, I felt crestfallen, as if the reef still eluded me—as if it were too vast and intricate to be perceived.

In the late afternoon I walked along the beach at Palm Cove. It was September, early spring in Australia. The water was chilly and the offshore winds kept it turbid, discouraging bathers. In the distance, the crew of the local Surf Life-Saving Club rowed over the crests of the waves, their white bathing caps bobbing like buoys. Indian mynahs hopped about the casuarina trees, and from a telephone wire hung a huge electrocuted bat, its black tongue dangling out of its mouth.

The next morning I drove to the airport in Cairns and boarded a milk-run flight heading south. My destination was Heron Island, a lone microdot of a coral cay 550 miles to the south. Unlike most of the other resort islands, Heron is perched near the reef's outer edge. Standing on it, I felt I would be standing unambiguously on the Great Barrier Reef itself.

The propeller-driven plane flew low over the coast, and from my aisle seat on the right-hand side I could see the Australian continent rolling by: the rain-forested foothills of the Great Dividing Range, the endless pristine beaches strung between craggy headlands, and, finally, stretches of dry coastal country that marked the probing edges of the Outback. Looking across the aisle through the other window, I glimpsed the reef as it followed faithfully alongside the great landmass. Island after island passed beneath the plane's wings. From the air, the reef showed up as a series of aquamarine patches fringed with white surf—holes in the ocean through which a radiant light seemed to shine from below.

We landed at the coastal city of Gladstone and took a helicopter out to sea, coasting over aluminum refineries and coal-loading bins and the murky waters of an industrial port. Twenty minutes later, Heron Island showed up on the horizon, a half-mile-long patch of white sand and green vegetation.

At this height, it was clear that the island itself was merely the exposed summit of something much larger, which seemed to have risen up from the depths like an immense, basking whale. It was low tide now, and the reef was barely covered with water. In fact, with its faded greens and yellows, it looked like a parched lawn. The only hints that it was submerged at all were the whitecaps dancing around its borders and the sharks swimming, as if suspended in air, across the austere sand flats. Looking down, I saw sea turtles as well, and schools of rays that looked like fallen leaves.

It was early afternoon when I landed. Like almost all of the islands regularly visited by tourists, Heron has a single resort, whose amenities—from pricey beachfront villas to utilitarian cabins—take up about a third of the surface area. Beyond the resort, Heron is a national park, with a marine research station occupying the site of a former turtle cannery. I arrived in time for lunch, taking my seat at an assigned table next to a stalwart elderly woman from England who appeared to be on a solo excursion into the known tourist world, from Uluru to Las Vegas. "A lovely island," she proclaimed. "Absolutely lovely! Submarine boats. Snorkeling. Bingo. Lovely food. Can't seem to develop a taste for this Vegemite, however."

After lunch I stopped off at a small museum next to the resort's gift shop and studied a display depicting the life cycle of a coral polyp. "Hello!" an Australian-accented voice blurted out from a speaker in the wall. "I'm a part of the coral colony... We corals use stinging cells to capture minute animals called plankton. Chemicals in the water coming off my prey let me know that food is about...Can *you* see my mouth? It's in the middle of my ring of tentacles!"

I listened as the polyp gave an unembarrassed accounting of his reproductive methods (sexual *and* asexual), and then I took a quick walking tour of the island, following the trail that led from the resort into a strange forest of pisonia trees ("pronounced just like it's spelled," a cheerful guest told me, "piss on ya"). The pisonias' large green leaves made a shady bower of the center of the island. Their trunks were contorted and powerful-looking, though the trees are as soft as pulp and vulnerable to cyclones. The branches were crowded with thousands of black noddy terns fashioning nests out of fallen pisonia leaves and gluing them to the branches with their own droppings. The air was filled with the birds' anxious creaking.

September is high season for the area's wildlife. Not only were noddies beginning to build their nests, but so were other birds, like the shearwaters and reef herons for which the island was named.

Out beyond the reef, male green sea turtles were clambering onto the slippery backs of their mates, and in another month or so the gravid females would begin to crawl up onto the beach to dig nests in the sand—sometimes slipping into the swimming pool on their way back to the ocean. Humpback whales, accompanied by calves born during the Australian winter, were beginning to head south toward their feeding grounds in the Antarctic, where, after their months-long breeding-season fast, they would consume a ton of food a day.

Reef walking late that afternoon, I kept glancing up at the blue water, hoping to see a whale come crashing up, its long white flippers waggling in the air. No luck, but smaller wonders were close at hand. Reef walking is a prime activity here. When the tide goes out, it exposes the shallow coral banks, making it possible to saunter along in a vast tide pool teeming with crabs, sea anemones, snails, and sea stars.

On this day, the tide was unusually high, and conditions were not ideal. Still, resort guests were out in force, carrying walking sticks for balance and wearing tennis shoes to protect their feet against the sharp coral and poisonous sea creatures. They would take a few unsteady steps, then bend over and peer into the shallow water through a face mask or a glass-bottomed bucket.

---

*T*he sense of endless space was intoxicating: Queensland's lush coast sprawled on one horizon, the Coral Sea extended across the other, with only a few scattered islands bobbing in the desert of blue.

Before long, we slipped past Bedarra, whose beaches were scattered with golden boulders like giants' marbles. Next came the "Twins," then the smaller "Triplets." Captain Al found a clam anchorage at the second-to-last sibling, "Bowden," which rose smooth and round like a big green billiard ball. As we pulled the dinghy ashore, a foot-wide stingray skimmed between my feet.

Perhaps because this was my first truly deserted island there seemed a Peter Pan feeling to the whole place—Neverland in the tropics.

◆

—Tony Perrottet, "Always Go North," *Islands*

Walking carefully along the sand channels between the coral boulders, I could see small rays and epaulette sharks scurrying off at my approach. The bottom was littered with sea cucumbers, sluggish relatives of the starfish that feed by filtering sand through their bodies. Recalling that no less an authority than Charles Darwin had termed them "slimy (and) disgusting," I reached down and picked one up. I took the precaution of studying it at arm's length because, according to a book I had recently consulted, "this species can eject toxic thread from its anus." When I returned the sea cucumber to its place on the sand I saw a blue sea star nearby, and the velvety mantle of a burrowing clam.

"Going out today?" said a man as I came up to the water's edge with my diving gear the next morning. He was an elderly American, stringy and toothy, with a booming voice. "I won't go out myself," he said, "terrified of the water! Have been ever since I stepped off a landing craft in France in 1942 with thirty pounds of equipment on my back. Sank right to the bottom. That'll cure you of ever wanting to go into the water again."

But when I boarded the dive boat the man was still standing there on the shore, shading his eyes against the morning sunlight and staring out at the water with a peculiar satisfaction, as if he were counting on the beauty of the reef to lure him back out into the sea.

I spent most of the next two days underwater. The water was colder than it had been farther north, but the marine life was even more abundant. Schools of blue-green chromis swept across the coral fields like a spangly curtain. Big coral cod hung motionless beneath ledges, their mouths open as if in ecstasy as small "cleaner fish" wriggled in and out, ridding them of parasites. When I looked up from below at the sunlit slopes of staghorn coral, I saw a dozen different species of schooling fish, swimming in tiers and wending columns, their movements accentuated by dancing light beams that seemed as frenetic and concentrated as strobes. There were green-spotted nudibranchs—brilliantly colored sea snails without shells—and moray eels that could be coaxed out of their lairs.

Once, swimming along at thirty feet, I saw what I took to be an odd, smooth boulder five feet long. When the boulder moved, I swam closer to investigate and saw that it was a sleeping logger-head turtle, its flippers tucked up beneath its shell, its head hidden in a coral crevice. Cautiously peering into the crevice, I saw the turtle's huge cranium and its horny parrot's beak.

Diving at night, among the extended golden polyps of daisy coral and the narcoleptic parrotfish wedged into rocky fissures, I came across something I had only seen in books and never ex-pected to encounter. It was a type of nudibranch called a Spanish dancer, one of the largest and most florid of its species. This one was the size and shape of a serving platter, and in the beam of my underwater light it was a sumptuous shade of red. Its shapeless body wafted through the water, flamboyant and ghostly. Every mo-tion it made seemed to pump more redness into it, so that its vivid color had a dynamic quality, like a rising blush. One of the divers I was with reached out and stroked it, as if it were a thing that needed comfort. I touched it too. It was slick and satiny, and though it was light as a veil I could feel its strange organic heft. After a while four or five other divers had gathered around, and one by one they extended their hands to touch it.

The next morning I woke early and walked through the piso-nia forest to the windward side of the island to watch the sun come up. The tide was out and the water calm, except for a neat rolling line marking the edge of the reef. A heron sat on an exposed coral rock, its long neck tucked into its body. Brown noddies were sweeping out of their nests and cruising low over the placid sea, searching for fish. I walked down the beach and out into cold water up to my knees.

The sun came up at 6:38 A.M., a ferocious disk slipping out of the ocean so quickly and brightly it startled me and hurt my eyes. The sky turned yellow all around it. Only when the sun was higher, and its laser intensity diffused, was I able to look out com-fortably toward the reef again.

Spreading from the beach to the reef crest were acres and acres of mustardy coral and beige sand—and that was only a speck of the

Great Barrier Reef. It was too vast, finally, to behold. To see it at all, you had to become a part of it. Standing here with my feet wedged between two spurs of coral rock, watching a sacred kingfisher fly over the water, I thought of that Spanish dancer glowing in the cold ocean night like some unquenchable flame. Eager to see something that wonderful again, I turned toward the shore to get my mask and fins. On the way to my room I heard a terrific splash beyond the reef crest. I swiveled around to look, thinking this was my humpback whale, or a leaping manta ray, but I was too late—all that was visible was a circle of white foam marking the place where the creature had slipped back into the ocean.

Stephen Harrigan's essays have appeared in many major publications, including The Atlantic Monthly, Outside, The New York Times Magazine, *and* Condé Nast Traveler. *His novel,* The Gates of the Alamo, *was a* New York Times *bestseller and Notable Book. He has also written many movies for television, including HBO's award-winning* The Last of His Tribe *and a biographical film for CBS entitled* Beyond the Prairie: The True Story of Laura Ingalls Wilder.

JAMES G. COWAN

✦ ✦ ✦

Rai

The author visits an ancient place,
and an ancient knowledge.

"You're in luck today," the librarian remarked, peering through the doorway into the wide, sunlit street beyond. "There's Mr. Rouse now. I see his vehicle pulling up outside."

Harvey Rouse was a small, wiry sort of man who I judged to be in his late seventies, possibly older. Wearing a bush hat that had been pushed out of shape years ago, he walked in a hurried manner that belied his age. He came toward us along the path, his shirt buttoned almost to the neck, his knobby knees protruding from a pair of faded khaki shorts. He reminded me of a gremlin or a garden gnome. It was hard to believe that he had spent most of his life working among Aborigines in some of the most remote places in the world. His mannerisms were most like those of a staff sergeant or hospital orderly than those of a scholar.

The librarian introduced me to the explorer, and we shook hands. Knowing that Mr. Rouse was the first European since George Grey to step inside a Wandjina cave made him, in my eyes at least, someone special. As an old bushman who had spent many years of his life sitting around campfires learning the Natingin language from the last of the Aboriginal elders, he was in a category all his own. I was keen to know to what extent they had shared their secrets with him.

"Why don't you come to dinner this evening and we can talk," Mr. Rouse said, generously extending the invitation when I explained the reason for my visit to Derby. He agreed to pick me up in his aging Toyota outside the hostel at around six o'clock.

Later that evening Mr. Rouse drove me to his place on the outskirts of town. I soon found myself gazing at the high wire gate guarding the entry to an earth-moving machinery site deep in the scrub. There were no lights in the place. Mr. Rouse unlocked the chain on the gate, then drove his vehicle past the shadowy bulk of front-end loaders toward a group of buildings in the far corner. The atmosphere in the yard was like that of a Roman ruin at night. I felt somewhat uncomfortable, especially when I learned that Mr. Rouse had been forced to live out his twilight years in three old workman's huts that he had managed to scrounge from the Department of Main Roads.

English explorer George Grey is credited with being the first white man to see Wandjina paintings, which he discovered in a rock shelter in the northwestern Kimberley in 1837. His colonialist mind couldn't comprehend that the paintings had been created by the local inhabitants, and it was a century before the source and significance of the art were accepted by Western science.

◆

—LH

"They travel everywhere with me," Mr. Rouse remarked with some pride. "The owner of the worksite offered me the land in return for caretaking duties when I retired. So I brought my huts over here from where I was living. You must think me a regular tortoise, carrying my house around like this!"

"You don't want to live in town?"

"I like the silence out here at night. Derby is too noisy for me. This place keeps me in touch with the bush."

Inside the first hut I was introduced to a world of cobwebs, large mosquitoes, a small table cluttered with food, a bed piled high with clothing, and a fridge. The bulb above our heads threw down a vague light, nothing more. A much-thumbed copy of the Bible lay by the window among assorted manuscripts and old newspapers. I immediately realized that "dinner" was likely to be a couple of cheese sandwiches washed down with a mug of tea. Old bushmen rarely linger over food; tinned beef and damper (bread made in a camp oven from flour mixed with water) form their staple diet when they're on the move.

"Tell me about the time when you found Grey's cave," I began as Mr. Rouse extracted a slab of cheese from a packet.

"During the war, it was," he replied. "I had been working on a mission in east Naringin country for a number of years. An anthropologist friend of mine in Sydney asked me if I might like to look for Grey's cave on his behalf. It was too far for him to come over here, and anyway nobody traveled in those days because of gasoline restrictions. Of course I jumped at the chance. I always wanted to rediscover those lost Wandjina paintings. But I needed a couple of good boys to help me find the cave. In the end I asked the administrator at the mission if he would give me my pick."

Mr. Rouse laughed at the memory.

"He agreed, but on the condition that I cut wood for him for three weeks. That's how I came by my Aboriginal guides. In the end they cost me a load of wood!"

"And a few blisters, I'll bet," I said. "Did they lead you straight to the cave?"

"Not at all. I had only a hand-traced map my friend had sent me. Trying to decipher this was no easy matter. We spent weeks wandering about the country hoping to find what we were looking for. Real rubbish country it was, too. The donkeys were a godsend, though. Horses would never have been able to cross that terrain. Too rough."

"You found the cave in the end, though."

"Yeah. But I tell you it was a spooky place to come upon. In all my life I've never felt so strange entering a cave. The Wandjinas on the wall were like figures from outer space. Here I was, in the presence of a group of beings looking down at me, almost as if they were interrogating me with their gaze. They had huge eyes and no mouths. I felt as if I had stumbled into a sort of living hell, like you see on church walls in Europe sometimes."

"Can you recall what color the figures were?"

"White, mostly. With black eyes surrounded by orange, ocher-colored circles. Their noses were the same color. But what made them appear really odd was a thick orange nimbus, like a horse-shoe, with rays radiating from above their heads."

"Like the ray on the signboard of a public house," I said, recalling Grey's description.

"That's about right," Mr. Rouse agreed.

"Did they have bodies?"

"Sort of, but all that wasn't very clear. They looked vaguely like ghosts, I suppose. The painting was in pretty poor shape, you must understand. The old fellas hadn't been up there to repaint them in years."

"The Aboriginal elders, you mean?"

"Yeah. In the old days, when the tradition was strong, they used to visit the cave each year before the wet season to perform rituals and repaint the Wandjina. According to Woolagoodja, one of my guides, they prayed to them when they wanted rain. That was their way of bringing on the wet season. He was good man, old Woolly. He knew his stuff really well."…

"Perhaps there's someone else in Derby you might recommend I talk to about the Wandjina," I said.

"Well, there's my principal informant on the Naringin language," he suggested. "His name is Waljali. He's what they call a sites officer here in town. Between him and his friend, old Kamurro, I reckon they know about all there is to know on the Wandjina these days. Most of the old blokes have died, you see. And the young ones know nothing. All they're interested in is grog and women, nothing more. Kamurro happens to be a sorcerer, which makes him rather special. He knows a lot about the old ways."

"He's a medicine man?"

"They call them *barnmunji* around here. I wrote a paper on them once. Hold on, let me see if I can find it for you."

Mr. Rouse went to a cabinet by the wall next to his bed and rummaged in one of the drawers. He produced a sheaf of papers at last and handed them to me. The title of the article was "The *Rai* and the Inner Eye."

"You can have it," he said. "I've got no use for it anymore. It could prove interesting to you if you want to know more about Aboriginal ways. Don't know why, though," he added dismissively.

Flipping quickly through the pages, I came across a Naringin text with an English translation written underneath. A few words caught my interest at once: *Wandjina djiri: ru; dambun djuman mana, yadmerinanganari.* Underneath was transcribed: "Wandjina is the important one. We say concerning him that he designed the world."

Later, when Mr. Rouse had dropped me back at the hostel, I wasted no time in beginning his article on the *rai*. It was a remarkable document, unlike any I had come across before on the subject. Not only did it describe the creation of the world to the Wandjina, but it also detailed the making of a *barnmunji* with the help of spirit beings known as the *rai*. It seemed that these *rai* had the power to transform a man into someone capable of seeing through the veil of ordinary reality with the aid of a so-called inner eye—that is, a quality of spiritual perception not available to the conventional run of men.

According to the document, the *rai* are spirit children who live in the bush and wander about at night. Men can encounter them only in their dreams. Furthermore, a *rai* is a sort of "spirit double" of the man, and is therefore capable of telling him how his country is faring when the man happens to be absent from it for some reason. According to the text, the *rai* feeds on its own arm blood and is therefore self-sustaining. The *rai's* main task is to give a *barnmunji* the power of visionary perception so that he can see with his inner eye, aided by the use of *gedji* or quartz crystals. These are pressed into the *barnmunji's* body in a magical fashion. But once the crystals are lodged in his body, he is equipped with supernatural powers that enable him to attend to the sick, perform new corroborees (sacred dances), and travel great distances through the air.

My first impression after reading about the *rai* was to ask myself whether Mr. Rouse had deliberately set out to mislead me. The concept of the *rai* seemed so preposterous that I began to wonder whether the old man had been affected by the sun. Spirit doubles, inserting quartz crystals into the body, vampirelike creatures that fed on their own arm blood, astral travel—these descriptions seemed to draw their inspiration from the shadowy realm of the occult rather than from any bona fide religious experience. Then I recalled the first words of the text: "Wandjini is the important one. He made the world." Such an emphatic statement made me reconsider my initial doubts. I decided to suspend my judgment, at least until after I had discussed these matters with the Aboriginal elders Mr. Rouse had referred me to.

The Mowanjum Aboriginal community outside Derby was my

first stop. Mr. Rouse had advised me to go there and meet with Waljali and Kamurro. He did point out, however, that these men often paid visits to their tribal country, and so might not be at home. Such was the nature of Aboriginal life today, where many tribes found it impossible to live in the bush now that much of their land belonged to pastoralists. The community had been founded for displaced Aborigines who wanted a secure place to bring up their children and be near to medical facilities. The word *mowanjum* meant "settled" or "on firm ground."

I bicycled out to the settlement early one morning. A collection of galvanized-iron shelters and abandoned motor vehicles met my gaze as I rode through the gate. People wandered aimlessly from one shelter to another as they attempted to put some order into an otherwise unvarying day. Hunting and food gathering activities had given way to weekly government pension checks for most of these tribespeople as they struggled to come to terms with their state of exile. I felt a certain sadness watching children roll bicycle rims across a clearing, knowing that in the old days they would have been out in the bush with their kinsmen learning how to hunt.

One of these children soon led me to an encampment lying in the shade of some trees. A number of women were sitting on the ground, their dogs asleep nearby. When I approached and asked where I might find Waljali or Kamuro, they fell silent. They looked at me as if I were only half there. It was the look all oppressed people offer to those whom they believe to be responsible for their plight.

Eventually an older woman in the group pointed rather diffidently to my right. I noticed a solitary figure sitting cross-legged under a tree, his head bent over some object in his lap. At no time did the woman speak. I thanked the ladies and made my way over to the man. He stopped whatever he was doing to observe my approach.

"Are you Waljali, or Kamurro?" I asked.

I estimated the man to be in his late sixties. His features were slender, rather refined in appearance. A loosely clipped beard covered his jaw, and his graying hair was swept back from his forehead to reveal partial baldness. His eyes appraised me as if I were standing some distance away. Though I had approached him in the spirit of friendship, I knew this man was considering his response with some caution, uncertain as to my motives.

"Maybe I'm Kamurro," the man replied, revealing his identity at last. Then he resumed carving a baobab seed pod, a popular pastime among older Aborigines who like to make money from selling their artifacts to tourist shops. Already he had etched in the outlines of a kangaroo hunt across the surface of the nut.

"Is it true that you're a *barnmunji*?" I asked tentatively.

"Who told you about me?" Kamurro's voice was edgy.

"Mr. Rouse. He said you gave him a lot of information about the *rai*."

"That was a long time ago, when things were good 'round here. Now all we do is sit about gettin' drunk."

"But nonetheless the *rai* still exist," I ventured.

"'Course they do," Kamurro replied gruffly, rubbing his fingers over the baobab nut.

"And they give you power to see inside a person," I added.

"Mr. Rouse, he tellin' you too much," Kamurro responded cautiously. Yet I could see my interest in the doctrine of the *rai* had aroused him more than he cared to admit.

"Is it also true that you can fly through the air?" I asked.

Kamurro glanced up at me. I was immediately struck by the change in his manner. The apathy and aggression that had marred his earlier attitude toward me had all but disappeared. Instead a look of grudging complicity had begun to appear on his face.

"I tell you: that missionary fella has been tellin' you too much," he repeated.

Feeling that my presence had been accepted at last, I sat down on the ground opposite Kamurro. Meanwhile the women were watching us from a distance. I could tell they were curious about what was happening because they sent one of their dogs over to investigate. The dog walked up, sniffed my arm, then lay down nearby.

"The women are real busybodies. They want to know what we're talkin' about," Kamurro began with a small smile on his face.

"But what they don't know is this dog understands nothin' about the *rai*. The spirits are too clever for 'im.

"Well, we Aboriginal people aren't much without the help of the *rai*," the old man went on. "They're the spirit people who made us. Without them we wouldn't be in this world."

"Not even as a result of a man and woman making love?" I suggested.

"That's white-man talk. Funny business with woman doesn't account for makin' a child. Your people only see things in one way. Always thinkin' 'bout sex," he added. His remark made me recall with some irony Mr. Rouse accusing Aborigines in much the same way.

Kamurro touched his temple and continued:

"The *rai*, they enter a man in his dream because they comin' from the Wandjina. That what important. They hop into a woman's body only after that happens, and make a baby. A man got to see the *rai* in his dream first. Everythin' goes on in our head, not down here." Kamurro patted his thigh to emphasize his point.

I gathered from Kamurro's explanation that in spite of his insistence on the *rai* being spirit entities that wandered about the bush at night, they were also much more. They appeared to be linked to the Wandjina in a spiritual way that could only be invoked in a dream. Physical paternity was so ingrained in my thought, however, that the idea of a person being dreamed into existence confounded me. Yet Kamurro was insistent that the "funny business" between man and woman was incidental to conception. A person was first conceived by the spirit of the *rai* before undergoing a period of physical growth in a woman's womb.

"If the *rai* are responsible for giving everyone life and making people who they are," I replied, "why is it that there are only very few *barnmunji* like yourself around?"

"Not everyone has the right to become a doctor-man. The *rai*, they give us special powers. These powers don't belong to everyone. The *rai* see you as being important. That's why they make me *barn-munji* and not some other fella," Kamurro explained.

"How do the *rai* enter you, and make you a *barn-munji*?"

"Only when the *gedji* crystals are placed inside you. Them spirit stones belongin' to the *rai*."

"Quartz crystals, you mean?"

"*Gedji*, they come from the *rai*," Kamurro insisted. "They don't come from the ground. To become a *barn-munji* you must have your insides taken out your body and replaced with *gedji*. Then the spirit of the *rai* goin' inside you. Once they're in your body you have power, what we call *kurunba*. You become a doctor-man, an expert. The *rai* make it possible for you to see all things. When you go out hunting, you can see through the bushes and know if a kangaroo is there. You can fly, too, that's right! Doctor-men can fly like birds. They can travel under the ground, too, like a lizard. Below the earth he rumbles along just like a goanna."

"How can you actually fly?" I asked, finding this revelation a little hard to accept.

I looked around, through the lacy filigree of the ghost gum leaves, out across the vast emptiness of the desert, falling away to horizons sheened in a soft dusk light. What to me was a beautiful but featureless flat plain would be, to many Aborigines, an infinitely complex interweaving of invisible songlines and sacred places, each one a vital part of a huge complex whole. Their earth, as they knew it.

Was it just one more way for man to deal with terrible loneliness of being, in a cold, disinterested universe, and particularly on this ancient, worn-down, empty land they now call Australia? The fear of the ultimate unknown—death—that makes us build elaborate fantasies of imaginings to convince ourselves that we are not alone, that we have a purpose, a function, a reason for being? The "walkabout" as the primary purpose of existence? Or was it something more?

♦

—David Yeadon,
Lost Worlds: Exploring the Earth's Remote Places

"That's a secret," Kamurro replied, not wishing to reveal too much to me. "But I tell you, the *rai*, they teach us, all we know. We can find out what's wrong with a fella when he's feeling sick, too. We look into his body and see the disease shinin' like a light. The healthy parts don't shine like the sick parts. Then we know what's wrong with a fella. The *rai*, they show us how to look inside his body. So for the *rai* to teach us how to fly isn't such a big thing."

"Are you ever called upon to cure people much these days?"

Kamurro glanced down at his baobab nut, as if embarrassed by my question.

"My people don't trust us doctor-men anymore," he said. "They go to white-men doctors in town and get pills. They like to sit in hospital beds and have nurses running around lookin' after them. My people like to have a white fella listen to their insides with something on his ears. A stethoscope, you blokes call it. They don't believe my inner eye can see what's wrong like they did in the old days. Much better than them white doctor-men with their shiny metal ears, anyway."

"Yet in spite of this your people still believe in the *rai*. Even though they go to white doctors, they haven't forgotten the old ways completely," I countered.

"They know they only born because of the *rai*, what's why. We teach them this when they're children. But that doesn't mean they want to listen to what I've got to say anymore."

Kamurro's dilemma was obvious. Not only did he find himself living on the fringe of white settlement, but it appeared that his skills as a *barnmunji* had been undermined by modern medical practice as a result. Sorcery and magic were no longer acceptable among his people now that they had become mendicants of the state. The old ways were considered to be inferior, little more that the remnants of their wild bush life, which for many Aborigines had become only a memory. To many of them, particularly the younger ones, Kamurro was an argumentative old man, out of touch with modern life.

"My people don't want to believe in my doctor ways because that would mean helpin' themselves. White medicine takes this away from us. It takes away our power," Kamurro added.

"You mean, white medicine and pension checks have stopped your people believing in the old ways," I said.

Kamurro barely nodded.

"*Rai*, they don't like people who don't believe in them. When they die, our people die," he added, a hint of bewilderment in his voice. It was clear that what might happen to his people once they ceased to believe in their culture had only just begun to dawn on him.

I was deeply touched by Kamurro's explanation of his people's logic that transcended any arguments that I might wish to put forth in reply. Here was a man who had seen his culture all but decimated by European settlement in the past 100 years. The power to see with X-ray eyes, to fly through the air like a bird, or walk underground like a lizard—these things were in danger of disappearing from the world forever. I had the impression that Kamurro felt that his culture and beliefs had been irretrievably damaged by the aggressive and often thoughtless ways of white men. Furthermore, the old men like himself were powerless to do anything about it....

"You be careful," he said to me as I climbed onto my bicycle.

"What of?" I asked.

"The *rai,* they got to like you first. Otherwise you be in trouble. They can trip you up pretty quick."

"Thanks for the advice, Kamurro. I'll keep my eyes open," I called as I rode away from the old Aboriginal sorcerer.

Kamurro, meanwhile, picked up his baobab pod and began carving again as if nothing had happened. Clearly the hunting scene he was carving on its surface reminded him of a time when men really did move about with the aid of spirits.

James G. Cowan is an author and poet who has spent much of his life exploring the world of traditional peoples such as the Berbers of Morocco, the

Tuareg of the Central Sahara, and the Australian Aborigines. He spent a decade living and traveling in Europe and North America, and then returned to Australia, where he embarked on a series of books and explored the agricultural peoples of early Australia. This story was excerpted from his book, Messengers of the Gods: Tribal Elders Reveal the Ancient Wisdom of the Earth.

JAN MORRIS

Sydney Reflections

*A renowned writer takes a close look
at the cultural history of Australia's
best known city.*

FOR MOST PEOPLE IN THE WORLD THE LOOK OF SYDNEY IS THE
grand-slam look, the whole hog, flag-and-fireworks look. This can
certainly be magnificent. Little in contemporary travel beats flying
down the coast from Newcastle on a fine spring day, following the
line of the northern ocean beaches and abruptly turning westward
at the Sydney Heads to make the home run down the harbour. It
makes you feel majestic even in an elderly, shuddering seaplane. It
gives you a triumphant feel, as though there ought to be incidental music in the air, preferably "Waltzing Matilda."

The Heads fall away below you, bashed by their Pacific waves,
the Middle Harbour runs off to the north, and then there are
wide red-roofed suburbs below, splodged with green wooded
protrusions, with the gleam of innumerable swimming pools, and
glorious splashes of flame trees and jacarandas. A couple of small
islands slide beneath your wings. The harbour is streaked with the
wakes of ships, freighters off to sea, hydrofoils rushing to and from
the city, and here and there stand fine white villas on desirable
sites. There goes Bradley's Head, with the *Sydney*'s fighting-top,
and there is the little island citadel of Pinchgut, and then—*tara!
tara!*—the heart of Sydney splendidly greets us, the great old arch

97

of the bridge, the splayed shells of the Opera House, the stunning green of the Domain, the skyscrapers of the city centre all flash and swank. Beyond it, as in diminuendo, the suburbs fade away dingy around the maundering Parramatta River, and beyond them again is the grey-blue ridge of the mountains, that ne plus ultra to the early settlers. Few cities on earth can offer so operatic an approach.

On the ground the purlieus of Sydney offer some histrionic vistas, too. Sometimes you can see nothing of the distant city but the arch of the Harbour Bridge, mysteriously protruding above thick woods. Sometimes you can so arrange your line of sight that the downtown structures are framed in green ridges, like a city among country hills. There are places on the harbour's north shore where the size and power of Sydney, ranged along its waterfront, is hallucinatorily exaggerated by sunshine and reflection, and on a very hot day from far to the south, from the brackish beaches of Botany Bay, the skyscrapers on the horizon shimmer like a towering mirage. Although the colours of Sydney are seldom gaudy, in the tropical kind, but more often hazed and muted, this is a city born for show, with a façade of brilliance, and a gift for exhibitionism.

Somebody once lent me five video cassettes of the bicentennial celebrations in 1988, which were the most spectacular of all the city's spectacular occasions. I played them at high speed, fast forward, and never was there such an exhilarating succession of images: yachts and symphony orchestras and flags and dancing Aborigines—airships, firefloats spouting, princes arriving, bands playing—vast cheering crowds, curtseys, soldiers saluting, gabbled speeches—now a wide shining shot of the harbour, now the Opera House from the air—gun salutes I think, helicopters certainly, flowers, children singing, and as the day rapidly changed to night before my eyes, a violent eruption of rockets into the sky, and a pyrotechnical waterfall over the lip of the bridge.

Speeding it up in this way seemed perfectly proper to me— aesthetically Sydney is made for the instant exciting impact, not five full cassettes of contemplation—but I slowed the tape down in the end when, as the city broke into a last tremendous blaze of rejoicing light, they really did play "Waltzing Matilda."

It is a nice paradox that Sydney, a city born in misery, should be blessed with a true gift for self-consolation. In 1850 Charles Dilke was already commenting upon its high capacity for personal pleasure, and it long ago developed a very different communal ethic from that of the more religion-bound and work-obsessed cities of North America. Nowadays the arrival of Friday *arvo* is a Sydney institution—the sanctioned moment when, at noon on the fifth day, much of the populace subsides into hedonism; but no matter what day of the week it is, or what time of the day either, more than most cities Sydney seems to enjoy itself.

There were few Puritans, of course, on Australia's First Fleet, and a general lack of religious zealotry or remorse has undoubtedly helped to foster the Sydney euphoria. It could never be said that religion is the opiate of the Sydney masses—I know of no city where it seems less

I learned "Waltzing Matilda" in the second grade. I was never sure what it meant, but once you translate it, the song turns out to be more violent than the average second-grade curriculum usually permits:

"Once a jolly swagman camped by a billabong…" (Once a drifter was camped by a small pond in the Outback.)

"…under the shade of a coolabah tree…" (A coolabah is a eucalyptus, home of the koala.)

"…Down came a jumbuck to drink at the billabong…" (A jumbuck is a sheep.)

"…Up jumped the swagman and grabbed him with glee, and he sang as he shoved that jumbuck in his tucker bag…" (A tucker bag is where a swagman keeps his food.)

"…You'll come a-waltzing Matilda with me…" (Lonely, celebrating the kill of the sheep, the swagman dances off into the night with "Matilda," the generic female name he has given his tucker bag.)

◆

—Daniel Burstein, "The Language of Oz," *Travel Holiday*

obtrusive. A century ago it was recorded that orthodox Christianity had little hold on the local mind, "neither belonging to the country nor yet adapted to its peculiar requirements": the 1986 census showed that apart from the faiths of immigrants the fastest-growing denomination was the one classified as No Religion. The Baha'i Temple stands proudly enough among the woodlands of the north, Greenway's St. James's church is prominent, the Great Synagogue is resplendent, St. Mary's Cathedral is vast, but on the whole places of religion play an unusually minor part in the city's aesthetic ensemble.

For some years they played no part at all. An outdoor Anglican service was conducted on the first Sunday after the landing at Sydney Cove, the text of Chaplain Johnson's sermon being taken from the Psalm 161—"What shall I render unto the Lord for all his benefits towards me?" No church went up, however, for another five years, until Johnson had one built at his own expense on the spot (in Johnson Place) now marked by a memorial. Its convict congregationalists were flogged if they failed to attend without good cause: wondering perhaps what they could best render unto the Lord for his mercies, they habitually spat, coughed and hiccuped throughout the services, and it was almost certainly some of them who burnt the building down in 1798. A second church was soon built—the one that looked like a prison—but in 1826 Barron Field was still complaining that Sydney was "a spire-less city, and profane." The first three Catholic priests, allowed into the colony at the start of the nineteenth century, were soon expelled on the grounds that they were inciting rebellion; the fourth arrived illicitly in 1817, began his underground pastorate under the protection of brave Mr. Davis, and was thrown out in 1818. It appears to have been only in the middle of the nineteenth century that religion assumed the social role it played in most English-speaking cities around the world, and even then it was largely an instrument of class—English Anglicans on one side, Irish Catholics on the other. Today it is administered by a Catholic cardinal, and Anglican archbishop, and countless ministers, rabbis and mullahs; yet it seems to me, as an agnostic outsider, relatively muted still.

Like any great English-speaking city, Sydney has its quota of cults and enthusiasms, encouraged here perhaps by the quasi-Californian climate, but it has never been a great place for revival movements or sectarian bitterness. There was however one famous example of religious ecstasy in Sydney, and its improbable focus was on the beach promenade in the suburb of Balmoral, on the Middle Harbour. This is now a very model of suburban contentment. It has a little white pavilion, a bathhouse and a rotunda for a band. An ornamental bridge leads to a public garden on a spit, and there a club of local friends meets every day of the year to have breakfast as the sun goes up. This modest esplanade was to acquire unexpected prominence when the mystical Theosophical Society declared it a site of profound sacred significance. The Theosophists were convinced that a World Teacher would soon be coming to rescue mankind from its ignorance, and some of their seers also believed in the existence of the lost continent, Lemuria, which lay beneath the Pacific and would eventually give up its ancient secrets for the salvation of mankind. After the First World War they determined that Sydney was central to these truths. It was, they said, "the occult centre of the Southern Hemisphere." They acquired a large, many-gabled mansion at Mosman on the northern shore, and Theosophist pilgrims came there from all over the world—including the young Indian, Jiddu Krishnamurti, whom some of them believed to be the World Teacher in gestation. They established a school and a radio station, 2GB. They arranged publicity in the press. They attracted influential sympathizers, including Walter Burley Griffin up the road at Castlecrag. By the 1920s their Lodge in Sydney was said to hold 2,500 people in twenty-six tiers of seats, and it looked magnificently across the harbour, through the Heads and out to sea. Here was a place of Coming, it was said, where the World Teacher would reveal all when the time was ripe; and through those mighty bluffs would flow the knowledge of Lemuria.

The conviction faded when, in 1929, Krishnamurti publicly declared that he was not the promised Teacher, and in 1939 the site of the Coming was sold—an apartment block stands on the

site now. Today it is hard to find signs of religious fervour in
Sydney. I once saw a shirtless boy march into St. Andrew's
Cathedral and fall in passionate prayer before the altar, but it
seemed forlornly out of character. I went to a lying-in of a much-
venerated Irish Catholic priest, expecting to find scenes of histrionic distress, but the mourners were restrained, tearless and
altogether devoid of black veils. A group of charismatic Christians
recently fed their conceptions of Jesus into the Sydney Police
Crime Unit's Image Generator—its Identikit. He looked like a
cross between the Bondi lifesaver and a small-time crook, with
short hair back and sides.

Spiritually the most rewarding place in Sydney seems to me
Rookwood Cemetery, which is one of the largest in the world,
and includes graves of every denomination. It was founded in
1867, and by the end of the century was the very latest thing in
cemeteries, eventually embracing 777 acres of land (well away
from settled areas, we read, "so that adjoining land would not be
devalued"). It had its own railway stations, and twice a day trains
from Sydney stopped at stations en route to pick up "corpses,
mourners or clergymen," the mourners and clergymen having to
buy tickets but the corpses travelling free. It was splendidly landscaped, with gazebos and canals, and was famous for its flower
beds—a green rose used habitually to blossom there. A park ranger
lived in a lodge with a tower, wore a peaked cap with RANGER on
it, and carried a revolver for the extermination of stray dogs and
goats. People of all sorts were buried in this ideal necropolis. The
very first was an eighteen-year-old Irish pauper, and among those
who followed him were politicians, artists, bushrangers, entertain-
ers and tycoons.

The trains stopped in 1948. The showplaces fell into decay, and
today Rookwood is a more realistic allegory of the natural condition. In its centre it is still well-kept, and the adherents of many
creeds lie there in trim oblivion—disciples of Shintoism, or
Assyrian Catholicism, or the Salvation Army, or Hinduism, or
Judaism, or Islam—Greeks and Latvians and Hungarians and

Assyrians and Italians—all in their own clearly demarcated and appropriately scripted plots. Joggers and cyclists pass among them here, and there are people tidying up graves, or laying fresh flowers, but as you wander away from the heart of the place an organic decay sets in. Obelisks become more tottery, gravestones are cracked, iron balustrades stand bent and rusted, until finally the great place of death is regenerated at its edges into life. The remotest parts of Rookwood are pure bushland, and there snakes, frogs, tortoises, ginks and geckos flourish, hares and foxes hide, figbirds and honey-eaters flutter vivaciously among the gums.

Secular consolations have been more boisterously pursued. Sex in Sydney, for example, began with a bang on the night of 6 February 1788, when the female convicts were disembarked to join the males already ashore at Sydney Cove. No doubt in the fortnight since the raising of the flag the married officers and wives had comforted each other in their beds, and perhaps a few people of initiative had already found comfort among the Aborigines. For the mass of the convict population, though, the barriers were lowered when the women at last came down the gangplanks on to Australian soil. It was a rough night. Violent winds and rain swept the settlement, lightning streaked across the harbour, but the moment the women stepped ashore the penal community threw itself into orgy. After eight months at sea, cooped up in sexual segregation and cruel confinement, both men and women were ready for it. The officials and marines were unable to control them—perhaps they did not even try—and the diarists seem to stand back aghast, as they view the commotion beside the Tank Stream. Tench preferred not to mention it at all. Arthur Bowes Smith, surgeon on one of the transports, said it was beyond his abilities to give a just description of the scene. We can only imagine it, reading between the lines and remembering human nature: around the soggy tents and shacks of Sydney Cove that night, watched from a cautious distance by officialdom and the less impetuous of the felons, several hundred couples writhing and twisting in the mud, while oaths, drunken songs, laughs, groans and the clankings of irons compete with the thunder.

It is a scene not at all appropriate to Sydney. This is not a very orgiastic city. In modern times the relationship between men and women here has traditionally been self-conscious, while homosexuality, though prevalent among the convicts and common now, has only recently become socially acceptable. It is true that the history books are full of licentious suggestion: "detestable vices" that could be satisfied in the Sydney of the 1790s, "scenes of immorality beyond description" in the Domain of the 1860s. However when in 1838 rumour said that Richard Davies was "doing something improper with a pig," his neighbour Mrs. Holland retorted indignantly that he was "not a man of that description," and most Sydney males today are not of that description either.

Wowserism has never been as powerful here as in Melbourne— its name, indeed, was invented by a Sydney man of permissive instinct, John Norton, the editor of *Truth*. Still, the city has had its share of killjoys, and anyway the general delight in the sun, the sea and the sand has perhaps kept libidos in restraint. I recently analyzed a column of twenty Strictly Personal advertisements in one of the suburban newspapers, and found that twelve of those seeking soul-mates required a commitment to sailing, bush-walking, surfing or simply the beach: the Cultured Lady, 49, who admitted that she was chiefly fond of anything fattening, expensive or sedentary seemed to me to be casting her bread upon unpromising waters. When the magazine *Tracks* asked its readers which was better, surfing or sex, 62 percent said surfing, but then 51 percent said they thought about surfing during sex.

It says something about the survival of innocence in Sydney that its people are so touchingly proud of Kings Cross. Originally called Queens Cross, in honour of Queen Victoria's Diamond Jubilee, the suburb was renamed when Edward VII came to the throne, and it used to be the centre of bohemia in Sydney, the one cosmopolitan part of town before the New Australians arrived. It was given a sleazy reputation by the American servicemen who flocked there during the Second World War, and later during the Vietnam War, and at night nowadays it suggests a red-light quarter in some kind of sociological exhibition, so compactly assembled are its strip shows, its pornographic bookstores and its upstairs massage parlours. The necessary hard-looking, unshaven men hang around the Alamein fountain, a whirling floodlit device like a dandelion head. The essential emaciated prostitutes parade the shadowy sidewalks of Victoria Street. There is the statutory scattering of drug addicts, transvestites, tourists, drunks, sailors and miscellaneous layabouts from around the world. You would have to be very unworldly to be surprised by the all-too-familiar sights of Kings Cross; yet Sydneysiders habitually recommend it to foreigners as a prime metropolitan spectacle, not on any account to be missed.

Anyway, if you go back to the Cross in the morning you will find it charmingly villagelike. The GIRLS! GIRLS! GIRLS! signs are out, the adult movie houses are closed, those jowly men are still in bed, and now you find flower shops and grocery stalls, pleasant houses in back streets, one of the best bookshops in Sydney and some of the most agreeable coffee shops. Along Victoria Street, now revealed as a delightful leafy thoroughfare, dropouts and addicts of the night before sit demurely beside the blistered Volkswagen campers they are trying to sell, before going home to be chartered accountants.

Far more than sex, the delight and the despair of Sydney has been strong drink. Hardly a passage of this city's history is without a reference to it, from the very earliest days when convicts always seemed to be able to get hold of it, to the fearful drunken-driving records of today. So far as I can discover the Australian Aborigines, almost alone among the peoples of the earth, never learnt to make fermented drinks—or perhaps never needed to, their elaborate otherworld of dreams, song and legend being quite intoxicating enough. Hardly had the British arrived, however, than alcohol became an essential adjunct to life, and rum, a generic name for hard spirits of all kinds, assumed the importance of money itself. Goods were bought in it. Labourers got their wages in it. Chaplain Johnson paid for his church in it. The rebellion against Bligh was named after it. The 44th Regiment mutinied for it. The New South Wales Corps, its officers having acquired their monopoly in it, became known as the Rum Corps, and for years the Sydney general hospital, which was largely financed by it, was called the Rum Hospital.

The original rum was all imported, from England or from India, but the settlers were soon making their own, together with wines, beer and more peculiar liquors. A spirit made of fermented sugar bags soaked in buckets of water proved popular among the Aborigines. The leaves of the Sticky Hop-bush, chewed by the Iora as a cure for toothache, were adopted by the Europeans to flavour their ale. A beer sampled at the Parramatta fair in 1824 was said to be so strong that "reason was de-throned and madness and folly reigned in its stead," while an early settler of the North Shore, experimenting with fermented peaches, reported that "one glas put parson in the whelebarrow."

In the nineteenth century there was a proliferation of pubs (called hotels in the city to this day). They were socially impor-tant in the early years because so many men were without fami-lies or decent homes, and later they became nests of mateship, being generally out of bounds to respectable women. With their quaint inn signs and particular reputations, the taverns greatly en-hanced Sydney's sense of picturesque antiquity, and they often had piquant names: the Help Me Through the World, the World Turned Upside-Down, or the Keep Within the Compass (kept by a former policeman). Sometimes they had resident fiddlers, often they were frequented by gambling schools and haunted by whores, and they came in many specialties. There were pubs where soldiers were not welcome, and pubs where convicts were not liked, and snug pubs that catered to the country trade, and rough pubs pop-ular among the boxing fraternity. The massed taverns and sly-grog houses of The Rocks were so uproarious in their heyday that their cumulative noise could be heard miles out to sea. The bar rail of the Shakespeare Tavern, in the 1880s, had an electric wire running through it, enabling its puckish landlord to galvanize his customers. The Marble Bar at Adams' Hotel was a prodigy of coloured marble from France, Italy and Belgium, supplemented by American walnut panelling, chandeliers, stained glass and lubricious wall paintings.

The pubs were open from six in the morning until eleven at night, and of course there were objectors to all this jollity. Temperance movements waxed and waned in Sydney—as early as 1837 the Quaker merchant John Tawell, whom we have met before, ostentatiously poured a large quantity of spirits into the harbour. The real blow to the city's drinking habits, however, did not occur until 1916, when there was a mutiny among the troops at a training camp in the western suburb of Casula. Objecting to a new and demanding training programme, several thousand soldiers raided the camp liquor stores, looted some pubs of their drink, and set off on a dishevelled progress across the city, smashing windows, breaking up food stalls, seizing cars and wagons, attacking clubs and stores and terrifying civilians wherever they went. There was no denying that drink was the cause of this rampage, and so there came into force one of Sydney's most depressing institutions, "the six o'clock swill." For nearly forty years every legal pub in the city shut its doors at six in the evening, leading not only to a plethora of speakeasies, but also to a headlong consumption of liquor in the last moments before closing time, when people came out from work. The Sydney pubs acquired a new reputation for lavatorial crudity and were mostly redecorated accordingly, with tiled walls for the easier cleansing of spilt beer and vomit. Everything most philistine, provincial and misogynist about Sydney was epitomized in the six o'clock swill: at the end of each working day (as citizens of vivid memory have described it for me) a tide of inebriated men came rolling out of their ghastly taverns, staggering into railway stations, barging onto buses or being sick over ferry rails.

The rule was mercifully abandoned in 1955. Nowadays the

pubs have mostly softened their ambiences, and welcome women with more or less good grace. Although beer and Sydney still go together in the world's mind, the per capita consumption of alcohol has lately declined, perhaps because of the new proportion of abstemious Italians, Greeks and Asians. Despite the neighbourhood problems of that former premier a couple of chapters back, for the most part public drinking in Sydney is temperate enough—even rather apathetic. I looked at one pub across a suburban street on a summery Friday, and this is what I saw: upstairs, in a window with a wilted potted plant in it, and a faded awning outside, an elderly, shirt-sleeved man with spectacles, all alone with a pint of beer; downstairs, through the open door of one bar, four slump-stomached workmen over the tankards at the counter, through the open door of another, two women watching an American chat-show on television. The general decorative impression was of a faded yellow. The television flickered dimly. A chalked blackboard offered Beef-and-Mushroom Pie or Chops with Mushroom Sauce. Catching sight of me scribbling these notes across the road, the man upstairs allowed his gaze to rest upon me for a moment or two, but soon lost interest.

On the other hand, Friday evening down on The Rocks, traditionally the quarter of chaos, can still be sufficiently rumbustious. Then the young people come into town from the outer suburbs, determined to live metropolitan life to the full, and the mounted police regularly move in to keep things in check. I was at a reception one evening at the Regent Hotel, the most luxurious in Sydney, which was a paragon of discreet conservative elegance. The older people were dressed expensively but not gaudily, the younger ones were in properly tempered derivations of street fashion. The music was provided, as is habitual at the Regent, by an elegant flute-and-piano duo. The refreshments were suave. Needing a breath of fresh air, I took a couple of sandwiches and wandered through the foyer into the street outside; and there, not a hundred yards away, in the shadow of the expressway, I found saturnalia in full swing. A couple of dozen young people, reconditely dressed and impossibly drunk, were singing obscene songs in the half light. There were beer cans in their hands, beer cans lined up for future consumption, empty beer cans rolling over the sidewalk. A youth in a wild and scraggly beard played the guitar. Three or four girls danced an abandoned go-go on a ledge. The men were husky and flushed, the women looked half-crazed, and they were all singing, shouting, waving their arms about, sloshing their beer and sometimes breaking into hilarious dizzy dances, like people in a dream.

I was rather sorry to leave this Bosch-like gathering and return to the reception in the hotel, where a waitress instantly offered me a small shrimp canapé, and the flautist was into a Telemann sonata, I think.

Except for that brief grim period in the 1780s, almost nobody has gone hungry in Sydney. The Iora were always capably self-sufficient, the convicts were quite well fed. Perhaps it was this tradition of general plenty that made the city for so long indifferent to cuisine. Even twenty years ago the food, whether private or public, was a desperate approximation of English provincial cooking, its one famous dish being the Pie Floater—a meat pie floating in pea soup which has been sold since 1945 at the Woolloomooloo food stall called Harry's Café de Wheels. Fish generally turned out to be fish and chips in the old greasy style, few Sydneysiders were keen on oysters and the cooking of kangaroos was illegal....

By now food has become almost a national symbol itself, and is certainly one of the prime Sydney consolations. The influx of foreign restaurateurs has changed everything—starting with the tea, now generally metamorphosed into espresso coffee. The restaurants have burgeoned sidewalk tables at last, besides climbing several hundred feet up the Sydney Tower and spreading themselves all around the harbour front. I can think of no national cuisine which is not represented somewhere in the city nowadays, and at private tables the food may be anything from roast beef to couscous. For a time the nouvelle cuisine in its silliest forms seduced fashionable Sydney, and everything was stuffed with artichokes or grilled over herb-scented charcoal. Today the fad is over, and the best of the restaurants have come to realize that the true Sydney specialty should surely be fresh fish and shellfish, simply served. At Watson's Bay, on the harbour, the Doyle family restaurant has been preaching this gospel for several generations; now it has been joined by dozens of others, to be dropped in at while waiting for a ferry at Circular Quay, or flown to by seaplane on the Hawkesbury River, and serving Moreton Bay Bugs, Mud-Crab Salad, Sydney Rock Oysters and all manner of fish washed down with good New South Wales wine beside lovely watery prospects.

It is sadly true, however, that to many foreign palates even the freshest and most straightforward Sydney food, even the juiciest Bug or most perfectly steamed Hawkesbury River Teraglin, seems disappointingly flavourless. It is glorious in the idea, enticing in the appearance, but it tastes as though it has been cooked in unsalted water—or in the case of the seafish, caught in unsalted oceans. Only the Sydney Rock Oyster, surely the best in the world, lives up to its promise. I am sorry to say this, because I first learnt the pleasure of gourmandcy in Sydney, thirty years ago. Until then I had been as indifferent to the subtleties of food as any six o'clock swiller, but I was given lunch one day by a friend in his apartment on the south shore, with a glorious view up the harbour to the city. The food was nothing elaborate—a crusty roll, as I remember, some pâté and salad, perhaps a cheese, a glass of white wine—but my host served it all with such sensuous grace, broke the bread with such crispy decision, drank the wine with such an almost lascivious slurp, that suddenly in Sydney I realized what a transcendental delight eating and drinking could be.

For years I remembered every detail of this seminal occasion—the food itself, my stalwart epicurean host, the blue Australian sky above and, crowning it all like a benediction upon the experience, the soaring white wings of the Opera House. Only quite recently did it dawn upon me that the Opera House hadn't been built yet.

Jan Morris has been wandering the world and writing about her experiences for more than fifty years. She is the author of numerous books and her essays on travel are among the classics of the genre. She lives in Wales, where she is helping to found a Welsh-language newspaper, Y Byd—The World. *This story was excerpted from her book,* Sydney.

PART TWO

SOME THINGS TO DO

CHRISTINA BOUFIS

On the Bus

*A tour of the Outback was
just the tonic she needed.*

WHEN MY HUSBAND DECIDED TO END OUR MARRIAGE, HE LEFT A
note. This was not all that uncommon I later found out; many husbands leave many wives with notes. When my cousin complained
to her spouse that their new house didn't have enough closet
space, he complied in a way she hadn't expected. She and her tod-
dler came home one day to find a single sentence scrawled by
what she assumed could only be some crazed burglar: "Boy, do you
have closet space!" was all it said.

My ex-husband's timing and behavior were equally unbelievable; we had lived together for ten years, six of them I thought
happily married, and the day I finished my dissertation was the
day he decided to leave, unannounced. "Too much of a feminist,"
he later told his (our) friends by way of explanation. What does
an academic feminist do after spending months crying in therapy
(and everywhere else), shocked, angry, and confused, yet yearning
only—in a very unfeministlike way—to be like the plastic couple
on the top tier of the wedding cake, frozen forever in smiling cou-
plehood?

I didn't know exactly, but in keeping with my newly formed
belief that people and life were the reverse of what they seemed, I

decided to visit a friend in Australia, a place where things are notorious for being upside-down. For a Victorian scholar, this trip also held a certain ironic appeal, for if you were a single woman living in nineteenth-century England and didn't have much money or family connections, Australia was the place you went to find a husband. Once there, it was believed, "redundant" women could find husbands, or at least live happy lives as domestic servants. These émigrés (at least in Victorian fiction) were mostly "fallen women" (those who had sex outside of marriage) or "distressed" (starving) needlewomen: both categories, I was certain, also applied to me. I wasn't a fallen woman exactly, but I felt like one. I had stumbled somewhere over my ideals about men and women and relationships. And like my nineteenth-century predecessor sisters, I thought a journey to the Southern Hemisphere might help fix what was broken. After first meeting my best friend in Sydney, I decided to explore the Outback in New South Wales, that part of the country that has probably changed the least in the last 150 years.

No one seems to agree on exactly where the Outback begins or ends or what it comprises. Basically, it is the huge interior of the country stretching over one million square miles from the cities along the coast. This is Aborigine territory, bush territory, where the nomadic kangaroos and emus outnumber the people, and where the dust of the road penetrates your face, your lungs, your clothes. There are signs warning travelers that there are no commodities for miles—no water, no gasoline, no services.

With this in mind, I booked a tour: Ando's Outback Adventure. Led by John Anderson himself, the tour promised "the real Australia all wrapped up in 7 days." The package also included panning for gold, fossicking for opals and sapphires, stays at remote sheep stations, "plus many strange attractions." This all came true, and the strange attractions were the things that weren't on any map, the things I least expected to find. This, I suppose, is what traveling is all about; it's the serendipitous finding of what you're not looking for, like love when you least expect it.

Ando himself had a Zenlike way of turning our attention to the journey as it was happening instead of always looking forward to the next destination. Responding to my frequent questions about where we were (there were few signs in the Outback), Ando would only reply that we were on the bus, which was perhaps all that we needed to know.

There were nineteen of us on a crowded bus, from Australia, France, Holland, America, Taiwan, and Guam. And we became close in the hothouse way you do when you travel together for six hours or more every day and none of you has showered for quite some time. We also came to depend on each other pretty quickly: there were few amenities in the Outback and even fewer places to find supplies (you're encouraged to carry your own gasoline) but we automatically shared food and water like the sole surviving members of a large extended family. There were other ways that traveling in a group fostered a sense of community that was different from anything I'd experienced before: you would think that traveling for miles and miles and seeing only the same red earth and dry grasses in various shades of brown might become monotonous, but it never was; for suddenly someone would point out a kangaroo or break into song, and arid landscape I had thought I had been so singularly viewing would look different.

What D.H. Lawrence wrote of Sydney—that it was "like London, but it isn't"—could be said less sarcastically about the Outback. It's like the American West, but it isn't. It's not only the kangaroos, which move incredibly fast (up to seventy-five kilometers an hour) when they're not staring at you, it's more a feeling you get from the people you meet there: they approach life with an ironic sense of humor that seems so distinctive it almost constitutes a national character. If you have red hair, for instance, the Australians will call you Blue, just to be perverse.

Maybe it's because life in the bush is inescapably hard (it rains only a few inches per year) that necessitates some kind of comic release. Because there is no physical escape from the extremes of cold and hot, the dryness of the cracked, dusty red earth, and the feeling you get that the land just doesn't want you there. It is telling that one of the most common ways people greet you is to ask how you're battlin'.

The other way people greet you is to ask what you reckon. This inquiry took me aback at first because I wasn't sure what it was I should be reckoning. But the question asks you to assess what's important and decide what you need, a directness that I found strangely comforting once I got used to it. And out in the bush it's important to distinguish the things you absolutely need, like drinking water or a good lover (according to some), from the things you don't, like showers.

The other half of reckoning correctly is to be able to distinguish the reality from what are often misleading appearances. This made sense especially to me as an American visiting a land where things are notorious for being the reverse of life elsewhere. To those in the Northern Hemisphere, Australia has always been the place where things are upside-down: the water runs down the facet in a clockwise direction; it is cold and wintry in mid-August when it is hot and steamy back home; the night sky is dominated not by the customary lights of the Big Dipper, but by the unfamiliar stars of the Southern Cross; and the swans are jet black, not white. Victorian novelist Charles Reade, having never set foot Down Under him-self, captures the sense of otherness that Australia evoked and still often evokes in the popular imagination. "Nothing is what it sets

---

I have never uncovered anywhere the same bonds of friendship as I found in certain small sections of Australian society. It has something to do with the old code of mateship and something to do with the fact that people have time to care for one another, and something to do with the fact that dissidents have had to stick together, and something to do with the fact that competition and achievement are not very important aspects of the culture, and something to do with a generosity of spirit that can afford to grow within that unique sense of traditionless space and potential. Whatever it is, it is extraordinarily valuable.

◆

—Robyn Davidson, *Tracks*

up for here," he writes in his 1856 best seller, *It's Never Too Late to Mend*, "everything pretends to be some old friend or other of mine, and turns out a stranger. Here is nothing but surprises and deceptions. The flowers make a point of not smelling, and the bushes that nobody expects to smell...they smell lovely," (sentiments which aptly captured my feelings about the way my marriage and ex-spouse turned out as well).

To Australians these are not oddities, but the way things are. Yet even Aussies, particularly those living in the bush, are wary of trusting too much to their senses. One Aboriginal legend, for example, (which still holds sway in the Outback) tells of a strange light that appears in the middle of the bush. Called devil's star, bushman's lamp, or more commonly by its Aboriginal sobriquet, *min min,* this yellow light glows brightly and invitingly to weary travelers. But if you try to approach it, according to those who've seen it, it never gets any closer. In fact, it moves as you do. Bushmen have gone miles out of their way or gotten hopelessly lost following the false promise of comfort from the *min min* light. How much like what I expected from marriage, I thought, and how like the *min min* light mine had turned out to be.

We didn't see any *min min* lights on our trip, but one of our "strange attractions" included an unscheduled visit to an elder hostel in Coonabarabran—an Aboriginal word that means inquisitive person in one tribal dialect and wild dog eating in another. Obsessed as I have been with marriage, I asked the elders mostly about their mates and about the hardships of life together in the Outback. One man, who was quite eager to talk, but very hard of hearing, responded to my question about marriage that he'd never been to America, an answer that struck me as somehow appropriate. Another told me her secret to a long life was her walkabouts in the Warrumbungle Mountains, a place she had roamed so often her boyfriend even named a peak after her. Her advice to my promptings on relationships was, "Just enjoy the trip," she kept repeating, "because you never know where you're going to end up."

Close to the intersection of Potch and Gem streets in the town of Lightning Ridge, we unexpectedly ran into Ando's first wife.

She was out on her morning jog. Curious about ex-spouses in general and about the first Mrs. Ando in particular (I could not imagine having such an itinerant husband) I waited to see what Ando would do, but he just waved and smiled and we kept going. Lightning Ridge is an opal-mining town of about 1,000 inhabitants, mostly miners who come from all over the world to dig through the slate that produces the world's only supply of rare black opals. Mining for opals is not physically that demanding, but requires a mental tenacity that is different from mining for gold or sapphires. It is genuinely difficult to find opal, in part because one most often finds much more potch along the way than gems. Potch looks like opal—it's grey and incandescent—but there's no real color to it. Yet finding "potch" is a good sign because it usually means that a seam of opal may be nearby.

But one can mine for months or years and not hit any opal. Stories abound of how a miner, fed up with working in one shaft, gave up, only to have another miner find a million dollars' worth of opal in the next pick of the ax. And like the close resemblance between potch and opal, it is also hard to distinguish, in any material way, those miners who have become millionaires from those who haven't. Everyone in the small mining community of Glengarry lives in corrugated iron houses, and no one, not even those who have become rich, has indoor plumbing.

Opal mining, I was pleased to find, can also be an egalitarian occupation. Both men and women could and did work the mines, sometimes together, sometimes alone. One older couple in Glengarry living in their self-described "Rocky Paradise," fondly recalled the years they spent mining together in the shaft. These years, she told me, were the best in her married life, because, she explained, "Down there, there's no competition between husband and wife. Down there you both work and hope for the same thing."

I never made it to the sapphire mines that we were scheduled to visit on the last two days of the trip, for Ando received word that his second wife had had a heart attack. Most everyone else continued on the tour in a different bus with a new guide. But

Ando, I, and a few others went back to Sydney, driving all night to reach the city by morning. We took turns sleeping and staying awake to keep the driver company, but none of us could sleep very well. At some point on that long journey back to Sydney, I later found out, we were all thinking or dreaming about our spouses or ex-spouses.

Perhaps it was some kind of holdover from what the Aborigines called Dreamtime—the twilight time when mythical elders created the world and established a system of beliefs that inextricably linked all life together—that produced this meshing of thoughts among us. Because as I was leaving the Outback, my thoughts returned again to those nineteenth-century women who had come to Australia dreaming of husbands-to-be. Did those hopeful travelers find fortunate positions? Kinship with the people they met there? Or true mates in every sense of the word? Or did they realize, as I came to, that marriage was not really a destination at all? That being married didn't mean you had arrived somewhere and that meant you could stop noticing where you actually were. I don't know for me when that time was, I only know that I had. Marriage, I now understood, was like traveling, and it was more like being on the bus than anything else.

Perhaps what I found in the bush was not all that unlike what those nineteenth-century women found when they arrived in a strange land filled with new customs: the chance to see with their own eyes, and to be able to judge, maybe for the first time, what was potch and what were gems.

Christina Boufis is a freelance writer with a Ph.D. in English literature, and an Affiliated Scholar at Stanford's Institute for Research on Women and Gender. She lives in San Francisco.

CLARK NORTON

Queensland Caravan

*Driving your own home presents unique
obstacles and opportunities.*

MY WIFE GULPED. YOU MEAN WE HAVE TO DRIVE THAT?

"That," to our bleary eyes, looked like a monster in intensive
care. A hose stuck out of its side. A long cord fed it electricity. All
its orifices gaped wide open, and we could see uniformed men
busily vacuuming out its insides.

It was the biggest motor home we'd ever seen. We had never
driven an RV (called a "motorized caravan" Down Under), much
less set out in one at eight in the morning in a foreign country one
hour after arriving from a sixteen-hour trans-Pacific flight. All we
wanted to do was go to bed.

Instead, a peppy young woman I'll call Miss Chipper—assistant
manager of the local Horizon Holidays/Newmans Sunseeker caravan depot—was about to give us the Grand Tour of the vehicle
that would be our lodging and transport for the next week in far
North Queensland, gateway to the Great Barrier Reef.

"Here are your pots and pans and dishes and sheets and towels
and sleeping bags and water tank and cooking gas and fridge and
toaster and shower and porta-pottie," Miss Chipper reeled off.
"Now your fridge and lights run on electricity and your hot water
runs on gas and don't forget to charge up every two days and

check the gas supply and voltage meter and put the chemicals in the porta-pottie...."

I tuned her out, trusting my wife to listen, while I tested the bunk beds. The caravan had six berths in all, counting the dining table that converted into a double bed, and I was ready for all six. Our children—a boy of seven and girl of four—clambered around the two-person upper berth over the cab and immediately staked their claim to it.

"And there you have it!" Chipper concluded, "It's all yours—have a super week!" She handed us some maps of the area and extensive lists of caravan parks. I asked her the name of the nearest park. "Oh, I'm afraid all the parks in Cairns are chock-a-block today," she told us, "but you'll have no worries up the coast. Here, try one of these. Both super." She circled Yorkeys Knob and Trinity Beach on our map. Only a half-hour drive. We could live with that.

I climbed into the front seat. The steering wheel was missing. "Wheel's on the right side here, you know," Miss Chipper chirped.

While I was locating the driver's seat, my wife was

That night in the nearby hamlet of Cervantes, we discovered the Australian custom of hiring caravans. We found these to be roomy, comfortable, well-equipped, and inexpensive. In fact, a night's lodging for two in a caravan park could be cheaper than a stay at a youth hostel. The rule was always BYO (Bring Your Own) bedding. That first night in our hired caravan, we both beamed like children who had discovered a wonderful secret. We were snug and warm and out of the wind. We had a fridge in which to refreeze our water jugs for our "esky" and a stove for cooking. All utensils and even detergent and Brillo pads were provided. Showers and toilets and laundry were mere steps away. And the glistening beach waited just down the slope.

◆

—Barbara Marie Brewster,
Down Under All Over: A Love Affair with Australia

securely belting the children in the rear. The nippers would ride in luxury: on padded cushions that surrounded a table on three sides, with panoramic windows behind all three. They could gaze at the scenery, read, play cards, work puzzles or lie down for a nap whenever they wanted. With six seat belts, they could switch from one seat to the next. If they started to bicker, we could separate them from each other. A good sixteen feet behind us, they could barely be heard in any event. Paradise…for both them and their parents.

Unfortunately, we couldn't sit in the depot forever; Miss Chipper would not have approved. I practiced shifting gears with my left hand. Then I stepped on the gas—and lurched out. I'd always wondered what it was like to drive a tank.

Eventually we reached the street, a good ten yards from where we'd started. "I'll get the feel of this," I told my wife. "Now, which way is north? Aren't the directions reversed down here?" I pulled out warily into an intersection.

"Watch out for that car!" she screamed. "Can't you go faster? The light's turning red!"

"Can't get it out of first gear," I screamed back. "These things aren't made for right-handed people!"

"You're driving in the fast lane," my wife noted after we'd finally reached the main highway out of town. "You've got ten cars stacked up behind you. And that man just called you a Drongo—"

"Daddy," a tiny voice piped up from the rear, "where are the kangaroos?"

I did the prudent thing, I pulled over to the side of the road and let my wife take the wheel. "I'll navigate," I announced. "You never could navigate."

"Fine," she replied. (I knew what she was thinking: "You never could drive.")

With my wife at the wheel, we soon left Cairns behind to follow the Captain Cook Highway north. A warm tropical breeze was in the air; fields of towering sugarcane lined the roadside; mountains loomed to the west. And then we saw a sign: "Trinity Beach Caravan Park—turn right 100 meters." We headed down a narrow road, and getting a bit of a second wind, decided to check out the beach before checking into the van park.

Trinity Beach was golden, palm-fringed and, at 9 A.M., virtually deserted. The sky was streaked with silver and black clouds; the Coral Sea was slate blue. Then it struck us: Australia! We were actually here; I was even ready to search for kangaroos. We hiked up and down the beach, climbed rocks, met a couple who invited us to look them up if we ever got to Ravenshoe. At ten we all had an ice cream, then headed to the caravan park. "I could sleep till supper time," I yawned.

The sign read "Full."

"Try Ellis Beach," the manager suggested. So we drove farther up the highway. "Sorry, sport," the manager at Ellis Beach informed. "But you might find something in Port Douglas." We had planned to go to Port Douglas—a resort town about fifty kilometers up the coast—at some point anyway. "What the hey?" my wife shrugged and off we lumbered.

The highway wound past a procession of sparkling coves, each with a beach more pristine than the previous, with sweeping vistas reminiscent of Big Sur. We considered pulling off and parking at one of the beaches, but we didn't know if local law permitted overnight camping in the area. Nor did we have any food. There wasn't a sign of a house or store within miles.

We arrived in Port Douglas around noon. A former gold-rush boom town, it was now charming, picturesque, and the home of four caravan parks—all "chock-a-block, mate. Have you tried Cairns?" We passed a string of motels. An insidious thought crept into my mind. Finally, I blurted: "You know, just for tonight...." My wife whipped the caravan off to the side of the road before I'd finished my sentence. "That looks like a good one," she said.

"You were lucky," the motel manager subsequently told me. "This is probably the last room in town. Mossman Fair, you know." Then, somewhat sheepishly, I asked where we might be able to park a caravan we just happened to be driving. She took one look and gasped. "Better bring it around to the rear," she said. "And watch those tree branches." Later, as we drifted off to dreamland, we were awakened by our daughter's plaintive cry: "Why can't we sleep in the camper van?"

We awoke the next morning with a new perspective on life, ready to tackle the vagaries of the open road. The motel manager recommended a caravan park some miles to the north called Pinnacle Village. "Super beach," she said. "No worries about space." I'd heard that before; I almost asked her to keep our room warm for us.

With my wife behind the wheel again—the arrangement was becoming permanent—we drove north through sugarcane country. It was harvest time, and smoke curled up from cane fires in the distance. We stopped for groceries in Mossman, center of the local sugar milling industry and site of the just-concluded fair that had packed the caravan parks for miles around. Like Port Douglas, Mossman still had the lingering aura of a gold-mining town. Trading posts, Victorian-era saloons and Aborigines were much in evidence.

Edible-looking groceries, however, were not. Besides rows and rows of sweets and a few barely fresh fruits and vegetables, the selection ran to items like "casserole mince" (unidentified canned substance), "camp pie" (a Spam-like product), and the ubiquitous sticky black Vegemite, Australia's national sandwich spread concocted from yeast. We opted for an exotic array of milk, eggs, ham, bread (white as Wonder), peanut butter, jam, crackers, and cornflakes.

North of Mossman we turned off on a long dirt road toward Pinnacle Village, located near the town of Wonga. No worries! A "power site" was available that could both accommodate and re-juice our home on wheels. With me waving directions, my wife skillfully backed it into its appointed slot. Everyone knew we had arrived; whenever in reverse, the van trumpeted a series of warning blasts rivaling the sound of elephants in heat.

A path led from our site directly to the beach a few hundred yards away. The tide was out, and the sand seemed to stretch for miles in all directions. The islands of Trinity Bay loomed offshore. Giant pelicans combed the shore for fish. Our son chased sand crabs and dug for tiny clams that left telltale gurgling bubbles in the sand. Our daughter joined him in the hunt. My wife and I searched for coral and seashells, which lay strewn by the thousands across the beach. The cares of the world had gone out with the tide. Was it possible we had been in Australia for only a day?

We remained at Pinnacle Village for three nights. Each morning at sunrise, the children scampered off to the beach on their own, cracking coconuts and collecting sand crabs, as we scrambled eggs and made toast. Later, before setting off to rove the countryside, we would kibitz with the locals, including many retirees who, during the Australian winter, had driven up from colder regions south of here to enjoy the tropical Queensland climate. They were extremely friendly and introduced us to the joys of interpreting "Strine"—the Australian language that vaguely resembles English as we know it.

"Emma Chisit?" a man asked me on the beach one morning.

"Emma who?" I responded.

"Emma Chisit?" he asked more loudly, no doubt thinking I was hard of hearing. "Emma Chisit to park your caravan per night?"

Our van park neighbor asked me in a Cockney accent how my "cheese and kisses" was. "You know," he finally said, "your missus—the one who always drives." (Strine, I was to discover, frequently induces Cockney-type rhyming slang. For instance, "cheese and kisses" equals missus.)

The van park itself was clean and efficiently run. It had a small store, playground, laundry room, swimming pool and, like all the caravan parks we were to stay in, ample community bathroom facilities with wash basins and private showers. At night, however, various of our family members chose to use the van's porta-pottie rather than wander outside in the dark to visit the WC. The first morning, we awoke to a certain pungency emanating from the tiny bathroom. It seems we had neglected to properly add the chemicals to the porta-pottie. "Weren't you listening to her instruction?" my wife asked me accusingly.

"You mean Miss Chipper?" I responded. "No, I assumed you were." I did, however volunteer to accompany the children to the

beach while my wife cleaned up. (She got her revenge; I drew latrine duty the rest of the way.)

With the aid of such trial-and-error experimentation—and
some prudent study of the written instructions—we soon caught
on to the camper van's mechanics and eccentricities. We learned
how to keep dishes from falling off counters while driving (put
them away, natch), how much water we could run in the sink
without overflowing the waste bucket, how to keep the fridge
properly charged up, and not to panic when the voltage meter read
"low." On our little propane stove, we began cooking feasts of
plump boiled prawns—bought fresh from a fish market in Port
Douglas—and broiled barramundi, a delectable local fish. We even
learned, somewhat too late, that it is perfectly permissible to park
a caravan at a beach or other suitable-looking natural campsite as
long as no posting indicated otherwise.

It took several nights to master sleeping arrangements. After
bedding down with her brother in that upper berth over the cab
for a night or two, our daughter decided she wanted to sleep with
Mommy. That sent me to the upper berth, but I found the tiny
ladder leading up to it so treacherous to climb that once there, I
adamantly remained there, till morning—no matter how urgently
nature called in the wee hours. From then on, I slept on one of the
fold-down bunk beds, while our son insisted on taking the other.
The first night of this arrangement, he chose the top bunk. In the
middle of the night we heard a gigantic crash: son had rolled off
the bunk and fallen several feet to the floor. His parents were so
shaken we didn't even wake up. Another night, during a wind-
storm, we discovered we had parked too close to some tree
branches. They whipped against the roof of the van, while we
swayed back and forth in the howling gale. We expected the roof
to cave in from the damage at any moment. In the morning, the
branches proved to be little more than twigs.

Each day we embarked on an excursion—to Port Douglas, or
to offshore coral islands to explore the reef, or on a jungle river safari. The latter took us to the end of the paved Captain Cook

Highway, where, to continue north toward Cape Tribulation and Cooktown, you need four-wheel drive, a change of dry clothing (in case you have to ford the Daintree) and shock absorbers from hell. This is still frontier country, and locals claim the place is going to ruination each time a new settler appears a few miles upriver. It is here you realize how much of Australia, away from the glitter of Sydney and the Gold Coast to the south, is still wild and untamed.

After our sojourn up north, even Cairns—with a laid-back population of 119,000—seemed glitzy. The managers of Pinnacle Village had made reservations for us at the Lake Placid Van Park a few miles outside the city, where we stayed two nights. We spent most of our time in town, however, Cairns (pronounced "cans" by the locals) has some of the widest streets in existence, perfect for maneuvering our behemoth. (The major drawback to a caravan is that when you

> ───── ✺ ─────
>
> *C*he only magazines on sale in Mt. Surprise (population 100) were *Women's Weekly* and *The Picture* which featured "Bi-Babes" on its cover. So I boarded the Savannahlander with nothing to read during the ten-hour journey to Cairns. Kangaroos played chicken with the slow poke train as mile after mile of scorched sameness slowly fell behind. A passenger poured martinis from the bottle he'd brought along. In the absolute middle of nowhere, a man flagged the train down. Hours later he got off at the first bar along the way, never having said a word to anyone, leaving us to wonder how much he intended to drink. There wouldn't be a train back for three days.
>
> ◆
>
> —Robert L. Strauss, "Making Tracks in Queensland"

need to drive to town for a quart of milk you have to take the whole house with you—and therefore we don't recommend them for touring large, crowded cities.) We explored Cairns harbor (famous for its marlin fishing) and multiplicity of shops, ate superb seafood and took off on a dramatic train ride through rain forest, up steep mountainsides and past waterfalls and gorges to the town of Kuranda perched high in the Atherton Tablelands.

Later we set off for our own caravanning through the Tablelands, a lush, fertile highlands within easy driving distance west of Cairns. Setting off in midmorning, we found a van park by early afternoon in the town of Malanda, the heart of the region. The van park adjoined the waterfall for which Malanda is famous, and included acres of grass and a playground for the children to romp in. We also took a jungle hike there.

We discovered, however, that the last grocery store in Malanda had closed tight for the weekend as of Saturday morning. We managed to grab some fish and chips before the only café shut down at 2 P.M. The sole establishments still functioning were the saloons, which were packed wall-to-wall with locals—mostly men "shouting rounds" of drinks for each other. We embarked on an expedition to Atherton, the largest town in the area, which we assumed would be well stocked with groceries—even restaurants. A sign proclaimed "Welcome to Atherton—One of Queensland's Tidy Towns." So tidy, in fact, that the one open store didn't bother to clutter its shelves with anything more appetizing than eggs and white bread.

The next morning, our last full day in Queensland, we drove past pastureland as green as Ireland, rolling lands where dairy cows grazed and neat white farmhouses lay tucked around the valleys. Country inns serving Devonshire tea and scones beckoned by the roadside. We stopped to gaze at waterfalls and hike. Then we headed back for the coast, where we spent a final few hours swimming in the warm sea waters before returning to Cairns.

Early the next morning we would fly off to Sydney, one of the great cities of the world, where we would ride ferries, taxis, and subways and stay in a splendid hotel. Further wonders awaited us to the south. But as we packed up our gear and folded up our berths for the last time, we sorely regretted having to leave

Queensland—and the "monster" that had enabled us to experience it so intimately. Miss Chipper would have approved.

Clark Norton, is an award-winning travel writer and screenwriter who divides his time between City Island, New York, and San Francisco, California. He is the author of two family travel guidebooks, Where Should We Take the Kids? California *and* Around San Francisco With Kids *and has contributed to several other guidebooks. He also writes frequently for magazines such as* Family Fun, Hemispheres, The Washington Post Magazine, *and* Parenting.

LUCY FRIEDLAND

✦ ✦ ✦

My Brilliant Surfing Career

After an age of observation, she becomes a participant.

I WAS WATCHING THE SURFERS AGAIN. ON BEACHES FROM PALM Beach to Pipeline, I had spent years watching the surfers. "Research," I had told myself. Before attempting anything new, I first had to do the research. Dozens of surf mags later, I had followed my fantasy to Sydney, Australia, but so far I was still just watching the surfers.

As I rounded a corner on the cliff walk between Bondi and Bronte beaches, I paused, transfixed by a wet-suited man picking his way up the rock face, like a mountain goat in black rubber, balancing a surfboard under his arm. He was an older "surfie." I knew he'd talk. Unlike the teenage surfers who don't exactly warm to a groupie pushing forty, the older ones would sometimes give me the time of day. I put on my best surfer-chick voice and asked him about the conditions. It was a stormy, overcast day. The water was dotted with bobbing heads, but the waves didn't look that great to me.

"It's a pretty typical day," he said. "But do you see that strip of sand down there? That's McKenzie Beach. I've lived 'ere seven years, and this is the first time, I've evah seen the sand. Two months from now, the water will wash back over the beach, and they'll be no beach 'ere for another seven years or more. Where ya from?"

"I'm from Austin, Texas. It's landlocked."

He snorted. "'Ow long y'ere for?"

"I'm leaving tonight for Byron Bay," I said, "to learn how to surf." This won me a smile.

"Yeah, the surf school's up in Byron, they'll take good care of ya," he said.

Byron Bay is a small resort town at the easternmost point of Australia, about 600 miles north of Sydney. It's known for long, sandy beaches and its neo-hippie lifestyle. Even though the beaches aren't netted to prevent shark attacks as they are in Sydney, I thought it would be a more hospitable place than frenetic Bondi to learn how to surf.

I took the twelve-hour night bus from Sydney, which pulled into Byron Bay at 10:30 the next morning. At noon, I found myself sitting in a beat-up van with Simon the driver. Simon had bad teeth, a moronic laugh, and judging by his eyes, he was stoned out of his mind. "Uh oh," I thought. We made the rounds to other local hostels, picked up five twenty-something international guys, and then drove to the surf shop where we met up with Simon's partner Gabby. To my relief, she was to be our teacher. "Yay," I thought, "a sister in surf. Maybe she'll be extra sweet to me."

We squeezed into our regulation wet suits, which were cold, damp, and sandy from the previous class—a pleasant start. Mine was obviously cut for a Laura Dern-type, with a mile-long torso. The crotch came halfway down my thighs. Gabby said, "No worries. Better too loose than too tight."

"Will it chafe?" I fretted.

"No, you'll be all right."

I believed her—I took everything she said as gospel. Gabby was a total surf goddess. She looked around twenty-two years old—wavy, honey hair to her shoulders, cherubic cheeks with deep dimples, and, of course, a lovely body. Even on this drizzly, cloudy day she radiated good health and happiness. She was like the sun; I could barely look at her. Since the five guys were silent on the ride over to the beach, in my nervous excitement I began rapid-fire questioning.

"I'm a Bondi girl, m'self," Gabby explained. "I've been surfing almost thirteen years now. While the other girls were layin' 'round the beach readin' dollies [women's fashion magazines], I went out with my brother and the other guys surfing."

"So you were a tomboy?"

"Yeah, I suppose so. Most of the city girls never take up surfing. The girls up here in Byron do, though. There's nothin' else to do. The boys don't pay attention to them 'cause they're so into surfing, so the girls surf along with the boys." I asked her why she left Bondi.

"In Bondi, it's too competitive with all those surfaholics layin' about, collecting dole. Since the beaches are less crowded here, it's a much easier place to run a surf school."

When we got to the beach, which was nearly empty since the weather was bad, we were handed surfboards off the trailer hitched to the back of the van. I was shocked to see that we were getting huge $8\frac{1}{2}$-foot-long boards, made of very dense foam, rather than the lighter short boards with pointy tips, currently favored for maneuvering in smaller waves. These were safer, Gabby said. A pointy board with sharp fins could slice your head in two like a melon if someone in front of you lost control of their board. She told us to tuck our boards under one arm and carry them 300 paces down the beach.

Now, the guys in the class were all tan and fit and looked like they'd been backpacking Australia for months. Clearly, they didn't spend their days sitting in front of a computer like I did. Not only that, I was willing to bet that they didn't suffer from chronic pain in their shoulders and necks and that they didn't have weak little robin wrists and taffy arms like I did either. Suddenly I thought, "Maybe Weightlifting 101 is a prerequisite for Surfing 101," and with all my mental preparations, I had left out that part. My arms were too short even to grasp the bottom edge of the board when I shoved it under my armpit.

Gabby saw me struggling to carry the board and shouted, "Whack it on your head!"

"What? Put it on my head?" So I visualized a mighty African woman carrying produce in a basket on her head, as the board teetered back and forth like a demented seesaw. I felt the sand from the board grinding into my scalp, and I hoped my neck wouldn't snap under the weight. At the halfway point from where the rest of the group had gathered, I thought my arms were going to drop off. I reminded myself that there'd be no surfing if I couldn't get the board to the water.

I finally made it to the group, where the boys looked like beached whales, lying on their stomachs on the boards and flailing their arms in the sand. Gabby was coaching, "Paddle now, paddle hard. You're going to point your boards to the shore and paddle as hard as you can. When the wave hits the back of your board, paddle once more, slide your foot out, shift your weight around to your other foot and jump up to a squatting position. Okay?" Yeah sure, Gabby, no worries.

She then instructed us to do a "Mexican Wave." We were lined up parallel to each other flat on our stomachs, and one at a time, we were to paddle sand and jump to our feet. I was last in line. I watched as each of these incredibly agile kids leapt to a crouch, like panthers preparing to pounce. Meanwhile, I looked like a bad excuse for a Twister player.

"Okay, in the water," Gabby said. Gamely, I paddled after them toward the ocean, board wobbling.

As I approached the break, I tensed with fear. I can never judge wave height until I'm right in the soup, the foamy white water at the water's edge. This surf was no joke. As an experienced swimmer, I wouldn't have even wanted to swim in this stuff, much less surf it. The waves were breaking so far out that the soup was over my head. The undertow was so intense it took all the strength in my legs to wade through the water without getting knocked down. Of course, I still couldn't carry the damn board. Gabby told me to drag it by the leash that stretched between the board and the loop around my left ankle. I tried that, but the surf would wrench the leash through my palm and burn it.

The littlest, scrawniest guy was already on his feet. "A natural,"

I sniffed with envy. The others were getting dumped right and left. I saw boards springing out of the water like blue-foam Shamus, while the guys splashed around gasping for breath. I tried to stay out of their way.

I began practicing the paddling part and riding the board on my stomach. As beginners, we were supposed to stay in the soup—not go out to the curls. The white water kept pulling me down, and I got dragged along the riptide parallel to the beach. It was a struggle to stay between the blue flags that were planted on the beach demarcating the rookie zone.

Most of my time was spent hauling the board around the white water, trying to stay on my feet, trying to keep the leash from ripping my hands or jerking my wrist. But every so often, I'd get my board in the correct position, catch a wave, scramble to my feet and ride into shore in a squat. When the water hit the back of my board just right, I'd see the tip propel through the soup at a tremendous speed, faster than my body alone had ever traveled. Just before hitting sand, I'd roll off, and the board would fly out of control. I'd tumble in the soup and come up laughing. To my amazement, I actually did this over and over like a possessed person. After two hours, my arms were throbbing, my knees were rubbed raw from scraping along the board, and I hurt all over. I had water down my throat and sand up my nose. I was ecstatic. After years of ogling surfer boys, I had finally launched my own surfing career.

Lucy Friedland quit her job as a travel editor in Austin, Texas to backpack solo across Asia and look for a new home. When she was last heard from, she had ferried out of the Perhentian Islands in Malaysia just as the monsoon was arriving, chickening out on another surfing opportunity.

* * *

Aussie Rules Football

*The game is easy to understand
after a few beers.*

AUSTRALIAN RULES FOOTBALL, ALSO CALLED "AUSSIE RULES" OR "Footie" is, according to an unemployed English actor named Barry who was staying at my youth hostel, "Australia's most popular national sport, right behind driving drunk and abusing the Aboriginals." Aussie Rules is a bit like American football, only, as the name implies, there are totally different rules, and they were invented by Australians. I was told by Barry that I had to see a game for myself to truly appreciate the difference.

I found I was low on cash when I arrived at the Melbourne Cricket Ground, a stadium built initially for cricket (another sport I don't understand) with a seating capacity of over 100,000, so I pulled out my press pass and walked from gate to gate, presenting it to each ticket taker until, after eight attempts, I was allowed entrance by an older man with poor eyesight who would have probably let me pass with my library card.

The first thing I did, at Barry's suggestion, was purchase a beer. I may not understand the game at first, but he assured me that after several beers it would make much more sense. I also ordered a meat pie, the Aussie equivalent of a hot dog.

"What kind of meat is it?" I asked the concession attendant.

"Meat," she replied.

In this match, Carlton, a top team, was pitted against Footscray, neither a top team, nor a shoe deodorant. I decided to "barrack" (root) with the Footscray fans because I like to support the underdog. I sat next to David, a farmer who drove into town specifically for this match.

The game started with an aggressive basketball-style tip-off in which the umpire bounced the ball (a cross between a football and a volleyball) in a designated square in the center of the field and let the players battle for it.

"What's that big square in the center called?" I asked David.

"The round one?" he replied. It seemed that David wasn't going to be much help.

Once the game got under way, I could see that the object of Aussie Rules is, quite simply, to clobber whoever has the ball, unless you have the ball, in which case you should run like mad, remembering to bounce it every ten meters and then get rid of it, preferably toward the opponents' end of the field, before you get clobbered. This is not as easy as it sounds because: 1) The field has no "end" as such since it is an oval, and furthermore it is approximately the size of a par-4 golf hole. 2) While you are holding the ball the opposing team may use any force necessary to stop you including—and I may need to consult the rule book on this—semiautomatic assault rifles.

And did I mention that the players are not wearing any safety equipment? Only sleeveless shirts and tight shorts, which need constant readjusting—just like American baseball players fiddling with the motorcycle helmet they wear in their pants—which may have accounted for the large number of female fans I saw in attendance.

Those are the basics. It only took me one beer to figure them out. The technical parts, like scoring, required another beer. The strategy took a third. But I found the history of Aussie Rules was the hardest to swallow. David told me it was originally played by cricket players who wanted to stay in shape in the off-season. Translated into American, this is a bit like saying the triathlon was created for golfers to stay fit.

I bought a "record" (program) to help me understand the game but it wasn't very helpful because it was written in Australian. And the positions had strange names. Plus, there were eighteen players per side and nearly twice that many people on the field and every player had a nickname that was not in the record. It would read something like this: "Hickmont and Spalding, the roving rucker and wing middie, have converted several high marks into behinds." Understandably, this didn't accomplish much in the way of explanation. So, I put the record down and ordered another beer.

I was, however, able to contribute in small measure to the continuous exchange of impassioned opinion. Umpires most commonly miss calling the holding penalty. In Aussie Rules, "holding" is not when an offensive player holds a defensive player; it's when an offensive player continues to hold onto the ball after he has been clobbered. So it's up to the fans, some of us sitting nearly a kilometer away from the play, to spell it out for the umpire by yelling "BALL!" This sometimes motivates the umpire to see the foul and make the call, which then produces a thankful roar of "YES!" So throughout the entire game I was able to yell these two words, and by the second half (and fourth beer) I had it down pat.

A few minutes into the game Footscray scored the first goal when a player, Ozzy or perhaps it was Lumpy, kicked the ball between two tall posts and put six points on the board. This goal was verified by the goal umpire who, dressed like Bogart in *Casablanca,* rapidly extended both index fingers at hip level as if firing two imaginary pistols. Then he picked up two white flags and started waving them as if to signal a commercial airplane over to the gate. This spectacle was by far my favorite aspect of the game.

Not much later, it looked like there was going to be a fight. One of the Carlton players was about to "make a high mark" (catch the ball) when a Footscray player jumped up from behind and kneed the Carlton player in the head to prevent the catch. This would be called pass interference and unnecessary roughing and might result in a jail sentence in the NFL, but in Aussie Rules it is highly encouraged. In fact, it was the Carlton player who was asked to leave the game because of the newly instated "blood rule," which clearly states that a player with a huge gash in his head is not allowed to continue play.

Between the gash in his head and getting thrown out of the game, the Carlton player was understandably upset. He started to exchange words with the Footscray player and several other players also entered this debate and exchanged words. But no one threw a punch. This, David explained, was because the "Melee Rule," also newly instated, strictly prohibits melees, which must have really gotten out of hand after the introduction of the blood rule.

When the game was over (Carlton won), David suggested I use my press pass to chat with the players in the locker room. David explained it is the dream of every Australian man, woman, and child to meet a professional Aussie Rules player, just as, I suppose, it is the dream of every American man, woman, and child to sue a rich professional athlete, buy a large screen television and watch "Wheel of Fortune." So I gave it a try and, sure enough, my press pass worked. This was my first interview with a professional athlete so I was a bit nervous, especially because I didn't actually have any questions prepared because I didn't think the pass was going to work.

I was allowed to speak with Mr. Rice, of Carlton, who seemed like a nice guy, though he wasn't overwhelmingly verbal.

Me: So how would you explain this sport to an American audience?

Mr. Rice: Lot of action.

Me: Anything else?

Mr. Rice: Not really.

We shook hands, took a photo together and I concluded this insightful interview. It was time to leave and concentrate on digesting the meat pie, which had blocked up my instestinal tract like a jackknifed semi on the Long Island Expressway.

Doug Lansky is the author of First Time Around the World, Last Trout in Venice, Up the Amazon Without a Paddle*, and the editor of* There's No Toilet Paper on the Road Less Traveled. *He lives in Sweden with his family.*

JOANNE MESZOLY

Bedrock City

Care to live in a cave?

"ARE YOU SURE I'M NOT INCONVENIENCING YOU?" I ASK CRAIG, as he dumps the remains of his coffee down the sink. Bending over to yank on his dusty, battered work boots he replies, "Mate, what else would I be doing? Costs me A$600 a week on diesel, explosives, and machinery, and even so, I probably wouldn't hit opal. You're actually saving me money to stay home!"

Lighting up his third cigarette of the morning, Craig slaps the layer of dust off his jeans. "I haven't found opal in a couple months," he says with a sheepish grin. "It's out there, but there's heaps of dirt in between."

Craig Stutley lives with his father Colin in Coober Pedy, a town in South Australia's Outback that calls itself "the opal capital of the world." Nearly 90 percent of the world's opals are mined here, the locals say, and it's the only reason to live and work in this brutally hot, dry, and desolate region, which averages a scant 10 to 15 cm of rainfall per year.

With its stony, almost treeless landscape, Coober Pedy looks like the set of a science-fiction movie. And no wonder: *Mad Max III*, and a host of other sci-fi movies, were filmed here. During the cooler months, Coober Pedy is dry and the soil is sun baked a dusty yellow color. Little is green and piles of rubbish lie everywhere. Sandy hillsides are marked by abandoned car shells and discarded appliances. Even the football field is without grass.

Summer, which lasts eight months, is even harsher. There's no relief in the still, dry air, and a piercing blue sky. Temperatures range from 35 to 48 degrees [95 to nearly 120 degrees Fahrenheit], and occasional dust storms scorch the place. Swarms of flies zero in on your eyes and nose, or cover the back of your shirt. Eventually, sunset ushers in a cooling breeze and the flies retire for the night. There is comfort for an hour, and then the mosquitoes arrive.

Early miners took shelter underground, moving their furniture into old mining dugouts. That inspired the town's Aboriginal name—Kupapiti, or "white man's burrow." Today, nearly two-thirds of Coober Pedy's 2,800 residents live, socialize, and do business underground and out of sight, adding to the town's unique air of desolation.

Less than fifteen years ago most travelers treated Coober Pedy as merely a remote petrol stop on the road to Ayers Rock and Alice Springs. But in the past decade, the paving of the only highway through the Red Center has been making it easier for tourists to get a taste of the Outback—and shop for opals, too.

Visitors to Coober Pedy can stay in an underground hotel, eat at underground restaurants, visit an underground museum and shop for opals. What's more, it's easy to socialize with miners here—maybe over a beer at the pub, or in their underground homes, and even down their mines.

That's how I landed in Craig Stutley's kitchen. Craig learned to dig deep underground for precious stones from his father Colin, who now buys uncut opals from miners and sells them to wholesale dealers. Brenton, Craig's older brother, frequently makes the eight-hour drive from his home in Adelaide to learn the trading business from their father.

Craig opens a few beers and we join Colin and Brenton in the dugout's family room. The red sandstone walls give off a musty, earthy smell, and the artificial light takes getting used to. A fine white layer of dust covers every table and couch. "Even though there are ventilation shafts, it tends to make you congested," Colin says.

Brenton adds, "Coober Pedy's the only place where you shake your laundry out *after* it's been hung on the line."

Colin pops open a plastic bag of jagged, white rocks and spreads them on top of a black table. He squirts the uncut stones with a fine mist of water, and they sparkle with glints of green, red, and blue under the strong overhead lamp.

Glasses perched on his nose, he hunches over the tiny mound, his fingertips sifting through, pushing the opals around the black table. After a few minutes' inspection, he weighs the lot, then jots down the weight, the grade of stone, and finally, a price. "It takes time and heaps of experience to learn the value of a pile of opal," he says. "Also takes good eyesight and keen business sense."

The opal fields surround the township in a 40 km radius, marked by the pointy mounds of "mullock," now-useless soil that's been pumped from the mines by giant, truck-mounted blowers.

These grayish mountain tops, like piles of dirty rice, stretch for miles against the cloudless blue sky. Along the road, signs warn visitors to hold onto children and step carefully since working and abandoned mines are left open and unmarked.

"You reckon you wanna do this? It's a bit of a drop." Craig holds out a narrow plank, secured by a cable. The owner of this mine, Arthur, busies himself repairing the handle of his lucky opal bucket, while his dog gingerly picks his way around the gaping mine shaft.

I ask Arthur how long it has been since their last find, and he answers, "About three weeks. But me and my son Bradley have gotten A$160,000 out in eighteen months."

Perched on a plank, I dangle over the open mine as a rattling diesel-powered winch lowers me down an oversized rabbit hole, twenty-three meters into the earth. Bracing my boots against the red-and-white-striped tunnel, I keep the seat straight as sandstone crumbles off and rains down the shaft.

At the bottom, the main tunnel has been drilled by machine,

but the jagged edges beyond suggest the rest has been dug by hand. Feeling like a character in a 1950s thriller, waiting for the approach of a giant spider or a swarm of killer bees, I look away from three dark chambers and peer down the only lit passage.

Walking through rubble, I duck and enter a long tunnel. Bradley stands at the end, inspecting the sandstone with a work lamp. Craig and Arthur quickly join us.

As the three survey the crumbly soil, I point to a clear line of sparkling rock. "That's only gypsum," Arthur explains. "Like fool's gold."

Unplugging the light bulb, Bradley shines a purple ultraviolet light against the sandstone. Red and white rock break apart as Arthur pulls off a piece of sandstone, carefully prying off chunks of earth with his callused hands. He touches the rock to his tongue and holds it up to the light. "Eh, it's just potch." He hands the creamy white rock to me. "See, it doesn't have any colour. It'll be opal…in about a million years," he adds with a smile.

With no visible line of opal, Arthur drills with a machine-powered pick, which works like a small jackhammer. During breaks, Bradley disposes of the discarded sandstone through the blower, a giant vacuum cleaner that sucks earth up to the surface and spews it into what looks like giant white anthills.

*O*pals are one of the more admirable gemstones because they don't flash all their beauty at you at once. At first glance an opal is just a milky stone. But bring one close to your eye, and look beneath the surface into its pearlescent depths. Cold fire flashes out at you as the stone is rotated: ribbons of dawn pink, electric blue, and cat's-eye green. The shifting iridescence within creates an illusion of dimension, like the ghostly image in a hologram. This is the "color" that the opal diggers strain their eyes for, the prize that becomes an obsession, almost a disease with some people.

◆

—Stuart Young, "Coober Pedy: Notes from Underground"

"I think we're going to use some explosives," Arthur comments, heading back to the tunnel opening. He flips open a cardboard box and casually shows me how to make a small bomb.

"May wanna put your fingers in your ears," Arthur warns a few minutes later as the four of us crouch at the farthest end of the tunnel. Forty seconds creep by, and suddenly the ground rocks with two quick blasts—much like explosions on cartoons where the television screen seems to shake. Long after the earth stops moving, little rocks and pebbles pour down on us.

With a pick and renewed enthusiasm, Arthur chips away at the underground wall. "More potch," he says. "What's this?" As he pries the extra earth off, Bradley and Craig eagerly crowd around. Arthur licks the stone, which fits into his palm, and holds it in front of the light. Under the lamp, lines and specks of red and green gleam against a shiny white background. That's about three grand," Bradley says.

It's their first find in weeks. "Now what?" I ask.

"Now we go to the pub," Arthur smiles.

Joanne Meszoly is a staff writer for Equus Magazine *and lives in Rockville, Maryland, with her husband and their border collie. Of all her travels, she calls Australia her true love, "for its people, hard landscape, and great beer."*

Looking for Dinner

*The locals teach an introductory lesson
in hunting and gathering.*

LEARNING HOW TO HUNT AND GATHER MY OWN DINNER WAS never a big priority until I went to Australia's Bathurst Island. But it didn't take long to get into the swing of things. My first morning on the island, two Tiwi Aborigines turned up on my doorstep to take me out chasing furry marsupials. Ready or not.

This was the end of Bush Camp month, when the Tiwi head out into their traditional lands and eat native foods, and I was being invited along.

Located at the very top of the island continent's Top End region, splaying out on maps like a giant Rorschach stain, Bathurst Island and neighboring Melville are all but unknown to the outside world. Even friends of mine in Sydney had never heard of them; when I explained at a barbecue where I was off to, one wit suggested I might be "hunted and gathered" myself.

Well, I was about to find out what was in store.

"First we pick up some Tiwi people," announced Bosco, as I climbed into the minibus, cautiously picking my way over axes, billy cans, and sacks of flour. Bosco was a beefy character with an unshakable grin. The driver, Theodore, was the more somber type, with a wild shock of white hair.

"Then we head out bush," Theodore said laconically. "Chase up some tucker."

Theodore pondered the menu: "Might catch some possum," he said. "Wallaby. Bit of goanna. Some carpet snake, maybe."

Bosco was beaming. "Oh, carpet snake's beautiful, mate."

It began to dawn on me that "tucker" on Bathurst apparently meant anything that moved.

For the next half hour we drove around, picking up Bosco's extended family—brothers, sisters, an uncle, an aunt, and ten kids—who all screamed at the top of their lungs in Tiwi. At the last minute a four-wheel drive full of Theodore's relatives joined us, and before long we were all roaring down a road into the endless Bathurst bushland.

It is territory that looks entirely different every season. This was July, the height of the dry season, and some of the bushland had been freshly burned off. Vibrant green cycads were poking like feather dusters through the black dirt, while clouds of smoke drifted eerily across the flat landscape.

Hunting and gathering, I can now report, goes like this: First, stop at a roadside car wreck to pick up some shards of mirror. (You will use the mirror pieces to reflect the sun into hollow logs to spot hiding animals.) Next, pause occasionally to take potshots at wallabies hopping across the road. Eventually, take your axes and buckets and hike off with your "skin group," or clan, into their "country." The time-tested Tiwi hunting method? Find a hollow tree. Listen for contents. Chop it down. Get ready.

On our second attempt a small animal bolted out in a gray blur. Fast, to be sure, but it never had a chance against the lightning-fast Tiwi kids. Mary Margaret, who was wearing a Bob Marley shirt, soon had the possum dangling by the tail. She swung it above her in a great arc and whacked its head onto the trunk.

"Good tucker, that one," Mary said, as I peered at the critter in the bucket.

"Ah, one possum won't go 'round," Bosco said, shaking his head. "Not for this mob."

Two more trees came down, both empty. Then Theodore spotted

a swarm of insects around the top of a trunk. That meant bush honey, the perfect dessert. There was only one problem: this was a hardwood tree. It took about two hours of us all hacking away before it fell. (I must admit that I was heartily put to shame by the Tiwi women, who slashed at that trunk like Canadian lumberjacks.)

This Tiwi hunting was getting to be a bit too much like hard work, especially as the winter sun was now high in the sky, and the temperature was hitting ninety degrees. We rinsed off in a water hole—taking care that no crocs were around—and then began preparing lunch.

The idea, Bosco told me, was to throw the possum onto the fire for a while, then peel off its blackened skin. That would go with "damper," a ball of moist bread dough baked in tinfoil like a potato.

As Bosco was explaining all this, the multitudes were getting hungrier. "One possum won't go round," he said again. "No way, mate."

And so we did the only logical thing: We broke out the ham-and-cheese sandwiches.

The romantic vision of Australian Aborigines—painted islanders sitting around the fire in loincloths, playing the didgeridoo—has largely long been supplanted by a blend of traditional and modern life that is no less intriguing. White-bread sandwiches aside, visiting the Tiwi islands could be the most intense cultural experience Australia has to offer.

Traveling around Bathurst Island, I discovered that the coastlines alternate between crocodile-infested mangrove swamps and great white beaches, which stretch for mile after mile with nary a soul about. Inhabiting this expanse, somewhat larger than Maui, are only 1,200 Tiwi—which explains why chopping down a few trees and eating a few possums won't dent the environment.

Isolation has always defined these islands. Although the Australian mainland is only about fifty miles away, for 40,000 years or so the Tiwi culture developed separately from that of other Aboriginal groups. Even the Tiwi language is only loosely related to other Australian tongues, and when written down looks like ngngngngngn with a few vowels thrown in.

Their remoteness has helped the Tiwi escape the sort of scorched-earth colonization suffered by Aborigines in the rest of Australia. Early Dutch explorers largely avoided them. When the British set up an outpost on Melville in 1824—the first settlement in northern Australia—it lasted about five years, thanks to an unbeatable combination of diseases and Tiwi sieges.

Catholic missionaries arrived in 1911, but unlike their nineteenth-century Protestant counterparts on the mainland (who tried to eradicate Aboriginal beliefs throughout Australia, breaking up clans and devastating whole societies) the Catholics here allowed many Tiwi beliefs to coexist with their imposed religion.

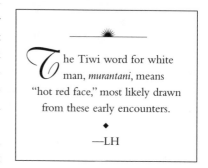

The Tiwi word for white man, *murantani*, means "hot red face," most likely drawn from these early encounters.

◆

—LH

Since the 1970s the Tiwi have managed their own affairs, and permits are required for non-Tiwi to visit Bathurst and Melville, where tribal law applies. And while mainland Aborigines still have to fight bitterly for legal title to their territories, Tiwi land rights have never been disputed. This confident sense of possession may be why the Tiwi are such an outgoing bunch. Despite a once-fearsome reputation, they now bill their homelands as the "Friendly Islands," and promote native-guided tours.

"If you go for a three-day hike with a lot of the mainland Aborigines," explained Anthony Venes, the manager of Tiwi Tours, "they're likely to be so shy they won't even start talking till the third day. The Tiwi'll open up with you straightaway."

A wiry, hard-bitten character with a bone-dry sense of humor, Venes was hired to set up the Tiwi-owned tour company. (The Land Council lets an outsider run the operation, he added, because complicated clan obligations would make it almost impossible for a Tiwi to refuse to lend out company 4WDs to relatives.) Profits from the tours go into health programs and a cultural fund for the islanders.

Now everything on the Tiwi islands is basically owned by the Tiwi people," Venes said. "The money doesn't leave the islands."

We were driving through the streets of Nguiu, home of the first Catholic mission and now the main settlement on Bathurst. Government houses on stilts were lined up in neat rows. Outside the houses, groups of Tiwi women were sitting in circles, smoking and playing cards. In workshops, artists were carving wooden sculptures and painting fabric with traditional designs. (After dark, families sat around open fires, with their TVs next to them plugged into extension cords.)

I spent the night in the government guest house, listening to coconuts thud down from trees—and distant screams. ("Domestic disputes are very public here," I was later told—part of the Tiwi expressiveness.) Nguiu, I learned, is also famously safe.

Left to my own devices, I probably could have appreciated the beauty of the countryside, with its lush eucalyptus and casuarina forests, dotted with orange grevillea, yellow wattle, red ceiba trees, and haunted by laughing kookaburras and pink-chested parrots. But seen with the help of Tiwi guides, the islands felt like a different universe, where every aspect of nature operated under its own rules.

A friend of Bosco's named Sidney, an earnest, religious bloke, took me to the lily-covered Lake Moantu, where the Rainbow Serpent is said to live. He showed me how to go digging on hands and knees for wild pumpkin and taught me that the orange nuts of the *samia* palm are deadly poisonous when eaten straight—but if left three days in running water and then cooked, taste deliciously like ricotta cheese. Later he took me to the two-mile-long Pawunapi Beach, where sea turtles nest, surrounded by piles of multicolored seashells.

The kids who came along on these trips made sure there was never a dull moment. They had names like Romeo, Juliet, Fidelio, Colistus, and Valentine, and after about five minutes were hanging on my arms, demanding to be "chucked" into water holes and asking probing questions about my marital status, my parents, sisters, and cousins. (Earlier, I had asked a teacher what it was like working here and he'd laughed. "Out of the classroom, they're the best kids in the world," he cackled. "But inside, they're absolutely shocking. I say that with great affection. But they're *shocking*.")

At times I would get an intimation, however superficial, of the Tiwi world beyond the visible. At Pawunapi Beach the two girls who came with us soon ran back and sat in the car: they'd seen a spirit on the beach.

Another time, walking with Bosco silently through the bush, we came upon some burial poles. About ten feet tall, the ironwood posts were carved and painted in geometric patterns. They marked the grave of a famous warrior from earlier this century. I'd seen similar poles in the Darwin Museum, but the experience was nothing like coming across them in the bush.

Bosco explained a little about the traditional Tiwi burial cere-mony—how the body would be wrapped in bark, while mourn-ers expressed grief by beating their chests and heads; relatives would then walk away, never looking back, lest the dead person's spirit chase and haunt them. These days the Tiwi, all Catholics, use coffins.

Out near the mangrove swamps on Bathurst's west coast, Barra Base fishing lodge is owned by the Tiwi but run by mainland fish-ing guides. I was picked up at the ramshackle dock by a bloke named Geoff, whose peeling nose and stubble-covered chin jutted sharply from beneath sunglasses and a cap. As we navigated the maze in a motorboat, a twelve-foot saltwater crocodile was sitting on a bank, sunning itself with its mouth wide open. It took one look at us and disappeared like a bullet.

"You wouldn't believe what I've seen crawl out of that water," Geoff chortled, in that slightly deranged, Jack Nicholson manner common to the Outback.

At the open-air wooden bar of the lodge, fishermen were watching the sun set over one of the most gorgeous beaches on earth. But nobody in his right mind would ever take a dip at that beach because of the crocs. One of the animals approached the lodge as darkness fell, but I could only see its red eyes, glowing like Captain Hook's nemesis in *Peter Pan*.

When I got up the next morning, the crocodile was still there, watching and waiting. Later, as an added fillip, Geoff told me he'd also seen teams of sharks cruising a few feet from the shoreline.

A family of Tiwi were camping a mile away, so I went to meet them with the only woman at the camp, Jodie, a chain-smoking, air force vet who spent her spare time bottle-feeding an orphaned wallaby.

The Tiwi were cooking up yam roots on a fire and gave us a few to try. They tasted almost like coconut. Two middle-aged sisters, Edwina and Dehlia Puawtjimi, said they were about to set off mud-crabbing and didn't mind if Jodie and I tagged along. So, we all took a boat over to a gray expanse of mudflats to help them dig.

Dehlia was the expert. She poked a stick in several holes before she finally hit pay dirt: a huge orange claw came snapping out of the clay at her.

"Baby crab!" Dehlia soon announced, pulling one out by the body. It was followed by another ("Mother crab!"), and then an orange monster whose carapace was a foot across. ("Father crab!") As this patriarch's vast pincers swiveled to nip a piece of her, she just chuckled at it: "Cheeky one!"

One snap from even the baby crab's claws might have taken off a finger, but Dehlia and Edwina hardly paid attention. Holding the crabs from behind, they gently folded the claws forward to be tied; the crabs simply obeyed, as if they were hypnotized. Dehlia put them in the bucket and tossed in a leafy branch.

"Make 'em sleepy," she said.

Afterward, encrusted in mud, we sat around in the shade, drinking cans of lemon soda. Dehlia told how, during World War II, when Zeros were on their way to attack Darwin in 1942, they strafed Bathurst first. One of the Japanese pilots crashed on Melville Island, and Dehlia's uncle took him prisoner. (A priest radioed Darwin to warn them of the surprise attack, but the warning was ignored, and some 243 people died.)

Edwina, who had helped her husband give up grog seven years ago, has since been lecturing on alcohol abuse in Aboriginal communities all over the Outback. Women are powerful on the Tiwi islands, and they do everything they can to get their families "out bush," away from the temptations of Nguiu, where alcohol abuse and domestic violence are common. Thanks to the women's vote in the Land Council, for example, the town's two pubs are closed on Sundays and for the whole of July, Bush Camp month.

"Edwina, mate," Jodie asked, "how's about some mangrove worms, eh?"

"*Yuwurli?* No worries." The worm hunt was on.

We all piled back into the boat, picked up Edwina's husband and son, then headed down a tiny inlet where I was soon sloshing through foot-deep brown mud in a mangrove swamp, clutching onto rotting trees to keep my balance and nervously looking about for crocs. The Tiwi bounded ahead, hacking away with axes at black roots.

Dehlia let out the first cry—"*Yuwurli! Yuwurli! Yuwurli!*"—and pulled out a long rubbery slug from the tree root.

White, fat, and covered with clear mucus, it came out with a truly sickening slurp. Dehlia smiled, threw back her head, and dropped it down her throat as if it were a strand of fettuccine.

I wish I could say that I tried one of these treats myself, but I'd be lying. I just couldn't face it. Jodie, however, was made of sterner stuff, and she gulped a decent-size worm.

Later, back at the base, I asked her what it was like.

"Oh, mate," she said, screwing up her face. "A bit like mud, eh? A bit salty. A bit like an oyster."

Geoff, standing nearby, just laughed. "You want to know what they're really like? Foot-long crocodile snot."

Anthony Venes was training a young guide, a Tiwi named Jamie, who looked properly cool in psychedelic Rasta clothes and wraparound sunglasses. The three of us bounced off in the 4WD to go camping in the north of the island.

On the way, the landscape seemed more remote than ever—deserted and strangely prehistoric. Flocks of cockatoos screamed overhead as fiercely orange sandstone bluffs appeared, fringed with spidery pandanus trees. This was the very edge of Australia, facing out toward the Timor Sea and Indonesia.

Jamie took me spearfishing. As we were stalking through the ankle-deep water, he suddenly grabbed me, saying "I almost stepped on a stingray. They're all around us. Hundreds of them."

I couldn't see the rays for the life of me, so I carefully followed his footsteps back out of the murk. I got even more uncomfortable when we stopped to examine some huge tracks in the sand. The tracks went into the trees and didn't come out.

"So, uh, Jamie, mate," I asked, "what do we do if we see a croc?"

Jamie pondered this for a moment, before replying with the apparently approved Tiwi solution: "We see a big croc, we bloody run."

We'd come back to camp empty-handed, so Anthony fried up steak and veggies on the campfire, using part of a giant nautilus shell to turn the steaks.

As the sun sank into the sea and the sky turned the color of ruby grapefruit, Jamie began to lose his good cheer. Whenever he came here as a kid, he told us, he had bad dreams caused by a witch. They only stopped when one of his relatives made the witch lift her curse.

"She's still there, that witch," he said bitterly.

As we rolled out our sleeping bags under the stars, Jamie built a huge fire—and he kept it going all night to ward off bad dreams.

One morning Jamie and Sidney took me across the strait to another burial site on Melville. A dozen elegantly carved poles were leaning in a clearing, their paint flaking, slowly weathering away. It was near noon, and we sat down in the shade and talked about ancient myths until my head began to swim.

Then Sidney wanted to talk about names. The surname on his birth certificate, he said, was Puruntatameri—his father's name—listed by the Australian welfare agents for the purpose of identifying citizens. Yet his traditional name should be Kurrupuwu (after Sidney's great uncle, an important man who had seven wives) or perhaps Maralimpuwi (after his grandfather). Sidney stressed he was a good Catholic but wondered if the church would mind him using his traditional name.

I mentioned that a lot of American Indians, for example, now use their traditional names. He nodded at the news and stood up.

"I know my country. I know my family. I know them very well. But," said Sidney, "I want my real name back."

Here where the present seems only partly successful in trying to nudge aside the past, the notion sounded perfectly reasonable to me.

Tony Perrottet is an Australian-born writer who lives in New York City. After graduating with a degree in history from Sydney University, he headed off to South America to work as a newspaper correspondent, and lived in Buenos Aires for two years. His travel writing has appeared in Esquire, Outside, Escape, Islands, Civilization, *most Australian magazines, and the* London Sunday Times. *He is the author of* Off the Deep End: Travels in Forgotten Frontiers, The Naked Olympics: The True Story of the Ancient Games, *and* Pagan Holiday: On the Trail of Ancient Roman Tourists.

Platypus Hunter

*Our intrepid correspondent is on a quest
for the Meaning of Life.*

HERE IS THE WILY PLATYPUS HUNTER, STALKING THE FORESTS OF
the night. He steps carefully into the pulsing darkness, feeling for
the trail with his foot. He breathes. Steps again. He doesn't want to
use his light yet, so he is moving slowly, slowly. The great eucalyptus trees all about soar 200 feet and more into an inky blue-black
sky, but the canopy itself is unseen above, a grand weight of leafy
life vaguely delineated by the unfamiliar stars of the southern
Australian sky. He steps again, and there is a muffled thud, which,
he deduces from long experience, is the sound of his own body
colliding with the trunk of a tree. It doesn't even hurt. Not that
much anyway. The bark is peeling off the tree in great long strips:
a stringy bark tree.

In less than four hours, the Platypus Hunter will be another
year older. He feels the seasons of his life slowly flapping in front
of his face like the beating of some great dark wing. You're born,
he thinks, you live, you die, and to what end?

Is our journey through life a quest? For enlightenment, perhaps? For nirvana? For a Union with the One? This is why the
wily Platypus Hunter is out walking into trees in the middle of
the night. He's pretty much clueless in the what-does-it-all-mean

department, but figures that a series of small highly defined quests—see a platypus in the wild, for instance—will one day accumulate into a critical mass and then there will be a blinding light like the collision of suns. In that radiant moment, the Platypus Hunter believes he will be able to see into the Very Core of the Universe.

I was about fifty miles north of Melbourne, on the far southern reaches of the Great Dividing Range, near the headwaters of Yea River, where the platypus, so I imagined, frolicked. The sun had set some time ago. The moon had not yet risen and the Hour of the Platypus was rapidly approaching.

Fear wasn't a factor. There wasn't much that could hurt me in this forest. Pigs, feral for generations, might leave me bleeding from a myriad of six-inch half-moon-shaped cuts, the scimitar tusks and upper teeth gnashing together like scissors in a cacophony of snorting grunts. Local tiger snakes are venomous and potentially deadly, as are all Australian snakes, but I'd yet to see one in two weeks of prowling the parklands above Melbourne. What they had here were koalas dozing in the trees, shy swamp wallabies—a kind of junior size kangaroo—as well as lyre birds, cockatoos, and burrowing wombats, an animal that can weigh up to 100 pounds and that looks a bit like a cross between a tiny bear cub and a Sherman tank.

I felt for the trail with a foot, took another step, and considered the idea of wombats in combat. Pursued by the native dingo, or by introduced dogs and foxes, a wombat retreats into the nearest burrow, dug for just such a purpose. There, secure under its home turf, the wombat waits. The predator who follows is in for a nasty, and, it seems to me, particularly marsupial, surprise. The fox or dingo or dog nips away at the wombat's bony rump, moving even deeper into the burrow. And then, in a narrow spot, the annoyed wombat simply pushes with its short stout legs, exerting tons of pressure, and crushing the skull of the would-be predator against unyielding earth. Wombats are brain smashers.

And so I was feeling around with my feet for wombat holes, but not because I had anything to fear from the creatures. In fact I hoped to see one. I just didn't want to break a leg stepping into a burrow without a light in the middle of the night. You could drop a volleyball down a typical wombat burrow.

My eyes had adjusted to the darkness, my confidence expanded, and I began taking two and three steps at a crack. Which was when I stepped on the tiger snake.

Everything happened very quickly. I was somewhere two or three feet above the trail, suddenly and involuntarily airborne. Gravity had no dominion over me. The tiger had twisted under my foot and the rest of its body thrashed in the foliage four feet away to my left. Big snake, I thought urgently, five or six feet long. Lotta venom.

In the fullness of time, I found myself some distance away, straddle-legged on the mute forest floor, where I dropped effortlessly into a gunfighter's crouch, right arm extended. The trigger seemed to pull itself and the night exploded into light.

And what the beam of the large handheld spotlight I carried revealed was not, in fact, a tiger snake. It was a wide, seven-foot-long strand of stringy bark shed by one of the eucalyptus trees. Had the big rechargeable halogen spotlight been a gun, I would have fired blindly into the night. The realization was a form of enlightenment I didn't care to contemplate. Even worse: had anyone seen me blow away the menacing strip of stringy bark?

I raked the forest with my spotlight. All the night things that crept and crawled below, that darted or soared above, were staring directly at me, in my solitary embarrassment. Their eyes, in the white-hot beam of light twelve inches in diameter, seemed vaguely demonic, as if the creatures in this southern Australian eucalyptus forest were burning up from within, all their hearts on fire. Literally dozens of sets of radiant eyes were focused on me, some of them red and demonic, like glowing coals; others shining a pale poisonous-looking yellow; and still others gleaming a cool and luminescent green. When I snapped off the spotlight after only twenty seconds, the eyes in the forest faded into a darkness that was more impenetrable than before, more absolute. It would take twenty minutes or more for my own eyes to readjust. For the moment, I couldn't see my hands in front of my face. I stood alone and still and silent. Listening.

Frogs along the riverbank grunted out their lust in an ir-regular bass beat that croaked along in counterpoint with the high-pitched chirping of bats. Owls—there were sev-eral of them—worked the horn section, hooting out short soft calls, which seemed to arouse a kind of rage in various species of possum who traded off in a series of angry solos: high in the trees, I heard the strange strangled gurgling of a possum called the yellow-bellied glider, and then the piercing bark of a sugar glider.

Above and unseen, there was an air war in progress. A "flying" possum, like the greater glider, can soar the length of football field on a wing called the patagium, a flap of skin that extends from the elbow to the knee. Flex-ing at the elbow, with the forepaws tucked under its chin, the possum spreads its wing and leaps from a perch high in the trees, falling into

*K*angaroo Island is also one of the best places in Australia to see koalas—a statement that does not fall entirely into the good-news department. Introduced onto the island decades ago, they've now overpopulated their habitat, often killing the eucalyptuses that are their only food by strip-ping them of their leaves.

We set off into the woods near Craig's house one morning and, within minutes, spotted a koala in the fork of a river red gum, flaunting all the traits that have made it such a Australian icon: plush fur, button eyes, big fuzzy ears, receding chin, and W. C. Fields nose, all adding up to an expression of incomparable, endearing world-weariness. One study I read said koalas spend 14.5 hours of every day sleeping—and another 4.8 resting. Couch potatoes of the world, meet your natural-born totem.

♦

—Mel White, "Wine, Wildlife, and Song," *National Geographic Traveler* a gradually descending glide path, and sometimes swerving off at right angles to its direction of flight. Greater gliders are pursued, and sometimes even taken in midair, by the rufous owl. The possum lands as a hang glider might, by turning back upward into the night sky, and using gravity as an air brake. It lands on all fours against the trunk of a tree.

There were greater gliders in the trees above, feeding on the eucalyptus leaves. I'd seen them earlier in my light and marked them by their eyeshine, which was a brilliant whitish yellow. They were known to turn away from direct light. The brushtailed possums stared directly into the spot and theirs were the bright-red horror-film eyes.

Most animals native to Australia are nocturnal, and, like all nocturnal creatures, evolution has engineered their eyes to collect and concentrate available light. Night-adapted vertebrates have a reflecting layer of cells backing the retina called the tapetum lucidum, the bright carpet. What light there is enters through the pupil, and is partially absorbed by the retina, the inside back wall of the eyeball. Light that is not absorbed by the retina is reflected back into the eye by the tapetum lucidum, effectively giving the animal a second chance to see the image.

When a bright artificial light is directed into such an eye, it will seem to glow, as if from within. The phenomenon is called eyeshine. Various droplets of colored oil in the cells of the eye of different species give each a distinct colored eyeshine. Cats' eyes seem to glow green; rabbits' are yellowish, deer are a very pale yellow, and wolves' eyes are greenish gold. The West Indian tree boa's are red-orange, and the Nile crocodile's are bright red, as are the eyes of alligators and caiman.

I once believed that the eyes of all nocturnal predators shone red. This, until very recently, had been a matter of lifelong misperception. At night, in the wild, I did not want to catch the red eye, and, more to the point, I did not want the red eye to catch me. In my mind, the association of predators and glowing red eyes has been reinforced by any number of flash photographs I've taken in which my friends' true and blood-ridden souls seem to flash out of bright-red pinpoints in their eyes. Humans are predators, these photographs seem to say, and you can see it in our eyes.

The physics of the situation are not so damning. A flash is used in low-light situations, when the pupil of the eye is open wide so that the full force of blinding light enters the eyeball and reflects back out the still open pupil at the same angle. What we see in those burning and satanic red orbs staring back at us out of the latest batch of snapshots is not the predatory nature of the human soul. It is the reflection of the blood vessels in the back of the eye. Still, the camera companies have developed anti-red-eye technology in the hope, I suppose, that we will, in our photos, seem to be maturing into a kinder and gentler race.

It took nearly a century before Western scientists were able to conclude that an egg-laying creature could, in fact, be a mammal. Because the platypus is such a biological oddity—web-footed, fur-bearing, and duck-billed—I had assumed it was rare and endangered. In fact, the most conservative estimate is that there are tens of thousands of them inhabiting rivers and streams along the eastern seaboard of Australia, all the way from Melbourne to Queensland.

They are not, however, often seen. Platypuses spend their nights swimming and their days curled up in burrows dug deep into riverbanks and set a foot to ten feet above the water. They like it cold—the colder the better—and carry more fur per square inch than any other creature on earth. The little duck-billed guy can withstand lower temperatures than a polar bear, or so the research suggests.

A platypus dines on freshwater crayfish and worms, but the bulk of its diet consists of caddis fly larvae sunk in the mud at the bottom of the river. Diving with its eyes closed, the platypus roots around in the mud, looking for the larvae with its sensitive bill, which is soft and wet, blue-black in color, and more like a dog's nose than a duck's bill.

In Australia, the platypus is protected throughout its range, but it is threatened by pollution, riverbank erosion, and predation by foxes.

I'd seen a few platypuses at the Healesville Sanctuary, in Healesville, north of Melbourne. It's a place where injured animals—

wallabies, wombats, the whole panoply of southern Australian wildlife—are brought for rehabilitation. Platypuses, whose diets are not significantly different than that of trout, are sometimes, accidentally caught on a fisherman's fly line. Some few, trapped in the stream that flows through the sanctuary, are on display, in a nocturnal aquarium situation, where lights are dimmed and fragmented, like moonlight falling through foliage. There, the platypus seemed to frolic, rather like otters, and they were much smaller than I'd imagined: a large adult male would be about two feet long and weigh just over four pounds. The tail is broad and flat, like a beaver's, and is used as a rudder.

At Healesville, I spoke with the platypus keeper, a man who calls himself Fisk. Just Fisk. Handling a male platypus, he said, is problematic: it is the world's only venomous mammal. There are two six-inch-long horny spurs on the hind legs which are connected to venom secreting glands. Males tend to use the spurs during breeding season altercations, which can be deadly to one or both competing platypuses. The poison is not fatal to man, but it is painful. People stung on the hand won't be playing the guitar for several months.

In Fisk's experience, platypuses like to be stroked on the bill. They recognize individual humans and like to play. Sometimes, when Fisk is

---

*H*ealesville Sanctuary, about an hour's drive east of Melbourne, is situated in a forest of soaring manna gums and bisected by a creek lined with tree ferns. Healesville is just as much a wildlife sanctuary as it is a zoo. In fact, wild platypuses make their homes on the creek banks and occasionally can be seen by lucky zoo-goers. The zoo also has a fine platypusary, where visitors can come within inches of a dabbling duckbill. In total, the zoo houses 200 species of Australian birds, mammals and reptiles. Where possible, exhibits, such as walk-through aviaries, have been designed to allow visitors close access to the animals.

◆

—Paul Prince, "Not-So-Wild Wildlife," *Travel Holiday*

working, the platypuses crawl out of their aquarium burrows, prop their little elbows on the rim of the enclosure, and stare at him sitting at the desk. It's hard to get a lot of work done, he told me, when the platypuses want to party.

I had decided that, in Australia, the platypus would be my totem animal partially because of our mutual tendency to spend most of the day sleeping and most of the night frolicking about and eating. More to the point, there was something quintessentially "high school" about the creature, something endearing and adolescent and immediately accessible. Who didn't feel like a platypus in sophomore English: so strange, so different from the rest, so inherently dorky as to be unclassifiable by science. Platypus boys and platypus girls confined to Platypus High, mammals all and some of us filled with venom.

So the platypus hunt was a personal exploration into what I'd been and what I'd become. To that end, I'd scouted the Yea River during the day, looking for likely platypus habitat. The river flowed through a forest of mountain ash eucalyptus, the tallest hardwood trees in the world. Some of them were well over 300 feet high, and the leaves were all concentrated at the top of the trees, so that a good deal of light fell on the forest floor, which was consequently covered with chest-high grasses and prehistoric-looking tree ferns. The leaves of the mountain ash, seen from below, were silver, and they shimmered in the breeze against a cobalt-blue sky.

The river was very narrow, only five feet across and four feet deep where it burbled through its narrows. As the Yea wound through the forest, it created cut banks five and six feet high, and these were places where a platypus might dig a burrow, which can be 100 feet long.

Fallen trees, in various stages of mossy disintegration, spanned the Yea, and the river was a muddy golden color, its waters essentially a strong tea made of eucalyptus leaves. Shafts of sunlight fell on the water, and in those places, the Yea looked like a golden mirror. Caddis flies were hatching out of the sun-dappled river.

These were the places I'd marked in my mind's map, the places I'd spotlight well after full dark.

And so, in the Hour of the Platypus, and for reasons that seemed obscure, even at the time, I chose to drop to my belly and crawl through the night toward the river. No lights. At one of my intended observation sites, just off the trail that paralleled the river, a newly fallen mountain ash formed a bridge across the Yea. I knew I was in the right spot when I found myself entangled in the exposed root system. Crawling through a big muddy root ball in the dark is an annoying and time-consuming task. It took fifteen minutes to find a position on the trunk, over the river. I took a deep breath, held it, then hit the trigger on my spot. And, by God, there he was. The very first time I spotted the river: a platypus! Or at least something furry, swimming. A dark swirl and it was gone. The creature might have been a water rat, I suppose, but water rats don't sport beaverlike tails. At another site, I saw another platypus only two hours later.

The great dark wing has flapped once again, and here's the wily Platypus Hunter returning from the river, yet another year older, and perhaps one quest wiser. Suns have not precisely collided in an explosion of white-hot light. In point of fact, the rechargeable spotlight carried by the Hunter is rapidly running out of juice. Its light has become feeble and yellow, totally inadequate for the task at hand. Presently the damn thing simply sputters weakly and dies.

This makes walking difficult and the tallest hardwood trees on earth assault the Hunter at every step. Stringy bark snakes litter his path.

He resolves that, in the future, he will carry two sources of light into the forest at night. And that's it, he thinks. That's the extent of the evening's epiphany, lesson number one out of Platypus High:

Anyone who aspires to see into the Very Core of the Universe Itself is advised to bring along two sources of light.

Tim Cahill also contributed "Speak Oz" in Part One.

GARY A. WARNER

Bondi Beach

It's an Australian Malibu,
and worth a visit.

I'M SUNBURNED FROM THE TOPS OF MY EARS TO THE TOPS OF MY feet, there's a nasty scrape on my knee, and everything tastes like salt water since I inhaled the Pacific while bodysurfing without fins.

But there's—no kidding—shrimp on the barbie (yes, Australians do drop the "cue" when talking about outdoor grilling). A tinnie (translation: can) of ice-cold Foster's lager is balanced on a window ledge above my head.

Across the street, two bronzed women wearing sunglasses, bikini bottoms and nothing else but a sheen of suntan oil chat up a lifeguard in a tiny red Speedo who looks like a video box cover boy for *Buns of Steel*.

Just another Thursday afternoon on Bondi Beach, the famous sand strand in suburban Sydney. Wait until Saturday, everybody says. Then Bondi really rocks.

At Bondi, life is a beach. Every day. Sunup to well past sundown. It's my favorite beach in the world because it is so much itself, all the time. An almost surreal world of beach babes, boys, beer, and barbie.

It also is a greatest hits of my favorite parts of other beaches: it has the waves of Hawaii's Waimea Bay, the playfulness of Britain's

Brighton, the urban verve of Rio's Ipanema, and the proud, preen-ing sun-worship scene of Malibu's Surfrider.

Relaxing against the hood of a black Toyota Celica convertible after a grueling four-hour stint of snoozing in the sun, Scott Damnerer said he had been to most of the famous beaches around Sydney, but keeps coming back to Bondi.

"It's a great beach with nice sand and good waves," he said. "It's clean, close to everything, and has a much more eclectic scene that anywhere else—it's our Venice Beach."

His companion, black-bikini-clad Dleanne Lewis, was more concise about the appeal for her.

"I come here to see hot bodies," she said, a sly grin curling beneath her wraparound shades.

See them you do. Bondi is tops optional and about one-third of the women are wearing only bikini bottoms. And it's equal-op-portunity ogling. Many of the men wear brief swim-team trunks that look great if you have less than 3 percent body fat.

Like most places around the world, the bit of exposed flesh doesn't set off howls of outrage—the beach is also popular with scores of families.

A highlight of many summer weekends is the famous lifeguard contests, when well-chiseled blond men and women in red swim gear and funky bathing caps show their stuff when it comes to life-saving, swimming, and running.

The crowd favorite is the dory competition, when teams march, three on a side, with the heavy boat into the surf, then row out and try to navigate their way back through the crashing waves (which often crash on them, sending teams into the water).

Most visitors make Bondi a day trip from the city. I say flip it. Stay in Bondi and go out for part of the day on the tourist trail from The Rocks to the Opera House before heading back for sun-set by the sea. It beats the noise and hustle of the Kings Cross red-light district.

For dinner you can pick from a number of beachside cafés serving everything from cutting-edge Pacific Rim cuisine to grill-your-own emu steaks. There are numerous hotels and guest houses, the perfect place to dive head first into the up-all-night summer party scene. If you'd rather sleep, just remember to throw a pair of earplugs in with the sunscreen and Ray-Bans.

Gary A. Warner is travel editor of the Orange County Register.

$\ast\ \overset{\ast}{}\ \ast$

Link to Another World

A visitor experiences mail bonding
in the Outback.

THE RED–DIRT RUNWAY APPEARS AS A MIRAGE AMIDST A WASTELAND of barren mountains and endless desert.

Piloting what may be the world's most grueling mail run, Steve Davis readies his Aero Commander 688S for a landing at the Moolatwanna sheep station, in the heart of Australia's impressively empty Outback.

Seconds later, as the plane lands, tires screech on the sand, rocks and weeds of the runway. Off in the distance, a gray Land Cruiser rumbles toward the landing strip, sending dust from the Strezlecki Desert into the brilliant, blue sky.

"G'day, Steve. It's nice to see you again," says Audrey Sheehan, as Davis piles from the plane to deliver the Moolatwanna mailbag. In return, Sheehan hands him a bag of outgoing mail.

Wearing a blue blouse, sandals and a wide-brimmed leather hat, Sheehan owns the ranch along with her husband Mike. At 485 square miles, Moolatwanna is the smallest property along the Channel Mail Run—a weekly route that provides service to more than two dozen small towns and stations (or ranches) in the Australian interior.

Covered with dust, I step off the plane after Davis. I am just

along for the ride, taking part in a "tour" offered by Augusta
Airways, the carrier contracted by Australia Post to make deliveries to some of the most remote mailboxes in the land Down
Under. In all, there are about a dozen mail runs serving the
Outback, and a few tourists are allowed on each ride.

From my perspective, I've chosen the most intriguing of the
tours. Billed as the "world's longest," the Channel Mail Run serves
a forgotten, 1,800-mile stretch of desolate land, where distance and
isolation have created an environment that only people of the utmost strength and resourcefulness can call home.

As Davis puts it, "It takes a different breed to live out here."
Indeed, Port Augusta—the nearest population center as well as the
jump-off point for the mail run—seems a world away.

Every Saturday morning, the mail plane heads north from Port
Augusta's small airport, and
every Sunday night it returns. Along the way, it traverses the Great Artesian
Basin, perhaps the world's
greatest reservoir.

"That's why it's called the
Channel Mail Run," says Deb
Grantham, an employee of
Augusta Airlines. "When it
rains in northern Queensland,
the rains come down in channels and flood the inland
desert areas." This runoff—
along Cooper Creek and the
Diamintina and Georgina
river systems—occurs across a
staggering 800,000 square
miles of arid land.

As I later learn, the floods
are both an omen and blessing. While water is essential

*T*here's a rusty old refrigerator lying on its back
in the desert. It's the only sign of
human life in this burnt-orange
landscape. Matthew Poole lifts
the door of the fridge and drops
in a canvas sack full of mail. "It'll
stay dry in here," he tells me and
secures the door in place. This
fridge is the communal mailbox
at a remote cattle station in
Australia's Sturt Stony Desert.
The station is hidden from view
by the desert bush and undulating landscape, but Poole assures
me it's not far.

◆

—Kari Bodnarchuk,
"Outback Overview"

for raising cattle and sheep, it also leaves ranches and towns isolated for days, weeks, even months.

This is bad news for people such as John Talbott, who seems to embody the spirit of the Outback with his hand-rolled cigarettes, Blundstone boots, blue jeans and wide-brimmed cowboy hat.

Talbott lives with his wife and two children at Durham Downs, a 4,000-square-mile cattle ranch on the banks of Cooper Creek, at the edge of the Sturt Stony Desert. In a sentiment shared by many, Talbott says he treasures the isolation that comes with living near the center of the world's flattest and driest continent.

"I love it out here," he explains, offering a one-word reason: "peace."

Despite the seclusion, there seems to be an intense sense of community among the towns and stations along the Channel Mail Run. Most people I meet in this vast land either know each other, know of each other or have some common acquaintance.

"Out here you know everyone," says Allison Bammann, a gardener at the 12,500-square-mile Innamincka station. "Down at the pub, we're pretty much the only people there, and we can have parties just for the people who work at the stations around here. It's great."

Or is it? As Talbott points out, there is one obstacle to Outback life, and it's neither the intense heat nor the unbearable bush flies, which buzz around his eyes, ears, nose and mouth as he speaks.

For this cowboy, the one "crook" thing about life in the Channel Country is, simply, "I've got to drive 150 miles to the nearest pub."

That would be the Birdsville Hotel, a 112-year-old watering hole in the tiny town that bears its name. Inside is a wall decorated with dozens of wide-brimmed hats, all torn, tattered and frayed, with names of their former owners: Highway Jimmy, Chopper Tony, Bazaa Skolee, Dylan Stoddy, Pee Wee Clark.

"You've got to live out here at least a year before you get your hat on the wall," says Richard Calliss, bartender at the pub, which is just across the street from the airstrip.

Birdsville is one of five towns on the mail run, along with Leigh

Creek, Innamincka, Bedourie and Boulia—the unofficial extra-terrestrial capital of the Outback.

For decades, residents of this town (population: 250), where we spend a night, have been baffled by a strange phenomenon called the Min Min Lights. Apparently, the Min Mins are ghostly luminous lights, which float through the air as if someone is carrying a lantern in the mist. Yet no one has managed to capture or photograph them.

Talk to Tania Tully, coowner of the Australian Hotel, and she'll tell you the Min Min Lights are merely liquid-induced lies. "The best way to see the Min Mins," she says, "is to grab a seat at the bar and start drinking the rum."

So I take her advice and even increase my odds by drinking a stubby (or bottle) of Australian lager. But much to my dismay, after climbing atop the water tower on the outskirts of town for a panoramic view of the surrounding landscape, I see nothing.

Tania's husband John has had better luck. "Yeah, I've seen them—twice—when I was a little boy," he explains. "I was camping with a bunch of my friends. At first we thought it was a car coming toward us in the distance, but it never got any closer."

Over the years, there have been many guesses, theories and explanations (fire flies, birds covered in fungi, moon mirages...), but as of yet, none have disproved the Min Min phenomenon.

As John Tully says, with not a shot of rum in his hand, "Yup, the Min Mins are out there. They're definitely out there."

Some might say, though, that the only thing "out there" are the folks who live in Australia's interior. Yet for all its isolation and hardship, the Outback is becoming more mainstream for some of its inhabitants.

"Up until a few years ago, all the communication was by high-frequency radio, which wasn't all that good," Davis says. "It used to break down a lot. Now they have television, radio, and last year they got telephones. Some people even have fax machines."

But make no mistake—this is a wild, unpredictable country, and there are still times when Mother Nature takes the upper hand. Our return flight from Boulia is a case in point.

Sudden rains on the Queensland coast have triggered floods in the Channel Country, and the muddy waters of the Cooper River are threatening to keep the town of Bedourie and a few ranches isolated for months.

During such a crisis, the mail runs take on added importance. As Bedourie's Jim Smith says, "We've got telephones now, but apart from that, we really got nothing. We don't even have newspapers. Most people rely on the mail service. They call it an essential service."

Pee Wee Clark, station manager at Glengyle, which is also besieged by floods, echoes the sentiment.

"Mate, we would really be stranded without the mail runs," he says, after Davis flies in mail, as well as disaster supplies such as groceries, newspapers and, of course, beer (courtesy of The Birdsville Pub). "Seriously, if we ever lost this service, we might as well roll up our swags and leave."

Which is exactly what Davis plans to do. Leave his job, that is. Once Davis, 36, makes his final pickup at Leigh Creek on the way home, he is officially an ex-pilot of the Channel Mail Run. His new job will be with the Royal Flying Doctor Service, working out of Alice Springs. He admits that exhaustion played a role in his resignation.

"This mail run is crazy," Davis says. "By the time I get home, I've made fifty-six landings and takeoffs in two days. And by the end of the weekend, I've used up as much adrenaline as most pilots do in a year."

Personally, I am just along for the ride, but by the time we touch down in Port Augusta, my pillow is calling. Yet I feel exhilaration as well—from the stark, almost haunting beauty harbored in the huge skies and timeless landscape of the Channel Country; the opportunity to share time with a community of people who don't get many visitors; and the chance to see how vital communication is in a place such as the Outback.

As Steve Davis explains, with bags under his eyes and sweat on his brow, "The thing we try and get across to people is that this really isn't a tour. It's a mail run. A fair dinkum mail run. And our first priority is the mail."

Andrew Tarica is a writer and editor living in New York City. Armed with only a backpack, fly rod and laptop computer, he traveled in 1995 along the "left bank of the Pacific Rim," from Tasmania to Kamchatka.

ROBERT L. STRAUSS

Cutting Teeth in Queensland

All he wanted was a home on the range.

THERE'S A LOT OF THINGS THAT WILL KILL YOU IN THE FAR NORTH-eastern corner of Australia known as tropical north Queensland. The Australians who live there never tire of telling visitors about the many hazards present in their state, famed as home to the Great Barrier Reef. It's as though once you've made the fifteen-hour trip from California the locals inadvertently intend that you should never leave your hotel room.

Despite its perils, Queensland does have something for every-one. There's the famed Australian Outback—millions of acres of barely inhabited nothingness. There's the Reef, with its thousands of islands and countless dive spots. There's the tropical rain forest which cascades down to the very edge of the ocean. And there's the beach, hundreds of miles of brilliant white sand, utterly un-peopled and unspoiled. Aside from snowcapped mountains, Queensland has every possible setting a tourist might want. And every one of them has something sure to kill you.

Steel fencing encloses vast stretches of beach to keep them safe from the great whites that prowl offshore. During Queensland's early spring and summer, a second, inner net is dragged out to keep the swimming areas clear of box jellyfish or "stingers" as the locals call them. One well-meaning Queenslander told me that should I get stung I'd have ninety seconds to get back to shore, find some vinegar, and splash it on the stingers. This would neutralize their deadly toxins. Fortunately, he explained, there are bottles of vinegar left out at all public beaches. Unfortunately, if I didn't make it in time, I'd begin to lose consciousness and death would quickly follow.

Of course, he reminded me, that while deranged and racing panic-stricken from the surf, I should try not to attract the attention of any of Queensland's thousands of enormous crocodiles that regularly drag inattentive bathers to gruesome and bloody submarine deaths. And don't get them started about scorpions, spiders, deadly rain forest plants, or Queensland's famed

> The rain forests of northern Queensland have had plenty of time to work on security precautions, about 100 million years. That's 90 million years before the Amazon rain forest raised a respectable tangle of branches. While this ancient forest squawked with life, the jungles of Africa were just a glimmer in distant seedlings. But as we trekked through the dense biomass, the cast of deadly characters faded and I lapsed into a Deep North mindset: don't step on it, and you live.
>
> ◆
>
> —Tony Perrottet, "Going Off the Deep End," *Escape*

and endangered cassowary bird, which, unlike its relatives the ostrich and emu, is aggressive and can kick a grown man twenty feet through the air, splitting his chest open in the process.

I'm a reasonably adventurous traveler. I've bungee jumped. I've stepped out of a perfectly good airplane 15,000 feet above the ground. In one twelve-month stretch I visited four different countries all claiming to be the world's most destitute. I even rent an apartment in San Francisco. There's not much that scares me. But this constant confrontation with nature's deadly side gave me the idea that boldly probing Queensland's many wonders might result in more adventure than I wanted.

After a few stunning dives on the reef and with "stinger" season about to begin I decided that the dry Outback might be a bit less hazardous than the wet and wild coast.

Ha! I was told by each and every Queenslander. Had I never heard of the taipan, the brown snake, the death adder, or the tiger snake? Didn't I know that Australia was home to eight of the ten deadliest snakes in the world? No, it's eighteen of the world's twenty most deadly snakes another well intended, proud and chauvinistic Aussie informed me with the same zeal New Yorkers once used when bragging about the crime problem in their city. (Just so I shouldn't miss the point, during my visit one of the local papers reported that fatal snake attacks had risen 600 percent in 1998 alone.)

Well then, maybe just a daytime bush walk in the Outback, I suggested. Fine, I was told. Just be careful of the black spear grass, an innocent-looking plant with a seed that catches on one's socks and then slowly corkscrews its way into one's ankles where the body's natural humidity causes it to germinate. The well-meaning man who guided me through the eerie lava tubes of Undara National Park told me that occasionally very nasty infections result, with a plant eventually erupting on the other side of one's leg. Clearly this was something I wanted to avoid because bringing live plants back from Australia would violate USDA and Customs Department regulations.

Having survived the reef, rain forest, and Outback, I was ready to see more of Queensland's nonfatal side. "What about a farm stay?" I asked of the tourism people. "Well, ah, okay," they said.

Nearly all Americans come to Queensland to dive the reef. My request for a home-on-the-range experience had them ruffling through their brochures.

"What kind of farm?" they asked.

"How about an alpaca farm?" I said.

"Al-what-a?" the woman said.

If nothing else, the Australians are persistent and not long after I was headed toward the Willow Park Alpaca Stud and Albion Farm Stay, home to a herd, rather "mob," of fuzzy, funny-looking, and, most importantly, nonvenomous alpacas. The worse they could do was gob some spit at you, I was told. *Nonvenomous* spit.

I didn't know much about alpacas. A few years earlier I had seen a mob of them in the San Juan Islands of Washington State. Their fur was the king of all fibers I learned, more prized than cashmere or pashmina. Alpacas and an alpaca farm, I thought, might be the way out of my confined, urban apartment existence and to a long-held back-to-the-land fantasy that once had me and my wife working on a goat farm. But unlike goats or cows, alpacas don't require milking twice a day. Aside from an annual shearing, they pretty much take care of themselves.

Driving through the Australian countryside, I passed towns with names that only Fred Flintstone could have conjured up. Towns like Biddaddaba. The welcoming sign for the city of Warwick informed me that I was passing through a "tidy town." Albion was not far away. I began to daydream about my future as one of America's great alpaca barons, rocking away on the porch of my alpaca Ponderosa, contemplating the fortunes of my mob with my feet up. Far away from the perils of sharks, and stingers, and spear grass, and crocodiles, I began to relax and enjoy Queensland's gently rolling farmland.

My daydream came to an end at a small rural junction outside Warwick where a sign pointed to the town of Albion. But a few minutes down the road I had more than covered the distance with no sign of a town. After turning around, I quickly arrived at Willow Park Stud, realizing that in rural Australia you don't have to be as big as a town or village to have your own road sign. You can just be a house or a farm. Albion and Willow Park were one and the same.

Forty furry, long-necked, absolutely goofy-looking alpacas stood quietly clustered together in the large paddock. A few had been shorn and their odd, camel-like features must have inspired George Lucas and his production designers when they first imagined some of the creatures that inhabit the world of *Star Wars*. Out strode Harry Liaubon, who together with wife Jen, owns Willow Park and has been in the alpaca business for more than ten years.

Harry, with his stiff gray mustache, head of perfectly silver hair, and a broad, gap-tooth smile, looked more the retired Buckingham Palace guard than alpaca tycoon. On the "barbie" he had a six-inch-thick, butterflied leg of lamb that easily weighed ten pounds.

"Do you have other guests?" I asked Harry who easily juggled cigarette, beer, and grill tools while swatting at the flies that should be Australia's national bird.

"No, Robby," he said. "Just the three of us. It'll cook down. You'll see. No worries."

"Australia," I thought. "Big country. Big food."

Over dinner Harry and Jen gave me a brief tutorial on alpacas. They're a high plains animal from the Andes whose wool was once coveted for royal garments. Now they provide the yarn for the finest of woolen goods. An alpaca sweater at Neiman Marcus, for example, can go for $500 or more.

At Albion, Harry and Jen raised the more common *huacaya* with its coat of puff-ball wool as well as *suris* whose wool hangs in long, tightly curled locks like the tassels of a flapper's dress. "Just feel this, Robby," Jen said. I plunged my hands in a large bag of alpaca fiber. Until someone begins weaving feathers or baby's hair it will have no challengers.

I told Harry and Jen that I had come to Albion for a hands-on experience. I wanted to know if alpacas were in my future. They shouldn't coddle me. "Right," Harry said, "No worries, Robby. We can cut some teeth tomorrow."

That sounded good—until the next morning when I learned that Harry really meant cutting teeth—alpaca teeth. For an alpaca, life at Willow Park is the gravy train. Without having to forage

> *T*he "Australian Wave" is a skill all visitors develop if they leave the urban areas. Flies are so prevalent and irritating in the bush that you are constantly waving them away. The best way to maintain your sanity is to wear a net over your face.
>
> ◆
>
> —LH

among the rocky plains of the Andean altiplano their teeth grow indefinitely, like beavers or woodchucks without wood to chuck.

"Problem is," Harry explained, "that when the *machos* (males) are battling for mates they tend to bite each others' testicles. So we need to cut their teeth." I briefly put myself in the male alpaca's place. Have my teeth cut with a garden shears or have my testicles bitten by a romantic rival. It was a choice that made me want to forget about dating altogether.

Like goats, alpacas are gregarious animals. They like company. Trying to separate one from the mob is like trying to split a drop of mercury. Jen, Harry, the dog, and I eventually penned half a dozen animals in a small corral and then went after our intended, long-toothed quarry, a pure, all-white *suri* named "Whitewater." Chasing the quick, fuzzy, jumpy animals on wet grass pebbled with slippery alpaca droppings was the kind of activity guaranteed to appear on a "stupidest home videos" program. I, of course, had brought only one pair of pants.

Once we had Whitewater in his own corral, it was time for a bit of dental hygiene. But first, of course, we had to get ahold of him. Harry, 59, strong and wiry, demonstrated, walking slowly behind Whitewater before grabbing a fistful of wool under the neck while going for a headlock with his other arm. "Right," he said freeing the animal. "Now you try it, Robby."

In my still semipresentable pants, I cautiously approached Whitewater from behind as Harry had done. We stood about the same height, 5'7". Harry told me the larger *machos* weigh about 180 pounds so Whitewater had me by 40 pounds. "I can do this," I told myself.

With the animal in reach, I lunged. My hands found nothing to grab. The first six inches of an unshorn alpaca is utter fluff. While I tried to reach deeper, Whitewater saw his chance and landed a crushing, backwards upper cut of the foreleg to my ribcage. As I struggled to hold on (and get my breath back), Harry quickly pried open Whitewater's mouth to take a look at his testicle-tearing teeth. "No," he said, "this one can wait. But let's give 'm a pedicure since you're so cozy and all." Harry quickly clutched Whitewater's feet and snipped off the overgrown, claw-like hooves with the same garden shears he would have used on Whitewater's teeth.

Over lunch, Harry and Jen explained the economics of alpaca ranching. In Australia, an alpaca can live for twenty years while producing seven to eleven pounds of wool each year. The wool sells for about $20 a pound so a good producer might earn a few hundred dollars annually. Yet a highly prized female or *hembra* can sell for $50,000 or more. Although I have an MBA from a prestigious business school, I couldn't quite figure out the bottom line in this.

"Well, you see," Jen said, "nowadays the business is in the breeding, not the wool."

"You're lucky if the wool pays for the feed," Harry added.

Evidently, for years alpaca farming has been a coming thing. There are said to be only 10,000 alpacas outside South America, and ranchers have been waiting for the animal's day to arrive. Meanwhile, long-term alpaca breeders like Harry and Jen, he a retired automotive engineer, she a retired oncology nurse, have become well-to-do beyond their dreams. It all started because Jen saw an alpaca for sale that was so cute she couldn't resist it.

"You're looking at three quarters of a million out there, Robby," Harry said to me as we quietly rocked on the porch of *his* forty-acre Ponderosa.

"Really?" I said, amazed that so few animals could be so valuable.

"Course, I don't mean to big note myself," he said.

"What do you mean?" I asked.

"Big note myself?" he said. "Oh, I don't mean to wave the flag is all," he added as a way of explanation before taking a drag on his cigarette and a pull on his beer.

Australians possess a bewildering multitude of peculiar expressions. It's as though, separated from the rest of the world, the English language has evolved much in the same way Australia's fauna has, resulting in expressions as unusual as the koala or platypus. Harry was simply trying to explain that he didn't mean to boast about his and Jen's success. These two unassuming alpaca farmers had become wealthy on an animal that costs far more to buy than it can ever recover with its fleece. I realized I could afford to become an alpaca rancher just about the same time I could afford to buy a home in San Francisco.

A few years ago Harry and Jen's mob numbered 160. That was when they ranched near Melbourne. They moved north in search of peace and quiet. Rural Queensland is a quiet, slow-moving place. Something like agricultural America thirty or forty years ago. And in this vast quiet, Albion was very quiet. Not much more sound than the occasional bleating of a sheep or the wind rustling through the eucalyptus.

With my fantasies of an alpaca empire dashed, I resolved to learn what I could in the time I had left at Albion. With the animals so expensive, why, I wondered, wasn't there more artificial insemination, which might bring the price down to where I could start out with an itsy-bitsy mob of two or three animals.

"Can't do it, Robby," Harry began. "They've spent millions researching it. You see, the *macho*'s a dribbling ejaculator. You just can't get enough of the stuff."

"Well, I suppose you could try to catch some of it—you know—afterwards," Jen said before going on to describe a process that could only interest an alpaca breeder or, possibly, a member of Ken Starr's staff.

"And you see," Jen added, "the *hembra*, well, she's an opportunistic ovulator. You can't really know when she might be ready."

"She needs that warm and fuzzy feeling," Harry said, before she'll release an egg. Apparently a turkey baster just isn't what fires a female alpaca's libido.

For several days Harry and Jen had been anxiously awaiting the arrival of a baby alpaca or *cria*. Every couple of hours we went out to a small corral to see if Tammy, the pregnant *hembra*, had "unpacked." I was scheduled to leave that afternoon but decided to stay another night, hoping to witness the *cria*'s birth. Jen said there was nothing cuter than a newborn alpaca. I didn't doubt it.

Over dinner that evening Harry and Jen confided to me that what they most like about alpaca farming are the clear nights when they go out into the paddock, hand in hand, lie down beneath the stars, and listen to the alpacas. "They make this delightful murmuring sound," Jen explained.

Tammy didn't unpack while I was at Albion but during my last night I did walk out into the paddock. Fires glowed along the dark horizon where farmers were burning their fields. The night sky was black and filled with unfamiliar stars. Huddled together against the slight chill, the mob lay quietly murmuring, their soft rumblings like a chorus of small brooks cascading through a mossy forest. Maybe I never would be able to afford an alpaca ranch of my own. But I had found a wonderful place in Queensland—a place where there was nothing to kill me but the quiet.

Robert L. Strauss has worked in more than fifty countries. His articles have appeared in the Los Angeles Times, Chicago Tribune, Saveur, *and other Travelers' Tales books. He is currently serving as country director for the Peace Corps in Cameroon.*

TONY PERROTTET

Fraser Sand

*It's easy to get stuck on the world's
largest sand island.*

I NEVER REALIZED THAT REAL MEN WERE EXPECTED TO HAVE AN innate understanding of four-wheel drives until I got bogged on Seventy-five Mile Beach. At low tide the wet sands of this spectacularly wide—and, yes, seventy-five-mile-long-stretch of coastline on Fraser Island are as hard as asphalt and much smoother, so 4WDs full of vacationing Aussies tear up and down past the pounding surf at fifty miles an hour as if it were an immense golden highway. (In fact, it is a legally designated road: on busy holidays the police are said to breath-test drunken drivers.) But I had foolishly strayed onto the drier part of the beach, where the sand was soft. In about two minutes my wheels were spinning; the more I gunned the engine, the deeper they sank.

Somehow, I hadn't absorbed many of the instructions on how to drive my tanklike rental Toyota Land Cruiser, which had been summed up in about twenty seconds by a laconic old character at the agency in Brisbane. So now, apart from exotic details about tides, wheel locks, and tire pressure, I was wondering what to do about the other gearshift, which had 2H, 4H, and 4L etched into it like hieroglyphics. I did remember the agent's smirk when I asked him a few questions.

"Yer'll figure it out," he'd said. Only here I was, poring over the Land Cruiser's instruction manual, and I wasn't figuring.

Getting bogged on Fraser Island isn't just inevitable, it's an integral part of the social scene. It was only a few seconds before another 4WD bounced across the sand and stopped. Out stepped a lobster-pink couple, Neville and Sharon. With his savagely peeling nose, half-shredded shorts, and silver reflective sunglasses, I could tell Nev was an old Fraser hand.

He didn't say a word as he pulled out a rope, tied together our bumper bars, and helped my car out of its hole; it was apparently too embarrassing to see another bloke humbled like this.

But Sharon, hitching up her bikini and sarong, broke the ice in a shrill voice: "It's pretty humiliating getting stuck in the sand, don't you reckon?"

"I reckon I'll survive," I said as nonchalantly as I could, but Nev wasn't going to let my battered manhood off so easily.

"Did youse ever start to wonder," he asked with some relish, "whether the tide was coming in or going out?" If the tide had been coming in, of course, the 4WD would have been swept out to sea (which, as everyone knows, voids the rental insurance; there was a photo at the agency showing one car in the waves, with the legend, *This cost the customer $16,000*). We had a good laugh about that, and went on to a virile discussion on tide movements and the finer points of sand driving. It turned out that the most powerful gear on sand is low range second, not first. How could I not have known?

"Put it in low, whack it in second, and *give it to 'er!*" Nev said, thumping me heartily on the back. "Doesn't matter if yer wreck 'er. After all, she's only a bloody rental."

Sand, Sand, Sand. It's not a substance I'd ever given undue thought to, even while I was growing up in Sydney, a city more infatuated with the beach than Rio de Janeiro. But on Fraser Island you can't exactly help but ponder the stuff. Located off the Queensland coast, a few hours drive north of Brisbane, the long, thin, crooked finger of Fraser is the world's largest sand island.

But Fraser Island is quite unlike any other mass of sand. Its ecology is unique, a fact that eventually placed it on the UN's World Heritage List in 1992. Instead of barren desert, the island's entire interior is covered with a rich patchwork of forests whose muscular masses of vegetation manage to survive on the nutrients in only the top six inches of sand.

The landscape changes every few hundred yards, from classic Aussie scrub of eucalyptus trees to reed-filled swamps surrounded by 200-foot-high satinay trees to astonishingly vast expanses of lush, dripping rain forest, with plants so thick and sinuous that they almost block out the tropical sunlight.

Nestled in the forests are some forty freshwater lakes, both "perched" (set above sea level) and "window" lakes (at or below sea level). Some of these giant, sand-floored swimming pools hold water the color of tea or almost red, while others are perfect blue, with blindingly white sands— a picture straight out of the Caribbean.

Fraser has been reshaping itself again and again over thousands of years. Enormous dunes creep across Fraser's

The best thing about Cape Tribulation is the sand on the beach. It's very, very fine. The finest. It gets all over you: in your hair, on your skin— practically inside your pores. But the thing is you don't mind. You actually kind of like the rough-smooth feeling of countless tiny, clean grains scraping lightly across the back of your hands, your fingertips tickling almost electrically.

And that fine, fine sand never really leaves you. Maybe in a few months or years, when you've forgotten all about it, you'll absently rub the back of your neck and you'll feel a gentle rustle. You'll take your hand from your neck and see, caught in the whorls of your fingertips, tiny pieces of beach sand. You'll remember being on the beach at Cape Tribulation and you will remember being happy.

◆

—Sean Condon, *Sean & David's Long Drive*

landscape like silent yellow glaciers, consuming entire forests and leaving behind petrified and ghostly remains; several of the dunes are like small mountains, moving grain by grain with the blasting sea wind. But plant life always revives in their wake: there are more independent dune systems—showing sand and vegetation in different stages of interaction—on Fraser than anywhere else on earth.

But for all its natural splendor, the human history of Fraser is strikingly bitter. The island won a permanent place in Australia's psyche in the 1830s, when some British sailors were shipwrecked here. A survivor named Eliza Fraser spent several months living with Aborigines before being rescued. (The story was turned into a novel by Australia's Nobel Prize-winning author Patrick White and perhaps the country's worst movie, *Eliza Fraser.*)

English settlers then used the island, also known as Great Sandy Island, as a sort of natural prison camp for Aborigines, transporting hundreds here from the mainland. Soon afterward, loggers eyeing the fine forests herded the Aborigines off again—killing many, it's said, by driving them into the sea.

For the last twenty years Fraser has been at the center of Australia's most vicious environmental disputes. In the 1970s a successful battle was waged against sand mining (the island's sands are rich in rutile and zircon), while in the early 1980s the focus shifted to a campaign to ban logging....

One of the hottest subjects of debate is how to cope with the booming number of annual visitors—10,000 in the early 1970s, and more than 350,000 today. The island has only about 300 permanent inhabitants but receives thousands of tourists weekly from every corner of Australia.

And they are given almost total freedom. There's surely no other World Heritage site so available to the public: anyone can bring a 4WD over from the mainland, bounce along the island's trails, and camp pretty much anywhere they like. On a crowded weekend this reduces the island to a kind of leafy, dodgem-car course. But at its best, it makes for the Great Australian Holiday.

My stay on Fraser began at its top end (socially, not geographically) at Kingfisher Bay, the ecotourism resort on the western coast. At dinner the first night, I found myself seated with a group of journalists and a crew from *Playboy*. The *Playboy* photographer had the air of a dissolute English aristocrat in the style of Peter O'Toole; the model was an office secretary from Queensland's Gold Coast. All I remember are the enormous plates of mud crabs, the mountains of prawns (call them shrimps, on or off the barbie, and you'll be laughed out of Australia), and endless bottles of white wine.

For the next couple of days I made sallies into the forested interior, navigating the rutted sand tracks to the likes of Lake McKenzie, perhaps the finest of Fraser's perched lakes. Its crystal blue waters reach almost thirty feet deep, but you can while away hours just wallowing like a hippo in a foot of pure water by the shore, pouring wet white sand that is the consistency of thick cream through your fingers.

Farther afield was Lake Wabby, squeezed between a giant sand dune on one side and a magnificent eucalyptus forest on the other. (Signs warn that you might break your neck if you run down the dune straight into the lake, which, of course, is just what everyone does.)

At the end of each day's wanderings, I returned to the resort and its split-level swimming pool and gourmet smorgasbord. From my veranda I could watch the sun set over the water. Nothing wrong with that, but the idea of sleeping in a hotel room seemed far removed from Fraser's other social world, which revolves entirely around camping.

So I loaded up my 4WD, bought a few supplies from the hotel's grocery store, and set off with my tent into Australia's most popular wilderness.

Fraser's basic division is between its forested interior and the long, eastern seacoast. Inland, you wind along sand tracks at about 15 mph constantly feeling that the steering wheel is about to be torn from your hands. The tracks are narrow, so if two cars meet, one has to back up until there's passing width. After a while, this starts to feel a bit like hard work, which is why on my first night out of Kingfisher I headed straight for the coast.

Emerging onto Seventy-five Mile Beach for the first time, I felt as if I were escaping from a coal mine.

Bathed in the golden afternoon light, the coastline ahead dissolved in a fine mist of sea spray. I could just barely pick out the rusted wreck of the *Maheno*, an ocean liner that washed up in 1935 and is now the beach's major landmark.

The tide was at its lowest, so I joined the file of 4WDs whipping along between the thundering surf and cliffs of twisted sand formations (locally dubbed Cathedrals), their curlicues looking even more hallucinogenic in the setting sun.

Seventy-five Mile Beach is the preserve of Aussie holidaymakers on Fraser, including those happily referred to, even by one another, as Drunken Yobbo Fishermen. A yobbo is an Aussie redneck, and during peak periods, such as school holidays and Easter, this whole coast can be bumper-to-bumper with 4WDs and fishing families, who set up tents at ten-yard intervals. (Last December one reveler brought a giant Christmas tree and an electricity generator to blaze up the lights.) But I was visiting in low season, and the yobbos were largely confining themselves to an area called Waddy Point.) A defining feature of Yobbo Fishermen is that they only fish where one species, the tailor, or bluefish, runs, thus crowding the same stretch of beach.) With my choice of campsites, I turned into a small alcove above the sand line.

Idyllic? Not quite. As night drew closer, I was battered by a driving sea wind. Whenever the wind died, I was attacked by giant horseflies, the bane of Fraser's east coast. Next morning the high tide trapped both me and the Land Cruiser in the alcove. The sun beat down mercilessly. I ran out of wood, and my kerosene burner clogged up when I tried to make tea. By noon I was staggering about like a shipwrecked sailor, muttering deliriously to myself.

That was when I snapped, took down my tent, and tried to drive along the beach before the tide had gone down. Which was when I got bogged in soft sand and was saved by Nev and Sharon.

After that, I studied my charts to make sure I never went near the beach at high tide, using the time instead to loll by a lake or hike through a rain forest. Occasionally I moved my camp. At Lake

Boomanjin, I set my tent between enormous eucalyptus trees, where clouds of red, green, and blue parakeets called rosellas squawked and cavorted at dusk; at dawn I was awakened by the maniacal laughter of kookaburras.

Dawn is the time when the Australian bush is at its finest, and the advantage of camping most obvious. Down by Lake Boomanjin, there was an absolute stillness in the air. The sand beneath the claret-colored waters was combed into the concentric ripples of an Aboriginal painting, as yet untouched by currents or wind.

One morning, as I slowly submerged into the cool, placid water, the sun broke over the eucalyptus trees, bathing the bush in Australia's famously clear and golden light. It was the sort of morning that D. H. Lawrence, visiting the country in the early 1920s, found "so soft, so utterly pure in its softness," that "one went into a dream."

But certain practical matters have to be taken care of, even in a dream. Worked somewhere into my daily ramblings was a shopping visit to one of the few small settlements on the island, sand-logged clusters of houses with names like Happy Valley and Dilli Village. Each boasted a single kiosk with a selection of tinned tuna, instant casseroles, Vegemite, white bread, and frozen snags (sausages). I found that while you can't buy green vegetables for any money on Fraser Island, you can always pick up an iced six-pack of XXXX ("Fourex") beer or excellent bottle of chilled Chardonnay.

Australia is notorious for its cornucopia of venomous animals, but in that department Fraser is unusually benign. There are six poisonous serpents, but they are shy and seldom seen, so I walked barefoot in the bush around Lake McKenzie with a confidence unheard of in the rest of the country.

Of course, that doesn't mean that weird animal encounters aren't part of the Fraser package. At a serene picnic site by Lake Garawongera, for example, the silence was broken by screams, followed by hysterical laughter. A couple of Australian travelers were standing on a wooden table as four goannas—black-and-yellow-speckled lizards, about a yard long from tail to nose—charged one another beneath them.

"I dropped a bloody egg," sighed one of the Aussies. Although goannas are basically harmless, they look vicious—in part because the goanna's head movements are disturbingly similar to a velociraptor's.

Skulking around the fringes of every campfire are lone dingoes, the wild dogs that gained international notoriety in the Meryl Streep film *A Cry in the Dark* for stealing a baby at Ayers Rock.

Dingoes are notoriously cowardly and won't do much alone (one did take a rasher of bacon from the back of my car), but the problem on Fraser is a manmade one: the garbage they got used to eating is now being transported to the mainland instead of being buried, and dingoes have only slowly readjusted to hunting wildlife. The week before I arrived, according to rumors, a pack of dingoes had apparently turned on a woman with her young child, driving them into the surf and biting them, so authorities were about to start culling.

And, oh yes, there are the sharks. On my first afternoon on Seventy-five Mile Beach, I went for a swim—until a woman waded in to warn me. Later, from a rocky promontory at Indian Head I could see the shadows of hundreds of sharks cruising the coast. They're apparently well fed on fish, because there hasn't been an attack on humans. But, after that episode, swimming in the interior lakes started looking more appealing than ever.

Truth be told, the most fearsome creatures on Fraser are the horseflies, which pounce from thin air and leave a painful sting. Only slightly less annoying are the inch-long marchflies and flea-size sandflies. (The first company to market an effective dual-purpose insect repellent and sunscreen will make a fortune on Fraser, since everyone on the island is in a permanent lather of both, usually mixed with gritty white sand.)

But uncomfortable as Fraser can sometimes get, it only seems to make the island's gentler side more seductive. Everyone has a favorite among the natural "sacred sites" scattered at regular intervals around the island, and mine was Eli Creek—a large freshwater stream that runs down to the coast through a natural tunnel of rain forest. Whenever I had the chance, I'd wade a hundred yards upstream and float back down on my stomach, gently pulling myself along the pure sand floor. The cold water is so pure, filtered through the sand, that you can drink it as you swim. And at the Champagne Pools, some natural rock aquariums on a shelf by the sea, I could swim with colorful angelfish left behind by the tide.

At the end of ten days on Fraser, I fancied myself a master of the four-wheel driver's art. No sand blow could bog me. I knew the daily tide times by heart, and I could discuss tire pressure with the best of them.

But there was one last challenge to face. The far north of the island is one of the most pristine parts of Fraser, the place where the island's natural processes of formation are most obvious. It's also the hardest to get to, at least in February, when the rains slash great troughs between a series of coastal rocks known as South and North Ngkala.

I made a stop to get the latest news on the route. "No worries," drawled one of the locals after looking me up and down for about a minute. "Yer'll figure it out."

Before long I was edging the car over a monolithic obstacle course of wet rocks and sand gullies. The tide crashed menacingly near. One trail was so steep that I needed a ten-yard run-up to get over it.

Finally, I met a car full of Very Sober Yobbo Fishermen coming the other way. "I wouldn't bother, mate," one of them grumbled. "We couldn't bloody make it." So we all retreated to Waddy Point, to drown our sorrows in XXXX.

The bright side was that I've now got an excuse to go back to Fraser and, old four-wheel-drive hand that I am, put it in low and give 'er another go.

Tony Perrottet also contributed "Looking for Dinner" earlier in Part Two.

PART THREE

GOING YOUR OWN WAY

PAUL THEROUX

The Beachcomber

He was Robinson Crusoe, by choice.

THE BEACHES HERE WERE NAMELESS, BECAUSE PEOPLE SO SELDOM used them. Anyway, this was all Aboriginal territory. If they had a name for it they had not divulged it to the cartographers. The mountains and headlands had all been named by Captain Cook, 200-odd years ago: he had only been able to pick out the higher ground from his ship.

Back at my camp I carried my gear to the kayak and went farther along the coast, looking for a less windy spot. I struggled to get free of the surf zone but I saw—with dismay—that there were breaking waves all the way to the horizon: a wide, foaming sea. Nearer shore I dragged the kayak along and just ahead was a four-foot shark—the sort of sand shark that turns up every now and then on Cape Cod beaches. I splashed my paddle and he took off: no need to spear the poor creature.

I had lunch on a sandy shelf on the steep back side of a dune: no wind at all, but because it was so still the dune was very hot and rather smelly and it was teeming with mosquitoes.

Kicking along the beach, pondering where to camp that night, I saw a figure in the distance coming toward me. When he came nearer, I saw it was a small grubby man, moving slowly, looking down: beachcombing. His shirt was torn, his trousers rolled to the knees. Every so often he picked up something, examined it, then either put it into his satchel or chucked it away. A dejected-looking dog trotted beside him.

I said hello. We talked about the wind. He was eyeing my boat.

"Collapsible," I said.

He said, "Want some home-brewed beer?"

One of the warnings I had received in Cairns was: "Don't trust anyone who's very friendly. A mate of mine did. He ended up with broken bones." At the time I had put it down as just another strange Australian warning, in a class with the fat man shouting: "Those mackerel are bigger than me!"

But this beachcomber was small and weedy.

"Lead the way," I said.

He blundered straight up the dune and through a dense thicket, going a very circuitous route.

"There's no proper path," he said.

We walked on, bush-bashing.

"I don't want to make a path."

The pine boughs were snapping in my face and even the dog looked confused.

"Then everyone visits," the beachcomber said. "Especially officialdom."

He had a rather formal way of speaking, and I thought I caught a whisper of London in the way he swallowed the "l" and said, *offishoodum*.

Finally we came to his camp. It was a patch of disorder in the bowl between two dunes. At the center was a pallet, with the dimensions of a queen-size bed, with a tattered canvas canopy suspended over it by guy ropes. This sleeping place was surrounded by immense clutter, but what looked like junk and debris at first glance was, if you looked closer, a collection of glass bottles and containers arranged by size and shape—stacks of them, and ones in long rows set up against the sandbanks, cups and tubs nested together. There were also net-floats—the large plastic balls that broke free from the wicked, turtle-strangling, dolphin-killing drift nets of the Japanese. A rusted wood stove had been set up next to the bed—I could see how this beachcomber might recline and cook at the same time—the beachcomber's economy of effort.

"This is what I call home," he said.

There were blackened bones, animal bones, on top of the stove's grille. To the side of the stove a heap of magazines—the *Reader's Digest* dominating the heap; and on a log, looking prim, a large pink plastic radio.

The man fossicked among the bottles and drew one out, while the dog yapped at me. I hated being barefoot here; I had thought that the camp was nearer the shore. But it was quite a distance from it, obviously to avoid the scrutiny of officialdom.

"Try this," the beachcomber said, and jerked the cap off the bottle.

I said, "Oddly enough, I'm not thirsty."

He took a swig. "Not bad." He took another, and wiped his mouth. "I made this batch last week." He swigged again. There was froth on his lips. "Thing is, the bottles have been exploding."

I distinctly heard him say *bottoos*.

"You're English," I said.

"From Kent," he said. He licked the froth from his lips. "Which is near London." He took another swig. "I was born in Gravesend. It costs six dollars to make about forty bottles of this beer. You just use a tin of this"—he indicated an empty can—"and a few pounds of sugar."

He became very intent on finishing the bottle of beer. He drank the rest of it in sips, neatly, staring between sips at the mouth of the bottle.

"And now you live here?"

"That's right," he said, and glanced around at the clutter. "In actual fact, I'm constructing a raft. That's why I have those pipes and those plastic balls. That's all my flotation, see."

Any purpose or design of those balls and pipes had been hidden by all the clutter.

"What will you do with the raft?"

"I'm aiming to build this raft and sail it in a northerly direction," arly migrants came to Australia by means of a long sea voyage. If a passenger felt unwell in adverse weather, he may have felt a need to rediscover his breakfast. If he was on deck, and did this over the side, it was considered good manners to warn anyone who might be engaged on a similar exercise through the port-hole on a lower deck by shouting, "Watch under!"—which was soon abbreviated to "chunder," a word still used today to describe this action.

Not all of the first settlers came of their own free will. On some of the migrant ships, presumably well battened down below decks would be a considerable number of POHMs, or Prisoners of His Majesty. This was pronounced, and is nowadays spelt Pom, and today, simply means an Englishman.

◆

—Keith Kellett, "Ozspeak"

he said with a certain precision.

"How much more northerly can you get than where we are now?"

"Around Cape York."

Good God, I thought. "Through the Torres Strait?"

One of the worst currents in the world—twelve turbulent knots of ocean rushing like white water squeezed between New Guinea and Australia.

"Yes. Through there."

"Any particular reason?"

He was smiling. His hair was wild. He was unshaven.

"That way I can go to Darwin."

"On a raft across the Gulf of Carpentaria."

"And the Arafura Sea. Yes." He had finished the beer. He put the bottle neatly away with the empties and said, "I'm not in any hurry. I've sailed rafts before. Down the Cabrera River in Colombia. I spent six months in South America. That was about eight years ago. Lots of adventures. Some dangers, too."

"Dangerous Indians?"

"No. I traveled with the Indians. In the South American bush you can't do anything without Indians." He seemed a little tipsy now. He struggled toward the bottles, rearranging them. "Kept a diary. I always said I should write a book about it."

Somehow, even standing barefoot in his beachcomber's camp on the shore of an Aboriginal reserve in North Queensland, it did not seem so odd that he should express this writing ambition. After all, I had the same ambition, and I was barefoot and whiskery too.

"Why don't you write a book about your South American trip?"

"I would," he said, "if I was in a hospital."

He was scratching his dog behind the ears as he spoke, and looking into the middle distance.

"In a hospital, with two broken legs. Then I'd do it," he said. He reflected on this a moment. "But I probably wouldn't want to do it if I had two broken legs."

"You seem to have plenty to drink here," I said. "What do you do for food?"

"Fish. Plenty of fish in these waters. I've got a crab pot. That's what I do with these bones." He poked the blackened bones on the stove. "Put them in the pot. Crabs love them. Also onions."

A bag of onions hung from the limb of a tree.

"Onions will keep for months."

We both looked at his bag of onions.

"Also 'roo meat," he said. "Plenty of that around. Here—have some."

He handed me a brown strip of meat that had the look of leather, exactly the shape and size of the tongue of an old shoe.

"That there is smoke-dried. Done it meself. Lasts for a long time. Years, actually." He became reflective again. "I found some 'roo meat under a box once. Forgot I had it. Two years old, it was."

"What did you do with it?" I said, trying to egg him on.

"Ate it."

"Two-year-old kangaroo meat?"

"Smoke-dried. It was delicious. Wonderful in soups."

"You make soup here?"

"All the time," he said. "Lovely stuff."

"Do the Aborigines mind you camping on their reserve?" I asked.

"They don't make a fuss. The ones in town are a bit rough. But the Abos here are good people. They're losing their old ways, though. They caught a big turtle the other week down where your boat is. They took some of the meat and left the rest to the wild pigs. Years ago they would have eaten the whole thing."

That was very much a beachcomber's point of view, the obsession with other people's wastefulness.

I told him I was camping myself, but that I was looking for a place out of the wind.

"Have you tried Leprosy Creek?"

"No. But I kind of like the name," I said.

He gave me directions to the inlet. I paddled there and at a little bend in the creek, I found a good spot—no wind and quite sheltered, and there I pitched my tent and spent the night. My only moment of anxiety came in the dawn, when I heard big feet crashing through the leaves. I grabbed my rifle as the noise came nearer—very loud now. I peered out of the tent flap and saw two wild turkeys—brush turkeys, with bald heads and yellow wattles, sleek black feathers, handsome, strutting past my tent.

"You can eat them, you know," the beachcomber said, when I saw him at the shore the next morning. He had just checked his crab pot: nothing inside. "You pluck the turkey and put it into a pot with a brick. You put some water and boil the whole thing, until you can shove a fork through the brick. Then you throw the turkey away and eat the brick."

He did not smile.

"That's very funny," I said. "What is your name?"

"You can call me Tony," he said.

I was sure that Tony was not his name. He was, in spite of his apparent friendliness, deeply suspicious of strangers, and from time to time he lapsed into silence, self-conscious because of my persistent questions.

He was very interested in my gear—my well-made tent and

boat: He examined the stitching and the fittings. He looked closely at my pots and stove, the water bag I had bought in Sydney.

He said, "That's just what I need for my trip around Cape York on my raft."

I said, "Where do you get your water?"

There was no drinking water anywhere to be found on this sunbaked coast; the pools of water I had found were brackish.

"I go to Cooktown in my canoe when the wind drops," he said. He made a face. "But the Cooktown water is no good. They put fluoride in it."

It was completely in character for this beachcomber to be very fussy and complain about the quality of water in the town. Most tramps I had met in my life believed there was something profoundly unclean about towns and cities, and many of the homeless men I had run across in London—the ones who slept on the common land outside London in camps very similar to Tony's here in Queensland—many of them had spoken with disgust about the beetles and the filth in the charitable wards and dorms. The grubby beachcomber invariably believes he is living the cleanest life possible on earth, and personal hygiene is always a popular topic with tramps, who invariably boast of their fastidiousness.

I said, "Aborigines aren't very popular in Cooktown."

"That's because Australians are racists, aren't they?" Tony said. "If it wasn't the Abos it'd be the Italians or the Yugoslavians. They need someone to hate."

This lucid statement from a barefoot wild-haired man with a dog in his arms, standing in torn pants in the wilds of Queensland.

"There's some towns in Australia, like Katherine"—in the Northern Territory—"where whites and blacks actually fight all the time. But Cooktown is mainly a peaceful place. I get my beer ingredients there. When the road gets bitumenized it will all change."

"Tony, it seems you're well set up here."

"I reckon I am," he said, looking pleased. "I've got all the necessaries."

"See any crocs?"

"Only little buggers. There are pigs around but they don't bother me."

"Mosquitoes?"

I had mosquito net on my tent. Tony slept in the open air.

"When the wind drops there's mozzies. But the wind don't usually drop."

He hesitated a little—it was a sign that my questions were making him anxious.

"Catch you later," he said—the Australianism that means: this conversation is at an end. And he appeared to be heading back to his camp.

"Aren't you going for a walk today?"

He was carrying his beach-combing satchel. His shoes were inside, with his water bottle, his hat, and something to eat wrapped in paper. He never went out on the beach without this survival kit, and it gave him a look that was at once shabby and respectable.

He said he had been on a walk but that he had turned back. "The beach was getting a little crowded."

I looked down five miles of beach on the great sweep of bay and saw no one.

"I saw someone else on the beach. Besides you."

This was too much for him. He went back to his camp, and I fished from my boat. I caught nothing but it was a good excuse to bob in the ocean all afternoon. At one point I thought I saw some Aborigines fishing in the surf about a mile farther up the beach—perhaps they were the people Tony had seen?—but when I paddled toward them they vanished.

At dusk I made my dinner to the sound of pigeons' wings—they were making for the trees to settle for the night. There was wind in the upper branches, but it was quiet down below in my camp. Just before I crawled into my tent I saw, clinging to the fly, a large brown spider, about two or three inches long. I flicked it away ("You got some of the most poisonous spiders in the world here, mate. One bite and you're dead as a mutton chop.") and zipped myself in for my nightly ritual: drinking tea, writing my notes, and after lights out, radio programs from distant lands. This sound of bad news was mingled with the frog croaks from Leprosy Creek....

I encouraged Tony to visit my camp. I wanted to know more about his beach-combing. I began to see a kind of luxury in his life that would be very hard to buy—it was not just comfort but privacy. I was interested in his periods of activity, his plans, his days of total idleness, his total self-absorption, and in his pleasures.

There was something deeply respectable and orderly about him. There was his satchel, containing his day's essentials—shoes, hat, food, water. He always wore a shirt and trousers, though buttons were missing from his shirt, and his trousers were torn in half-a-dozen places. He never went anywhere without his dog, which was a tiny mutt with a hoarse and timid bark.

I asked him one day whether the dog had a name.

"No," Tony said. "Well, he's so small"—as though his size did not justify having a name. He went on, "Sometimes I say 'chop chop' meaning hurry up. Maybe that could be his name."

The dog loved him,

And the poor who got away had no intention of imitating those whom they had left behind; they were glad to be rid of the old world and its restrictions and refinements. They wanted Australia to be the land of the common man with a new lifestyle and new attitudes. Before long, the effete Englishman had come to represent all that was irritating about the old world, and when that Englishman came to Australian shores he was in turn irritated, and thus a stereotype was born and a battle begun which it is easy enough to trace in the pages of Australian literature. It was a battle between the genteel and the robust, the refined and the crude, the men of paste and the men of steel, the old world and the new.

◆

—Linda Christmas, *The Ribbon and the Ragged Square: An Australian Journey* needed to be picked up and hugged. I was especially interested in the idea of Tony's trying to survive in this difficult place, and needing to find food for a dog, but when I mentioned it to him he simply shrugged.

Tony's routines and opinions, and the way he ran his life, suggested respectability. He could not bear the proximity of other people, and I knew from his reactions to my questions that he had a real aversion to anyone's discovering where or how he lived. He was entirely self-sufficient, contemptuous, and selfish. The fact that he was a beachcomber did not mean that he was an exile. He had a place in the world, which was wherever he happened to be. Beachcombing, though, was his preoccupation: He needed bottles for his beer brewing, floats and cast-up line for his raft, driftwood for his stove. The rest of the time he went after fish, oysters, and crabs. He was proud of his soup making and his bread making. He was often very busy, involved in the process of survival—and he managed this without spending any money at all—but he also had immense leisure.

He said to me one morning, "I drank eight or twelve bottles last night, listening to the radio. I slept late. Had a bit of a hangover. Then I put out my crab pot. Now I'm going for a walk."

This was his whole life on the hot windy coast of Cape Bedford, and it amazed me, because it combined the most rigid discipline with an utter disregard for time.

And sometimes I seriously wondered: *Am I like him?*

The night before I left my camp, I asked him whether he had been back to London.

"Oh, yes, I went back once. About ten years ago. Didn't have no money, so I got a job in the post office, the central one, in West One." He smiled. "It was all Indians and Jamaicans. Blacks from the West Indies on my right, Hindus from India on my left. I couldn't understand a word they said, and they were always jabbering. I said to myself, What's this country coming to?

He was in his early fifties, small and rather slender, scorched by the sun that always burned in a cloudless sky.

"That's why I couldn't see any point in staying."

I was tying my boat to the mangrove roots so that the tide wouldn't take it away.

"And I'm not even a racist," he said, in a complaining way.

I aimed to set off for the Aboriginal mission, and I wanted to lighten my load, so I gave him some food I would not need and my spare water jug that held two and a half gallons.

"I'll use it on my raft," he said, "when I go north."

"I wish you luck."

"I'm not bothered," he said, and then in a casual way he summed up what I took to be his guiding philosophy, "What I find is that you can do almost anything or go almost anywhere, if you're not in a hurry."

Paul Theroux is the author of many works, among them travel books such as Dark Star Safari, Riding the Iron Rooster, The Old Patagonian Express, The Great Railway Bazaar, *and* The Happy Isles of Oceania, *from which this story was excerpted.*

* * *

The Red Centre

The gap is wide and sometimes unbridgable
between two cultures.

IN THE MIDDLE OF A MILLION HECTARES OF DUST AND SCRUB IS A large red rock. It's been the source of controversy, media attention, and political and cultural maneuverings for many years. It's featured on stamps, compact disc covers, tea towels, postcards, clothing, and most travel brochures and is as much an icon of Australia as the sails of the Sydney Opera House.

From the air, besides its size, it's difficult to imagine what all the fuss is about.

But the Aborigines who have lived on the Australian continent for 60,000 years have the answer. To them this rock is the source of their very existence.

For many years Ayers Rock, as it was known then, belonged to everybody. Its visitors left much more than footprints and took more than photographs. The Aborigines felt that this sacred land of theirs was being desecrated. It wasn't only the rock that was being affected. Many who climbed its steep face fell to their deaths; those who removed pieces of the significantly red rock returned them years later, apologising and asking for the curse which accompanied the stolen piece of rock to be lifted.

In 1988, after a protracted and bitter struggle, Australia's red monolith was returned to the Pitjantjatjara, an Aborigine group of people who have always lived there. They renamed it Uluru and celebrated. To the Aborigine, or Anangu, as they prefer to be called, their land is their life.

The Rock is in the Uluru Kata Tjuta National Park, a few hundred kilometers northwest of Alice Springs in Australia's Northern Territory. Uluru, on the World Heritage List, is ranked as one of the world's most significant arid ecosystems. Pilgrims in their hundreds of thousands brave Outback Australia's bizarre landscape, heat, and flies to see The Rock.

No matter how prepared you think you are, the first sight of Uluru will jar each of your jaded senses. The rock rises like a colossus out of the cracked red earth, visible from the air for several minutes before it looms like a sleeping monster on a barren landscape.

And on the ground, Uluru possesses a tangible spirituality. You can't help but be cowed by the colors that change from blood red to slate grey as a cloud passes; by a temperature that over an hour can freeze your fingertips and scorch your feet. Its sheer bulk challenges the adventurer in your soul but the ghosts that follow you about will have you walking on tiptoe.

And it seems to sing—a mournful dirge that careens through the cracks in the solid core of red. It sounds very much like the haunting Aborigine wind instrument, the didgeridoo, created from a hollowed out root; blown through till spit trickles out the bottom and the player's cheeks are grossly distended.

Eroded shapes catch shadows and resemble the earth's creatures; dried water trails leave silvery whiplike marks, gnarled, battered trees take on ghostly forms.

According to the Anangu, their origins are based in the myths and legends that surround a complicated belief system—the Tjukurpa—that refers both to their past and their present, and encompasses everything that is natural, lawful, and true.

But Tjukurpa also refers to ancestral beings and their fundamental part in the creation of the world of the Anangu. In their eyes, the world did not exist until their ancestors, in the forms of people, plants, and animals, traveled widely across the land and, in a process of creation and destruction, formed the world as it is known today. The Tjukurpa provides the Aborigine with a system of beliefs and morality through symbolic stories and metaphors to guide them through life.

Their tradition is primarily oral, recounted and confirmed in the many religious activities carried out through ritual ceremony, song, dance, and artistic expression. Because song and dance are such an integral part of their lifestyle, many people understand Aborigine mythology in terms of "songlines," the paths followed by the ancestors as they traveled the earth and sang the world to life. However, their society is a secret one, and difficult for the outsider to penetrate, much less understand.

Anangu also restrict secrets within their own group. Females may not attend male initiation rites, males are forbidden knowledge of "female business."

The Pitjantjatjara speak what is known as the Western Desert Language, a complicated grammatical structure using 10,000 words, uttered in 50 different dialects. Languages within these languages are often used in restrictive contexts such as secret ceremonies or talking to relatives. They also use sign language and whisper, to limit understanding to those who are privy to such information.

For these indigenous people, the rock is the centre of their mythology. Each depression, rockpool, or twisted bush has its own story—this pile of stones is where the evil doglike creature, Kurpany, killed many Mala people. That wedge-shaped stone is the *yuu*, a small shelter for the marsupial mole Itjaritjari from where she can see Mala women and children gathering bush tucker. And that triangular-shaped cave over there? That's Mala Puta, the pouch of the female hare-wallaby.

To photograph the many mythological sources around Uluru's nine-kilometre base is, according to the Anangu, to steal its spirit and insult its owners. To this end I was compelled to sign lengthy documents that I would not do so. I was not to photograph the east face at sunrise. I was not to photograph the impression of the skull on the right. I was not to point my camera towards the crack in the rock that resembled a woman's private parts. And when, at sunrise, I stood amongst a thousand people doing all these without licence, I wondered at the rationale of my ban. Was it because I was to make money out of the images, money that the Anangu would want for themselves?

But the Anangu work in mysterious ways: Uluru appeases itself and claims its own victims. From the infamous story of the dingo who took a camper's baby, to those who have died of heart failure or slipped to their deaths, Uluru continues to make its presence felt.

The Pitjantjatjara call those foolish and insensitive enough to climb the rock's massive hulk "*minga*"—ant—for from a distance the struggling climbers inching their way up the slippery track resemble a row of ants.

Look closely at the ground, the guides around the rock instruct, that seems as if it is composed of nothing. Iriya (tumbleweed) dance across the sand, *ipi-ipi* sting the skin, *wanari* (mulga) offers

---

*T*he resort operators have to explore every last tourism option.

In a way it reminds me of the many things that you can do to dress up the humble egg. You can boil it—just drive around The Rock and see it for yourself. You can fry it—pay to be guided around the rock by two rangers for three hours (includes a sandwich). You can make a fancy omelette—pay a lot of money to fly over it in a plane or helicopter (includes free risk of death). You can paint the eggshell, turn it into some ridiculous novelty piece and try to sell it—pay an absurd amount of money to be driven around The Rock on the back of a Harley. Or you can go all the way and have your *oeuf* Florentine style—drink champagne as you float over The Rock in a balloon at dawn (spinach not included).

◆

—Sean Condon, *Sean & David's Long Drive*

shade and firewood, and it's also used for *miru* (spearthrowers) and *wana* (digging sticks). Don't pick the *tjulpun-tjulpunpa* (pretty flowers) or the *paltu-paltupa* (parrot pea)—and respect the *kurkara* (desert oak), it's probably 450 years older than you are. You'll see some gentle mountain wallabies or a frilled lizard or skink, and if you're lucky, some abandoned stone flints.

But I wanted to know more. To further appreciate the traditional business of the Pitjantjatjara I had to travel deeper into their territory, a day's journey by heavy four-wheel-drive vehicle into the powder red dust and desiccated spinifex of Central Australia.

The waving palms, air-conditioning, and warm swimming pools of Yulara had lulled me into a false sense of desert security, for just beyond its boundaries the primitive environment is relentlessly harsh and forbidding. In the heat the land wobbles and everything becomes a sunburned orange red. At night the skies dazzle with light from the rest of the universe. In this bizarre landscape even the daytime sky was the color of evolution—streaks and swirls of grey and silver and red.

The OKA vehicle in which we were traveling transported us high above the potholes and slippery red dust, although kamikaze insects bent on a free ride suicided on our windscreen so that it had to be washed every hour or we wouldn't be able to see. At Mulga Park Station, a surrealistic desert outpost in the postholocaust barren moonscape, we stopped to stretch and buy a warm Coke. For desert dwellers, it's the only place to fuel and buy flyspray, McWilliams snake-proof boots, squeezy Kraft mayonnaise, three colors of plastic carnations used for funerals, rifles, floral cotton dresses, cowboy belts, and tinned food.

The entrance to the dusty, barnlike shop swung with long colored strips of sticky plastic to deter the insects seeking asylum from the sun; dizzy flies that would otherwise suck at our tear ducts. Some laconic pups were being teased by a couple of yellow-haired Aborigine kids; there was an old petrol drum filled with empty tins of Foster's. When we left, the kids waved and the dogs stopped licking themselves for a moment.

We collected Kunmanara, an elder of the Pitjantjatjara tribe, who was to be our storyteller for the next few days. She lived with her extended family in the Amata community just across the South Australian border. But Kunmanara wasn't her real name, just one she'd have to use until it was safe to use her own again. A living person cannot have the same name as a recently deceased Anangu—who assumes the form of their ancestors, whether it's a kangaroo, a skink, or a snake—because if they hear their name being called they become distracted on their return to the spirit world and get lost.

Kunmanara was accompanied by a half dozen of her dusty grandchildren, whose sticky snot ran down their noses like slugs. They scaled the mound of swags (all-in-one sleeping bags) that packed the aisle of the truck. Now the road noise was punctuated with bursts of Pitjatjantjara dialect, short staccato stabs of unintelligible speech to the outsider. But Linda, the driver, understood, and she translated above the din.

Abandoned, rusting cars littered the track for hundreds of kilometres like some alien vegetation. The government aids the Aborigine in the purchase of cars, so to take the time to repair one would seem a senseless occupation. "That's Kunmanara's brother's car!" shouted Linda, spraying water on the windscreen and pointing to a wreck at the side of the road. "He's going to come back for the steering wheel." Strange extraterrestrial cloud shapes hung like aliens in the sky; beams of gold sliced them and illuminated more techno-litter. "And that's her uncle's—he says the transmission's still good!"

She began to explain the desert's evolution, according to Anangu legend. "That mountain is really a Kurrajong tree man. He looks over and sees the entrance holes to honey ant nests—inside these entrances are chambers—all the honey ants are inside, he goes over to them and fills in the holes and kills them all. He's speared and he goes home." In these unfamiliar frames of reference, I've no idea what she's talking about, but her bizarre fables fit in with the grand scheme of the desert.

"And that tree is the man who's chasing seven sisters from east to west because he wants to marry all of them. He tries all sorts of tricks to lure them to him, like turning himself into a tree so they will sit in his shade or eat his fruit, or turning into a rock so they will sit on him!"

That first night, in the shelter of a *wiltja*—a canopy of spinifex supported on poles of desert oak—Kunmanara huddled near a blazing spinifex and desert oak fire and told more stories of her ancestors, in a lilting and sing-song cadence that complemented the very dark desert night, her voice fortified by the bitter tea that boiled on the blackened billy.

Used to the shush of the waves near my home, I couldn't sleep. The mournful howl of a dingo prickled my skin, owls called and hooted, and twigs, snapping like rifle shots under creatures that slither into swags, made me as alert as a commando on duty.

When the sun staggered over the thorny horizon, Kunmanara kick started the fire and fed the kids chunky sandwiches from a plastic bag. Our lessons continued. She found seeds on bushes, and ground them between two flat stones.

And then she began the epic saga of the Perentie Lizard, about a half-man, half-lizard who stole a grinding stone because he thought it was better than his own, and the hazards of his pursuit and escape until he was killed as punishment.

We followed this Anangu songline, as it was told according to tradition; three white people battling the heat and flies, trying to make sense of the bizarre red centre of Australia. Kunmanara walked in front, carrying her ground seeds in a curved piece of bark that had been decorated by burning dot patterns into its surface, following the little dust balls her flat, padding feet kicked up from the thorny ground.

Kunmanara pointed to some giant boulders and spoke. "See that pile of stones?" Linda translated. "That's where he spat out the mistletoe berries. And that cave? That's where he curled up to hide—you can see where his feet rested." Two dusty kids scrambled up the rocks to demonstrate, danced the way of the ancestors, and lit brush to smoke out the bad cave spirits.

A shot rang out, ricocheting against walls of rock. Kunmanara chattered excitedly with Linda's help. "They've shot a 'roo. Let's go find it."

The vehicle followed her ancient tracking techniques of listening, pointing, and inspecting the ground. We found Kunmanara's brother and several kids struggling to drag the wallaby, its leg snapped in two, down the hill. They hauled it by the tail, twisting and bouncing and flopping over rocks, impaling its bloodied fur on thorn bushes, until a sad trail of blood marked its descent. Occasionally the jubilant kids would rest, and kick the poor twitching wallaby.

When they'd managed to haul the battered body to the side of the car, the wallaby's eyes were glazing over. The final injustice was still to come: the kids reached into her pouch and pulled out their prize—a pink squirming joey that had been growing in the protective pocket for many months. Days after conception it had crawled the long precarious journey up her body, and attached itself to her nipple, there to feed and grow until it was mature enough to leave the maternal pouch for good.

The embryo had no fur, and its eyes were still sealed over. The limp wallaby's eyes were cloudy, and she'd stopped twitching. The

*L*ast night I'd hoped to show Ian the magic of camping in the Kimberley. The sky is deeper and the stars brighter than anyplace I've ever seen, and I'd raved about the tranquillity. Instead Ian learned where Australians store their irony when they're not using it. The bush is thick with it. You want magic? A poisonous centipede thick as a finger, long as a hand, scuttled past the toe of Ian's shoe. Tranquillity? A colony of fruit bats woke in a nearby tree and began their evening's foraging, their leathery wings *whump-whump-whumping* in the darkness. More tranquillity? A feral donkey began braying somewhere, its nocturne cut short by two quick blasts of a road train's horn and a terrible bang.

◆

—Roff Martin Smith, "Over the Top," *National Geographic*

elders heaved her blood-damp body and flung it unceremoniously into the back of the *ute* where it lay, its head resting on a spare wheel. They were happy, for there'd recently been a death in the large extended family, and now they would have something to feast on during the ritual song and dance.

The kids flung the embryo around by its tail, like a Frisbee. I thought I was going to be sick, and I had to turn away. And when the kids saw my distress, they played up to it; when I feigned a loss of interest, their interest waned.

Sensing my dismay, Kunmanara stage-whispered her concern at the killing. "I am sorry." And then she wanted to know whether I was going to put this part in my story. "Yes, of course," I said, and she was horrified. "No!" she whispered. "Cannot!" I demanded that she agree the carnage had indeed taken place, but that was not enough to convince her that a mere event could become written fact.

I asked why the 'roo could not be killed outright, and she said it had to die by being hit on the head with rocks, that was the Anangu way. I was furious, and struggling with tears, and beside me the little embryo and its mother passed into another, one would hope, safer, existence.

And then I realized I was in her territory, and this was the way things had always been done in Central Australia, and I had to keep quiet. I was struggling with my own conscience: did I have any more right to shoot a rabbit or transport live sheep across oceans?

The men disappeared with their booty and we didn't see them again. They made no comment to me or reference to the fact that I was even there: apparently my reaction had disappointed them.

We went bush to find the "tucker" that sustains the Anangu in their hostile environment. Fruits, berries, roots, insects, and worms complement their diet of rabbit, reptile, and kangaroo. There's no oasis here to grow green or red vegetables. Aborigines adapt the scarce spoils of the desert to their needs, whether they are medicinal or nutritional.

So again, they rely on their ancient traditional skills. Kunmanara—at least sixty years old—but who knows?—squatted on the ground, her dark scarred legs flat out in front of her. Her battered spade attacked the hard ground. She dug, and dug, and dug: dust and sand and roots flew up around her, covering her hair, her wide lap, and the grubby kids. She was sweating, and the dust stuck to her. Finally she shouted. "Here! Ants!" and dangling on the end of her long stick like preposterous Christmas baubles were ants, gorged with golden honey.

The kids screeched with excitement and almost fell down the deep hole. They poked their own sticks into the nest and hauled out several grotesquely bloated ants, desperately clinging to the stick. The kids picked them up by their spindly legs and dangled them over their open mouths and squeezed and squashed the bodies until the honey drizzled out onto their pink flicking tongues. "Here!" they offered, but I couldn't, preferring my sweetener in a teaspoon.

The real truth is that the ants live underground, in the soft dry soil of the desert, on tree roots which die when exposed to the sun. These trees would have survived scorching heat and fires, stinging winds and the on-

"*I*t's a carpet python. Nonvenomous. Now see these?" He pointed to the snake's triangular head. "Those are green ants, and they're biting it. That's why it fell out of the tree, I'd say."

I pointed out to Shaughnessy that a green ant was crawling on his face. To my surprise, the ranger grabbed the insect and popped it into his mouth.

"He wasn't very nice," he explained after hastily ejecting it. "We'll find some that taste good."

♦

—Paul Prince, "Off in the Wild Down Under," *Travel Holiday*

slaught of other animals. All it took was a spade and some digging to end their 500 years on earth. The ants were the booty but the trees were the victims.

We drove to a salt pan where the wild camels that roam Central

Australia often came to drink. Kunmanara again squatted on the ground, and with her spade dug another deep hole—promising us that when we returned a few hours later, the hole would be filled with fresh water. She covered it with sticks that she'd ripped from the desert oak—a hardy tree that lives a half century and makes excellent, long-lasting firewood.

Another day Kunmanara and the kids upturned some of those desert oaks and excavated to their roots to find fat, bulbous white witchetty grubs, as long as a finger, that squirmed in the unaccustomed sun. Ten witchetty grubs in exchange for an ancient tree. She made a fire of brush and oak lit with a flint, and sizzled the grubs like popcorn in the hot sand. I couldn't eat them; but the others said they tasted like peanut butter or coddled eggs. That we had tinned food and bread in the back of the OKA did not matter: Kunmanara was "teaching" us the ways of the desert.

The kids had found a long yellow skink sunning itself: shrieking with joy they offered it to Kunmanara who impaled it with a forked stick, gutted it and laid it on a hot rock to dry to eat later. Soon the bulbous blowflies hovered over it, and when we left, the skink was flung in the back of the truck where we kept tripping over it. A few days later, its stinking, rotting carcass was tossed out of the window.

She told us about the quandong plums that grow on bushes near The Rock, the wild figs, the herbs and fruits from which she makes beverages, the leafy mosquito repellent, the snake bite antidote. She tried to explain the obscure dot paintings of her people and their body decoration.

On the last night a massive moon, the color of old goats' cheese, rose over the spinifex. It was my turn to make the fire. I had matches, and twigs, and brush; there were chunks of desert oak, and there was no wind. After an hour I'd managed to smoke out the campsite and almost choke us to death. My skin was itching and had turned a peculiar color from the sun and the dust. I hadn't eaten meat since the 'roo episode. I dreamed, tucked in my swag, of smashing a dozen eggs with a spade, and rescuing the kangaroos that were trapped inside. When I woke in a cold sweat, it was to the dream that I had been trapped inside one of those eggs.

It was time for me to leave, to return to the culture I was familiar with. We drove from our campsite, past a community where a stark-naked man, sitting in the dusty shade at the side of his truck, was chattering into his two-way radio.

Kunmanara looked up to the sky and told me the plane was coming—I couldn't see it in the vast expanse of blue. It landed, ten minutes later, but she refused to go near the silver bird from the sky. She said she preferred walking.

She waved as we flew away, as mystified by my culture as I am about hers.

Below the dragonfly-sized plane was the desert of Central Australia, spread out like giant fossilized etchings on a corrugated red canvas: the living proof of so many myths. There were grooves where the ancestors had rested in the heat, the ridges left by their twitching tails, the scorched depressions that their tails carved across the land. It was suddenly easy to believe that the earth was indeed sung to life and to follow the songlines would make its understanding a whole lot easier.

I just wish that the music were different.

Susan Storm is a widely published photojournalist working for Australian and international magazines and newspapers. Born in Prague, she grew up in South Africa, and now lives in Australia. She has won numerous literary and photographic competitions, and runs travel writers' workshops.

GREG CHILD

✦ ✦ ✦

Report from Quinkan Country

A climber discovers the ancestors
of his heart's desire.

IT WAS THE FINEST CLIFF I HAD EVER SEEN, A LEANING SHEET OF sandstone, tungsten hard and glistening with a burnished patina of silica more orange than a sunset. Beyond it stretched a hundred other flaming walls—Buoux, Arapiles, and Smith Rock all crammed into one place. Ten lifetimes of climbing surrounded me. But there, in a remote place called Quinkan Country in an isolated part of the crocodile-infested tropics near the Cape York Peninsula in northeast Australia, there were no bolts, no climbs, no climbers.

I was not the first to eye these rocks with infatuation. At the base of every cliff, where rocky overhangs formed shelters, were "galleries" of ancient paintings left by the Aboriginal people who dwelled here aeons ago. Working with natural paints of ocher mixed with animal blood and fat they had decorated the rock with images of men and women, animals they had hunted, plants they had gathered, and the strangely misshapen spirits of their fears, the Quinkans, the poltergeistlike demons that the Ang Gnarra still believe inhabit the heart of the rock and slip out through cracks. They also left their signatures—hundreds of them—in every stony nook and cranny, in the form of simple stencils painted by blowing a mouthful of ocher over a hand placed palm-down against the rock.

I had seen such signatures before, but those—the chalky-white hand smears of rock climbers—belonged to a more modern breed of cliff dweller, a tribe with different ceremonies. And though it is a stretch to say that the dark-skinned ancients of Quinkan Country could have had anything in common with the sons and daughters of the white invaders who shot their way through this stretch of land a century ago—and in so doing blew away our chance to understand the deeper meaning of these paintings—the figures and hand stencils daubed around me made me wonder if, in some remote sense of the spirit, those long-vanished people and we climbers were distant cousins.

That the ancients were lovers of the rock was obvious. They chose only the most architecturally spectacular outcrops and caves to decorate and to shelter themselves from the seasonal monsoon and blazing sun. But the way they incorporated the natural shapes, pockets, and flakes of the rock into their Dreamtime murals suggested that they possessed a sensitivity to the tactile feel of the stone that comes only from handling it, from studying it, from climbing it. They didn't just paint rock, they interpreted it, as carefully as climbers feel out holds on a vertical path. Proof of this lay everywhere on the cliffs: beside an ocher emu, a row of deep, oval *huecos,* or potholes, had been utilized to represent the eggs of that huge, flightless bird. Farther on, a finger-size monopocket had become the eye of a kangaroo. Near that was a row of hand stencils. For those, the artist had made his clan members stretch high up a wall and, seemingly, cling to small edges while paint was sprayed over their hands. The hands appeared to be moving up the wall— perhaps depicting an ascent, a dyno from the dawn of time.

Just when these works were created is uncertain, but whoever decorated the thousands of cliff galleries of Quinkan Country had been doing it for millennia. The paintings overlapped one another, again and again, so that faded figures of great antiquity hovered like ghosts in the backgrounds of every gallery. Predating all of that lay the engravings of an even more ancient race, who chipped and pecked strange shapes into the rock. The descendants of these people, the Aborigines of the Ang Gnarra clan, believe most of the painting predates their arrival to this land. Anthropologists have dated relics in the shelters to 32,000 years ago, but other experts believe the engravings are 150,000 years old, making them the world's earliest known rock art.

Climber and sufferer of tunnel vision that I am, my eyes wandered from the painting to the wall above, where the monopockets and crisp edges peppering the 150-foot cliff carried me on an imaginary journey. Tracing the paths of my dream, I pictured my fingers stabbing into abrupt puncture-wound pockets, my arms lunging through rocky waves, my feet toeing sharply hewn flakes and ripples. All that was needed was a power drill and a dozen bolts. But evil-looking spirit-figures at one end of the wall and a lively scene of hunters spearing kangaroos at the other stood like guardians, warning me against touching this splendid wall. There could be no climbing here. The place was too sacred.

Years, before, in America, I had been strolling along the base of a sport-climbing cliff with a traditionalist friend who saw only ugliness in the bolts above. He was of the old school that believed a climb should begin at the bottom and follow a line using natural protection, so that after the climbers had left, there was no trace of their visit. I tried to persuade him that the bolts were okay, that the rock was the canvas where the next generation of climbers was pushing the art of climbing. He wasn't impressed. To him, the bolts had violated the cliff. "Some places just shouldn't be climbed on," he said.

Even so, as I pushed sweatily through thick scrub and walked from gallery to gallery and from one world-class crag to another, I found it impossible to imagine that these ancient people did not indulge in some form of climbing of their own. So, scrambling in an area outside the gallery, I looked for signs that the Aborigines had made vertical detours on their walkabouts. I didn't have to search for long.

The first hint came at a deep cleft in a wall where cool air rushed out of a jam crack. Twenty feet of 5.9 climbing led to a narrow, peapod-shaped cave entry. With cracks all around me, it seemed unlikely that I'd find traces of Aboriginal ascent so quickly, but immediately I saw that the rock was polished by many hands and feet. And sure enough, beside the cave entrance were two faded hand stencils. For whatever reason, people had found cause to climb this crack and enter the dark cave that disappeared into the cliff, probably for ceremonial reasons, maybe to communicate with Quinkans, whose mischievous shapes stood a few paces away.

The sun was low now, the cliffs amber, and dingo howls resounded through the valley. I walked at a brisk pace, wishing for more daylight, more clues. Farther along the scarp, below a long, easy chimney splitting a wall bedecked with the 5.12 face routes of my dreams, I bouldered onto a ledge and found a painting of a small man beside a hand stencil. The symbol looked like a sign for travelers, an ancient topo symbol saying "climb up here." So I did. Massive jugs blazed a 5.6 trail through the steepness. The holds were worn smooth. They had been here, too. Before I knew it, I was eighty feet off the ground, nearing the top.

As I climbed down I realized that for the agile ancients, even with spears in hand, this line would have been a highway to the hunting grounds atop the plateau, and a good escape route from the murdering whites of the British Empire who wiped out the last of these people in the 1870s. Ironically, it was around that time in Europe that the "first" climbers were venturing onto the crags of England and the European Alps. Those events are duly recorded in climbing histories. Unrecorded, of course, are the climbs of the peoples of antiquity: the Andeans who left the tree line and climbed ice-clad volcanoes more that 20,000 feet high to make sacrifices to their gods, the Native American hunters who climbed Longs Peak and left a small wind shelter there, the barefoot boulderers of Quinkan Country. I see no reason not to believe that these people—lean and sinewy as the best sport climbers and raised in the shadows of cliffs that would make a modern climber drool—indulged in some form of recreational bouldering. To create such a body of art, they had time to play, and what more obvious thing to do in a field of boulders than to try and climb?

Every civilization has its glory days, and every civilization declines into faded painting or the rubble of fallen castles. In the distant future, long after climbing has ceased to be fashionable and the last crag rat's bones have been eaten by worms, the anthropologists of another race will visit Buoux in France, Arapiles in Australia, and Smith Rock in America, and they'll stroke their beards in puzzlement over the age-pitted pieces of steel protruding from the cliffs. Maybe they'll declare them the trappings of religious ceremonies. Certainly, they'll say, "Here was a race of eccentrics who worshipped the vertical." Chances are the boffins of a future millennium won't understand climbers any better than we, today, understand the rock dwellers of Quinkan Country.

Greg Child began climbing as a teenager in his native Australia, where he established numerous rock routes before moving to the United States. He has climbed extensively in the Himalayas, with ascents of many new routes and significant peaks at high altitude, including those of Shivling, Lobsang Spire, Broad Peak, Gasherbrum IV, K2, Trango Tower, and Shipton Spire. His work has appeared in adventure magazines around the world, and he is the author of a number of books including Thin Air: Encounters in the Himalaya, Climbing Free: My Life in the Vertical World, Over the Edge: The True Story of Four American Climbers' Kidnap and Escape in the Mountains of Central Asia, *and* Postcards from the Ledge, *from which this story was excerpted.*

A Visit to the Wandjina

Many consider the Kimberley Australia's last frontier.

WE HEADED EAST OUT OF DERBY ALONG A BROAD RED–DIRT TRACK that cuts like a raw wound through the wilds of the northern Kimberley. The washboard corrugations in the hard-packed dirt set everything in the car to clattering wildly.

"Got to keep your speed up to seventy-eighty ks an hour or more and try to ride the summits of the corrugation," Mike said, expounding his philosophy of negotiating these bone-jolting Outback tracks. "That's the smoothest way. Go any slower and the bangs 'n' bumps'll only be worse. I've driven roads so bad the cans of Coke in the back of the car'll rub against each other till they finally wear through and explode. Makes a bloody mess, I'll tell you."

For hours we drove through a stultifying sameness of flat scrublands, seemingly endless kilometers of weirdly shaped termite mounds and stunted gum and wattle trees with occasional kapok putting out its fiercely yellow blossoms from yawning pods. Here and there wondrous boab trees, almost human in their individuality, gave sudden life to the landscape—some squat and as massive as sumo wrestlers, others as sinuous and slim as prima ballerinas. The land seemed nine-tenths sky—a hot, brazen sky that seemed not to vault overhead but to press down like a heavy hand, suffocating everything beneath.

Here in the Kimberley's antipodean otherland, the seasons oscillate between a steamy tropical Wet, when more than a foot of rain falls in a typical month, and a brain-poaching Dry, when temperatures routinely push into the forties Celsius—100 to 115 degrees Fahrenheit—for months on end. Heat-crazed locals "go troppo"—like a fellow Mike mentioned who had recently set a series of brushfires, proclaiming them to be "signal-fires for UFO's."

"Usually happens around Christmastime. Temps'll hit 45 degrees. Not a cloud or raindrop for three bloody months. Melts a bloke's mind. People start waitin' for rain, lookin' up at the sky with blank eyes. Sometimes you see lightnin' in the distance, but it seems forever before that first raindrop falls. Then, when it finally comes, usually in January—*whew!* You never saw rains and thunder and lightning like that, mate. Rivers and billabongs start to overflow their banks, and soon half the landscape is underwater. It's like a moving inland sea. Temps cool down to maybe 32, 34 degrees, real comfy. Then when the waters subside, everything turns green for a few weeks and the wildflowers pop like fireworks outa the ground! Few weeks later the heat starts buildin' up, and everything's all scorched again."

Millions of years of alternating Wets and Drys have cracked, scoured, and fissured the Kimberley landscape, exposing rocks more than three billion years old in some places and revealing immense deposits of gold, diamonds, uranium, zinc, iron, bauxite, and other mineral treasures. A gold rush around Halls Creek in the 1880s brought the first permanent white settlers to the Kimberley, soon followed by pioneer stockmen who drove their herds thousands of miles cross-country and divided the region's geographical immensity into million-acre cattle stations, virtual empires unto themselves.

Within a few decades most of the local Aboriginal peoples were usurped from their ancestral lands, many dying from white man's diseases, others killed outright or scattered to missions, cattle stations, remote camps, and isolated towns as fringe-dwellers. Of the mere 50,000 or so people living today in this California-size region, perhaps a third are Aboriginals.

The land in places has been almost entirely depopulated. Along many Outback tracks you can drive hundreds of kilometers without seeing a single habitation, a single human being, only perhaps an occasional vehicle dragging its gritty plume of red dust through the desolate emptiness.

Here and there low mountains of raw, red sandstone and silver-gray limestone—the remnants of a barrier reef some 350 million years old—erupt out of the terrible monotony of the bush. For all its geological antiquity, the landscape somehow looks temporary, the rubble of ages strewn about in utter disorder. Some colossal accident seems to have happened here. You have a sense of traveling through a vast construction site abandoned by its workers. It seems unfinished—as if the Ancestor Beings will surely be returning momentarily to complete their handiwork.

We camped that night beside a billabong.

"No salties here?" I asked Mike.

I was referring to the huge, massive-jawed saltwater crocodiles, some growing sixteen feet long or more, that often swim scores of kilometers from the sea up estuaries and rivers, occasionally getting stranded in billabongs when the Wet-season floods subside. Though much less common inland than the smaller, slender-snouted freshwater crocs, which may snatch a dog or calf or wallaby but rarely make more than a lacerating swipe at human beings, these grimly smiling man-eaters are the true terrors of the Kimberley.

"Always got to keep an eye out for 'm," Mike said. "But not likely you'll see any of 'm this far inland. Mebbe a freshie or two. No worries, mate."

In the distance something howled mournfully.

"Dingo," Mike said.

"They ever bother you?"

"You'll probably never see one. They don't much care for people."

The billabong resonated with life-sounds—chirps and whistles, thrums and rasps, gurgles and suspicious ripplings. A warm yet cooling breeze ruffled the heavy night air. In the upper branches of a silver-trunked ghost gum, a raucous flock of white cockatoos settled and resettled nervously.

Not twenty feet away a knee-high goanna—an almost Disneyesque long-necked monitor lizard—stood on its hind legs staring our way. I could have sworn its beady eyes caught mine. A moment later I looked back and it was gone.

"No Dreamtime story for this place?" I asked Mike.

"Probably, but can't say I know it."

After dinner our conversation turned to Mike's early days as a pitcher for a semi-pro baseball team in Perth.

"Those were *my* Dreamtime days, mate. Had a helluva fast ball, pretty good curve and change-up. An American businessman saw me play, liked my style. Had contacts with the Chicago Cubs, he said. Told me he could arrange a baseball scholarship in the States. I was only sixteen. Trouble was, I'd also been offered a fauna warden's job with the government. They'd had 400 applicants and chose me. It was a real opportunity, somethin' I dreamed of. So I had to pick between dreams. Toughest decision of my life. I decided to take the warden's job, but sometimes I wonder. Maybe it was a big mistake. Now my dream's to explore America Outback style…and see the bloody World Series!"

He'd served the government for nearly twenty years, the last ten as the only wildlife officer in the Kimberley.

"Spent a lot of my time trackin' poachers. Croc poachers. Fish poachers. Bird smugglers. I loved it. Lots of times I had run-ins with Aboriginals, but I always played fair with 'm. Won their respect. Got to know 'm…and they got to know me. They gave me

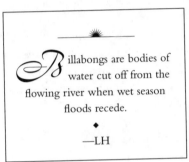

*B*illabongs are bodies of water cut off from the flowing river when wet season floods recede.

◆

—LH

the nickname Turkeyfoot. I had this knack, see, of creepin' up on 'm in the bush without bein' heard or seen just suddenly poppin' up in their midst…sort o' like the wild turkey does, you know? You don't see it, and then suddenly it's there, and then just as suddenly it's gone again, disappeared. I'm bloody proud o' that name!"

After retiring from the service in 1988, he'd started an Outback safari business called Kimberley Vision out of Kununurra, supplementing his income by catching rogue crocs on contract from the government.

"That was my second toughest decision—leavin' the service. It wasn't the work, I always loved that. It was the bloody bureaucrats in Perth always meddlin', always tellin' me what to do and what not to do, blokes who wouldn't know a king brown from a coil o' rope!"

His reference was to the king brown snake, one of the deadliest reptiles in the world. "They don't just strike once like most snakes." Mike had told me. "They'll come up and rat-a-tat-tat-tat, bite you ten, twenty times before you even see 'm. You'll likely be dead in a few minutes, mate."

"Any king browns out here?" I asked, eyeing the liquid darkness of the billabong.

"You bet. They're probably here, all right. But, like I say, no worries. They won't bother us."

"How do you know?"

He wiped a smile from his lips with the back of his hand.

"To tell you the truth, Harv, I don't. But I've been swagging out here all these years, and I'm still here to talk about it, right?"

A tough-minded realist, this Mike Osborn. Level-headed to a fault. His competence in matters of survival and good sense both amazed and humbled me. He was the perfect guide, the perfect companion. Though twenty years my junior. He treated me with a fatherly toleration and bemused concern, smiling wanly at my fears and imaginings. Many a time, stumbling up a rocky scree or clinging to a narrow ledge, I felt myself losing my balance only to sense the steadying grasp of his hand in mine and a calming "Easy there, mate. You'll make it."

His Fu Manchu mustache gave his movie-handsome face an appropriately ferocious aspect for a veteran "bushie." He'd reluctantly trimmed it at my impertinent suggestion during our trip the year before, revealing an underlying countenance as wholesome as a Norman Rockwell Boy Scout's. He'd hated it.

"Just ain't me," he'd snarled, looking unhappily in a mirror. "The blokes'd laugh me outa the pub." Within a couple of weeks the full-length mustachio had returned.

And yet I've known few men kinder or more considerate. Beneath that crusty macho exterior beats a sentimentalist's noble heart. Dozens of times during the 35,000-odd kilometers we've driven together, I've seen him come to the aid of stranded travelers, stopping for hours to jury-rig someone's broken axle or fix a rope to haul a broken-down vehicle back to the nearest road-house.

I remember the night we were driving along a lonely stretch of road south of Broome. Our headlights picked out some shadowy figures waving at us in the road.

"Could be trouble," I said, having heard of unwary travelers being mugged by groups of drunken youths.

"No worry, mate. We'll see what's the problem."

We stopped, and the group of shadowy figures approached the car. In the darkness they seemed definitely menacing.

"Just a family of Aboriginals," Mike reassured me. "Looks like their truck's conked out."

Sure enough, he was right. The family of eight or nine Aboriginals had been waiting for hours for the next car to come along. Mike worked at their vehicle for forty-five minutes, finally deciding it was "no go." After all but emptying our larder of provisions and passing them out to the grateful family, we roped their front bumper to the rear of our Land Ranger and pulled them all the way back to town, more than fifty kilometers out of our way.

"Outback etiquette," Mile shrugged as we headed back.

Another time we were tooling along an Outback track when a flock of birds suddenly wheeled low out of the sky directly across our path. I'd many times seen Mike slow down, even swerve to avoid hitting birds or other animals in the road. But this time one of the birds hit our front window with deadly impact. Instantly Mike braked the car, threw it into reverse, and backed up a hundred yards or so in a cloud of red dust.

"Have to make sure it's dead," he said. "Damn, but I hate myself when I hit one of 'm."

Jumping out of the car, he searched the brush.

"Here she is, she's still alive," he called.

He returned with the trembling creature, still fluttering weakly, cradled in his hands.

"Crested pigeon," he said, setting it in my lap. "Here, you take her while I drive. Hold her gentle around the wings, mate. Maybe we can take her home and get her well."

The bird was surprisingly warm in my hands. I could feel the beating of its heart.

"My God, it's beautiful," I murmured.

Its little head had a spiky crest of silvery feathers, each exquisitely formed with marvelously intricate interweaving patterns. Its body feathers were a lovely mother-of-pearl, almost iridescent. And its eyes...I had never seen such eyes, concentric circles of yellow and brown within an outer circle of brilliant, pulsating orange-red. I cupped my hands carefully around its wings to keep them from flapping.

But the bird struggled, terrified.

"Here, you take it," I said, feeling helpless.

Mike took the bird in his hands and held it maternally to his chest, softly stroking its back.

Still it struggled. Then, after a few agonizing seconds, it gave a convulsive jerk and went still. A greenish-gray nictitating membrane slowly slid over those lovely eyes with their glistening, pulsating concentric circles.

"She's had it, mate," Mike said softly.

He carried the now-limp body back to the side of the road and set it on the ground, covering it with brush.

"Dingo'll take care of it," he said, swallowing the crack in his voice.

We headed back up the road in funereal silence.

"You never get used to these things," he finally said.

Now, after a delicious meal of lamb stew cooked in an Aboriginal-style pit fire, I unstrapped and rolled out my swag—an inch-thin mattress wrapped about by a heavy canvas tarp with two flaps that can be pulled loosely shut to provide a modicum of protection against wind, cold, or rain. Mike was already sprawled out on his swag, snoring softly—pitching a no-hitter in some Dreamtime World Series, no doubt—and I was left to my own imaginings. I pulled the canvas flaps of my swag over my chest and stared up into the night sky. The Milky Way trailed across my field of vision like a twisted bridal veil of incandescent blue-white gas. Low on the horizon the Southern Cross hung pendant, reminding me of a gleaming crucifix intruding into the Aboriginal sky. My mind took flight into those stars, tracking the ghostly footprints of the Ancestor Beings on their celestial wanderings.

Someone—something—laughed aloud in the darkness.

"Kookaburra?" I called over to Mike.

He never answered.

And I didn't care.

We awoke with the flies and quickly broke camp.

"There's a cave not far from here I want to show you," Mike announced. "One of my secret places. It's around back and up the side of one of those cliffs out there. A big rock overhang with old paintings of the Wandjina. The Aboriginals seem to have forgotten all about it. Hasn't been touched for years so far as I can tell. Hold your hat! We're taken' a little ride!"

He swerved the Land Ranger off the red-dirt track, and we were off, bouncing wildly through a yellow blur of high cane grass whose seed heads rattled like buckshot against the windshield. Shattered cane stalks quickly covered the vehicle's front end, completely blocking Mike's view and forcing him to stick his head out the side window to see where he was going, which seemed to me to be absolutely nowhere. We lurched and jounced through a slalom of gum and wattle trees, narrowly missing scores of concrete-hard, chest-high termite mounds.

"Where the hell are we going?" I asked, desperately bracing myself to keep my head from banging against the roof of the car.

"Shortcut!" he announced.

At last, when it seemed we must be totally lost, we came to a barely recognizable track tunneling through the thick brush. This we followed for a few minutes, then plowed back through more high grass. The pattern repeated. I began to realize that there was an almost invisible network of tracks out here, a web of pathways discernable only to the practiced eye.

"You've been this way before?" I asked.

"Nope."

"Then how do you know there's a track out there?"

"You get a feel for it. There's always a track. Hard to find sometime, but it's always there."

"Always?"

"Always."

"Aboriginal tracks?"

At its tamest time of year, this territory is an environmental eye-popper. Deciduous boab trees—hollow, bottle-shaped lords of the bush, related vaguely to the baobabs of Africa and Madagascar, but found only in northern Australia—stand out on the horizon like solitary old geezers, their limbs frail, their girths measuring up to sixty feet. On the verdant Mitchell Plateau, almost as far north as you can go in the Kimberley, waterfalls spill from one eroded bowl into another, like outsized party displays. Herons, spoonbills, magpie geese, and brolgas cranes prance about riverbanks, while blue-winged kookaburras scope out coastal fish supplies. And you've not lived until you're jolted awake one morning, your blood pressure at an all-time high, by the cacophonous reveille of white cockatoos bickering in the mangrove trees.

◆

—J. Kingston Pierce,
"A Matter of Perspective"

"What else?"

"Dreaming tracks?"

"I suppose, mate. Maybe once. Now they're just tracks for bloody anyone."

We finally reached the base of some low, red cliffs and parked the Land Ranger.

"Up this way," Mike said. "Watch your step."

We scrambled up a stony path among large strewn boulders to a rock overhang and ducked beneath. The red sandstone walls and ceiling were covered with a ghostly gallery of large, white-painted faces, wide-eyed and mouthless, staring down at us as if startled by our arrival.

These were the Wandjina, or Cloud-Beings, of whom Daisy Utemorrah had spoken—uniquely haunting rock-art paintings found only in the central and west Kimberley. Mike had shown me several other Aboriginal rock-art sites in the east Kimberley, but in those the sinuous Rainbow Snake had been the dominant figure, surrounded by a panoply of red-ocher turtles, crocodiles, lizards, sticklike hunters with spears, and fright-figures called "devil-men."

Archaeologists have dated some of the Rainbow Serpent paintings to 9000 B.C. or earlier, which, according to Josephine Flood in her *Archaeology of the Dreamtime*, "would make the Rainbow Serpent myth the longest continuing religious belief documented in the world."

Even older Aboriginal rock drawings in South Australia have recently been dated back to 43,000 B.C., predating by more than 10,000 years the Neolithic cave paintings of Spain and Germany—hitherto considered the oldest in the world.

But these Wandjina figures of the Kimberley—some of them carbon-dated at "only" 8,000 years old, twice the age of Egypt's pyramids—are utterly unlike any other rock paintings elsewhere in Australia in style and psychological impact. They seem to be the work of an entirely different mentality and artistic tradition. Scholars have been chary of attributing them to so "primitive" a people as Australia's Aboriginals, speculating that they were the work of ancient Hindus, Egyptians, even the Lost Tribes of Israel. One pseudoscholar, Erich Von Däniken, in his controversial tome *Chariots of the Gods: Unsolved Mysteries of the Past,* went so far as to attribute the Wandjina figures to beings from outer space—interpreting the halolike fringes around their staring countenances as space helmets.

To local Aboriginal peoples, however, the halos fringing the faces of the Wandjina figures represent clouds and lightning. For generations beyond counting, they periodically visited these caves of the Wandjina to retouch or completely repaint their fading images, believing that by so doing they assured the return of the life-giving Wet. To them, these Wandjina figures aren't paintings at all; rather, they are the actual living images of the Cloud-Beings themselves, embedded in the rock for all eternity.

> For me, Windjana Gorge always will be the Kimberley's outer limit. It contains fossils of extinct crocodiles twenty feet long, and kangaroos that stood ten feet tall. There's a smattering of rock art that was old before its creators mastered fire. The graceful Bradshaw paintings and the mystical Wandjina heads have been tattooed into my dreams. In 30,000 years, when the Kimberley looks much the same as it does now, will there be anything so indelibly beautiful left of us?
>
> ◆
>
> —Neal Matthews, "The Back of Beyond," *Travel Holiday*

With the near-depopulation of the region's Aboriginal peoples over the past century, the Wandjina caves—like those of the Rainbow Snake and other Dreamtime Ancestor Beings—are no longer retouched, and they grow fainter and more weathered with each passing year. An attempt by the government in the late 1980s to have some Law Men retouch them resulted in a bitter outcry among Aboriginal traditionalists who insisted no one any longer possessed the requisite knowledge to do so. The attempt was abandoned.

But the Aboriginal art tradition continues, ever transforming it-self, in the modern bark paintings and canvases sold for upscale prices in galleries around the world (and for which the Aboriginal artists, alas, rarely receive more that a comparative pittance). New styles continually emerge, clearly demonstrating the extraordinar-ily resilient artistic genius of Aboriginal people—arguably the world's first artists—and making it, hopefully, no longer necessary for the doubting Gadia mind to attribute these wondrous Wandjina figures to ancient Egyptians or visiting spacemen.

Beneath the enigmatic wide-eyed stares of the Wandjina figures, I sat on a ledge of rock and looked out over the almost surreal Kimberley landscape—ranges of fractured red mountains inter-spersed with shimmering hard-scrub plains. So beautiful from up here, so oppressively monotonous at times when seen from the road below. Far on the horizon I could see a single small flotilla of black-bellied clouds drifting in from the Timor Sea, belching lightning. It takes no great leap of the imagination to picture the Wandjina and other Ancestor Beings on their immemorial travels down there, creating and re-creating the Dreamtime landscape.

Mike interrupted my thoughts.

"Hey, look at this,"

He directed my gaze to a shallow trough in the rock ledge; sit-ting on it were two almost perfectly round polished stones.

"Grinding stones," he said, picking one up and juggling it in his hand like a baseball. I half-expected him to pitch it out on a wicked curve into the abyss, but he set it reverently back in place.

"How old are they?"

"No idea. Maybe a few decades. Maybe centuries. And look here"—he gestured to the stone-littered floor of the cave—"see those stone chips? Some bloke made himself a spear point up here. And this one—see the polished edge?—that's a scraper. Stone Age stuff."

"And what's this?" I asked, picking up what appeared to be a petrified walnut.

"Quandong," Mike answered. "Aboriginals call 'm emu apples. That's just the pit you're lookin' at. You can eat the flesh around 'm when they're ripe. Aboriginal ladies still gather 'm in season. Bitter—pretty awful-tastin', really—but they'll keep a body."

"Maybe I'll take it for a Dreamtime souvenir."

"Sorry. Can't take anythin', mate. Not allowed. That's the law—whitefella's law, I mean."

Here I was, taking what wasn't mine again. Properly chastised, I set it down.

It was getting unbearably hot. Clouds of flies droning in the cave set up a resonant hum. At least a hundred of them had settled on the sweaty back of Mike's shirt. Reaching around to pat my own back, I raised hundreds more into the air.

We climbed down to the car for the long drive back to Kununurra, Mike's hometown in the east Kimberley, where he had arranged an appointment for us with the elders of the local Aboriginal community.

Harvey Arden was a staff editor and writer for National Geographic *for twenty-three years. He is the coauthor of* Wisdomkeepers *and the author of* Dreamkeeper: A Spirit-Journey into Aborginal Australia, *from which this story was excerpted. He lives in Washington, D.C.*

✦ ✷ ✦

Eco Trippers

The "Eco-Challenge" is not your ordinary race.

SHE HAS DIAMONDS IN HER EARS, GOLD ON HER FINGERS, LIPS tastefully glossed, blond bob. Petite, pretty—very pretty. Only the vertical grooves in her spandex-covered thighs and the surprising clamp when she takes your hand don't seem to square with the refined yuppie image. Then you take a closer look. There are traces of salt at her hairline from the Coral Sea breakers she's just been battling. A sherwood green sprig of vegetation is snagged in her shoelaces, picked up while she was careening through tropical rain forests on horseback and mountain bike. A contusion on her right forearm marks the sore spot where a Class IV rapid smacked her against a boulder. Her hands are scarred by a 300-foot climb, a 270-foot rappel, and a hand-over-hand traverse across a crocodile-infested river. And under it all, the faint ocher foundation of Outback soil. Louise Cooper-Lovelace has just completed a Discovery Channel Eco-Challenge, one of the toughest of a proliferating series of man-against-nature sporting events. She and her mates of the Endeavour team have raced nonstop for six days, eighteen hours, and thirty-three minutes across 334 miles of absolutely magnificent, utterly horrific Australian terrain. Yet Cooper-Lovelace doesn't look or act like the Iron Woman or

Marathon Man you'd expect. She has neither the aggressive lean-
ness of a marathoner nor the pumped muscles of a sprinter. At 43,
she is older than the top athletes in most other sports. And above
all, she is nice—no other word will do—remarkably nice, even to
the pale, flabby reporter who is questioning her now. No Albert
Belle belligerence, no Dennis Rodman attitude—in short, no
symptoms of sports ego. "I'm the team captain, but we don't really
have a leader," she says. "I'm just one of the merry little dwarfs."

Over the next hours and days, competitors of every description
stagger over the finish line. There are Australian go-go dancers and
French dentists, Mexican economists and German fashion models,
New Zealand geophysicists, Irish midwives, Finnish policemen,
and South African infopreneurs; there are New York cops and
Hawaiian lifeguards, psychotherapists from California and carpen-
ters from Ketchum, Idaho. Yet the groups are not as dissimilar as
they seem. Most good teams share maturity, an unremarkable
physique, and that most passé of virtues, niceness—qualities that
are even more crucial to success here than conventional athletic
merits like strength, endurance, and ego. And in the Eco-
Challenge, success means much more than finishing fast. It means
staying alive.

From a helicopter's air-conditioned bubble, the North
Queensland racecourse has an almost surreal beauty. At the start in
Undara, frosty eucalyptus trees whip in our rotor backwash, calming as we ascend, their white trunks marching out eastward across
a level grassland. The plain is punctuated by volcanic outcrops and
periodic water holes, blue pockets of sky in the orange earth.
Gradually the vegetation thickens and becomes green, tan spear
grass gives way to bottlebrush, eucalyptus becomes hoop pine. We
cross the Herbert River, gentle channels interwoven with strands
of dense scrub, between banks that steepen slowly to gorge, then
to full-fledged canyon. By the time the Herbert meets Blencoe
Creek, it is big water, running beneath 399-foot cliffs. Waterfalls
tumble over slick granite.

Northward the Earth's crust buckles in hills, heaves in full-scale
mountains. Rivers flow in long frothy rapids, impatient now for

the ocean. We fly over the wooded hills of the Cardwell Range, then the mountains of Bellenden Ker, which are blanketed by thick tropical vegetation. The topo map reveals creeks, swales, escarpments; from the air the terrain is an unbroken jade-green canopy. Cresting Mount Battle Frere, the tallest peak in Queensland, we see the South Pacific blue of the Coral Sea filling the horizon. We loop out over open water. Just visible seaward are palm tufts and the sheen of distant breakers—stars in the enormous galaxy of the Great Barrier Reef. Islands edged with golden sand slip by below us until we round a jutting headland and swing into Cairns harbor, where rainbow lorikeets flit in the mango trees along the waterfront promenade.

By air, the transition from Outback to tropical forest to Barrier Reef seascapes is swift and indescribably serene. On the ground, it is a very different story. There are extreme hazards and a very real danger: *Crocodylus porosus*, the estuarine or saltwater crocodile—or salties, as Australians jauntily call them. To a hushed audience of press and racers, herpetologist Steve Irwin recites the terrifying litany. Salties can grow to almost thirty feet and weigh over a ton, yet they can hide in a puddle the size of a birdbath. They leap six feet clear of the water, hold their breath for ninety minutes, strike as fast as a snake, and bite with two tons of pressure per square inch. They eat frogs, fish, dingoes, feral pigs, monitor lizards, taipans, cassowaries, *and* human beings. Crocodiles have been around for 200 million years and have pretty well perfected their shtick.

"What should a person do at close quarters with a croc?" a pale, flabby reporter wants to know.

"Look," Irwin explains helpfully, "if a saltie lines you up for a bit of tucker, honestly, you haven't got a chance in hell." Tucker is food. Hot food. Tucker is you. "The bright side," he concludes, "is that you'll never know what ate you."

Back at Undara, the countdown has begun. Tree trunks throw long shadows in the mellow evening light. The crowd of competitors falls silent as the last seconds tick away, then with a roar they lope over the line and into the heart of Australia.

Checkpoint 4/*Day 2, just before dawn.* The Southern Cross

glitters above the silent gum tree canopy, symmetry in an unfamiliar chaos of stars. Breath comes in clouds; the Outback cold is surprising. In absolute darkness the distant quavering howl of a dingo seems ominous. Somewhere in the trees a kookaburra clears its throat, then chuckles maniacally. Then another noise, faint at first and nipped off by the dark, slowly growing until head-lanterns slice the night: Frenchmen, moving fast.

Two teams, ARS and France Raid Adventure, stride to the checkpoint together, lean and very thirsty. They scan the roster impatiently and see that three teams, including Endeavour, passed through nearly an hour before. Another team arrives, Odyssey, members of the crack U.S. Navy SEAL unit. The French rise and push on.

The French have a long tradition in adventure racing, and they do well. The first major race, the Raid Gauloises, was founded by a Frenchman, Gérard Fusil.

Over the next few hours, as night pales to dawn, more voices roll in from the Outback: broad, twangy Aussie and Kiwi tones, burbling Swedish, staccato Japanese, singsong Spanish, California diphthongs, and Deep South drawls, as forty-eight teams from fifteen countries troop through the checkpoint, stop for water and to tend their feet, then proceed.

The Cherokee was due to return for me in an hour. On our way to the airstrip, Brian and I stopped at a local billabong. It was exactly the kind of place where, according to Steve Hughes, a person could expect to be devoured by crocodiles. I watched in horror as Brian stripped, waded in and swam to the center. He floated lazily, the picture of bliss, and peered at me with amusement.

"I'd be lying to you if I said there was absolutely no chance of a croc attack," he confessed. "But it hasn't happened yet—and my people have bathed here for many, many years."

◆

—Jeff Greenwald, "Australian Odyssey," *San Francisco Examiner*

At 08:10 hours Eco-Internet tramps in, twenty places and three hours behind the leaders—not at all where they are accustomed to being. Composed of a U.S. landscape designer and her New Zealand doctor husband, a Harvard computer guru born in Ireland, and a self-employed window cleaner (also Kiwi), this team dominates the sport. They have trademarked the team name. These people are serious.

And yet, they're not. "How many places back? Twenty, d'you say?" John Howard, the window cleaner asks. "The pressure's off, then—we can lie down for a while." Howard is an adventure racing legend, with multiple wins in almost every major event the world over. He fits the pattern. He is 41-years-old, has a sturdy but nondescript build, and is undeniably nice. He says things like, "[Other] people are faster and bigger, and I'm just an average all-around athlete." Robert Nagle, team captain, 38, stocky thighs, wry Irish grin, nice: "We are just trying to follow our own game plan, playing the cards we're dealt."

Throughout the rest of the morning and on into the day, more teams straggle in, battered and bleeding, dehydrated. They drop down beside the spring, fill their bottles and camel bags, drag off shoes and leggings and duct tape and spear grass-riddled nylon, then survey the damage. Beneath is a sight that would make even a saltie wince: toenails pried up by swelling blood blisters, vast tracts of raw flesh, shins slashed by razor-edged volcanic rock. Joints stiffen as contestants sit; many hobble painfully when they leave. Four checkpoints down; twenty-seven to go.

Checkpoint 11/*Day 4, 08:56 hours.* She scrambles over the rim, unclips from the safety rope, and does a little dance. "Waaaaa-hooooo!" she exults, red ponytails bobbing. "That was a blast!" Pippy Longstocking conquers Everest. Everyone smiles—stern race coordinators, battle-hardened photojocks. Nora Tobin's joy is contagious.

"What is it like to climb 300 feet through a waterfall after having trudged and canoed three days straight?" a pale, flabby reporter wants to know. "It was fabulous—what a view!" Vieuuu—her Alaskan accent sounds vaguely Canadian. "And the spray was really refreshing. You should try it!" Later the reporter will crawl to the edge and peer down through rainbow spray to the water far below, and decide once and for all: never. But right now he is questioning Tobin's teammate and fellow Alaskan, Chris Flowers, who has joined her on the summit.

Flowers sits cross-legged, arms cradling knees, the gentle smile and relaxed facial muscles of someone fresh from the sauna. "This is the ultimate vacation," he says. You can see it in his China-blue eyes: he's not kidding.

Just about now you begin to tell the successful teams from the unsuccessful by who's having fun. A day ago it might have been possible to fake it, but no longer. Most top teams sleep less than three hours a night for the duration of the event—some half that—and the mounting weight of physical exhaustion and sleep deprivation soon means your lips mirror your heart. You smile if you're enjoying yourself, scowl if you're not.

Three hours earlier, Louise Cooper-Lovelace, her team locked in a duel for first place with Eco-Internet, sat in the same spot and giggled about her climb. "I was terrified, slipping and sliding around that rock like a complete idiot." In a short time, Ian Adamson of Pure Energy Australia will arrive, wearing his own pack on his shoulder, and a teammate's on his head. "Like my sun hat?" he chirps. Later in the race, his teammate Jane Hall, hobbling on terribly swollen ankles, recalls repeated falls during the mountain bike leg. "Every time I came off my bike, the boys joked that I was trying to 'nest,'" she says.

If you want to win an adventure race, it helps to be a Kiwi or an Aussie. Something about the perennially sunny disposition and uncomplicated, unpretentious outlook of Down Under is perfect for the sport. Failing that, be from somewhere low-key: Ireland, say, or South Africa. Yanks are, by and large, too serious, too driven, too keen on winning to win. Some are learning, though. Alaskans seem to have a pronounced Kiwi streak.

Somewhere Beyond Checkpoint 26/*Day 8, 20:45 hours*.

People have been lost in the Bellenden Ker rain forests and never found. And as if this weren't enough, it has been raining for days now. East Wind, a Japanese team, makes its way painfully up steep slopes and down brush-choked ravines. Three pairs of weary legs slogging endlessly in the mud. A fourth pair dangles limp, flopping with every step. Three East Wind racers are carrying their fourth teammate, Nohoko Hayama, whose badly injured legs no longer support her weight. Piggyback. Over mountains. In a rain forest. Through the rain.

In one sense, the race is long over. Eco-Internet finished in first place three days ago, closely followed by Pure Energy Australia. Right now Louise Cooper-Lovelace is back in her snug hotel room in Cairns, after taking seventh place; so are Nora Tobin and Chris Flowers of Wilderness Classic, the top U.S. finishers in ninth. So this Eco-Challenge is finished. Yet the race is very much still on.

Clearly, this event isn't just about finishing first, or even just about finishing. It cuts to the core of human motivation, a force conventionally assigned to specific parts of the anatomy—heart, guts, backbone—but actually much harder to pinpoint. It drags out some interesting questions. "Is this race against others or against myself?" "What does 'winning' mean?" If the contest weren't so grueling, such questions would only seem like sports-speak.

Nohoko Hayama lies on a cot in the medical tent at the far side of the rain forest. "What was it like?" the reporter asks. She smiles and nods but does not reply. Perhaps she is too tired; perhaps they do not share a language. But he reads the answer in her eyes: "Magnificent."

She still has fifty miles of kayaking on a treacherous, white-capped ocean to look forward to.

Somewhere Between Checkpoints 29 and 30/Day 9, 13:30 hours. It is a seafarer's nightmare. The bruise-black wall of cloud rolls forward faster than any ship can flee, engulfing everything before it in ferocious winds and driving rain. Waves building to six, eight, ten feet...and building higher.

Four people are in deep trouble in the Coral Sea. They have lashed their kayaks together to form a raft; two of them are already overboard, clinging to the gunwales. Foam-crested waves toss them like driftwood. Wind blows raindrops like liquid bullets. The people in the water are losing feeling in their hands. The raft is sinking. The men in the boat break the seal on their emergency radio and call the rescue chopper.

Fortunately the team is Odyssey, the Navy SEALs. Others might not have survived the storm. Yet the irony of elite naval officers being fished out of the water like toddlers from a splash pool is unmistakable.

Ironically, all-military teams do badly in adventure races and always have. Precisely the people you'd expect to excel at such extreme physical and mental stress—the hardest of the hard, the toughest of the tough—frequently fall to pieces. It is difficult to say why, but it seems to come down to ego and teamwork.

"Ego prevents a lot of military guys from speaking up when they're hurting," says Andy Petranek, successful adventure racer and former U.S. Marine Corps captain. "If your Achilles tendon is killing you, you have to speak up, give up some of your weight. But in the military that's almost taboo. It's not manly." Military leadership may also be too rigid and hierarchical for adventure racing. "When you are told 'Take that hill!' you just have to do it." Petranek says. "You aren't necessarily taught to ask yourself why, or the best way; it's just 'Take that hill!'"

The Absolute Ruler approach may work well in other pursuits, but not here. Sir Ranulph Fiennes, schooled at Eton and honed at the British army academy Sandhurst, is one of the greatest living explorers. He has led numerous major expeditions, including an unsupported trek to the South Pole. "The only position that I can tolerate on an expedition is that of team leader," he says. "If others, whether or not they form a majority, favor an opinion which I believe to be stupid, dangerous, or unlikely to help attain the goal of the expedition, then I overrule them no matter how disaffected this may make them feel." Fiennes entered the 1996 Eco-Challenge in British Columbia. His team did not complete the race.

Successful teams use entirely different methods, employing what we might call the Cooper-Lovelace Merry Dwarfs Model. "We take a democratic approach to decision-making," Robert

Nagle says. "Whenever a tough decision has to be made, we all confer on it. Conflicts are brought out in the open and resolved as a team. We never resort to the one ultimate leader paradigm. We're here to learn and enjoy and will never sacrifice our friendship for a competition." A far cry from "Take that hill!"

The Finish/*After ten days, four hours, and twenty-eight minutes, it is over.* New York's Finest, a group of remarkably filthy, bedraggled, and radiant New York police officers, beach their kayaks and stumble over the line, the last team to complete the race. Of the forty-eight teams that started the race, only twenty-nine finished. New Zealand teams took first, third, and fifth places; Aussie teams finished second and fourth.

At the closing press conference, a flabby reporter raises a pale hand. "What can normal people possibly learn from the superhuman ordeal of the Eco-Challenge?" He asks the question, yet over the last ten days he has begun to sense the answer. Keith Murray, a member of the winning Eco-Internet team, looks genuinely surprised. "People shouldn't be put off by the strenuousness of what we've done," he says. "We're just normal people with normal jobs, normal families."

Yes and no. Flaying yourself alive for a week isn't normal. Few aspire to it, or even should. But Murray—deprived of sleep and buzzed on victory champagne, with enough beta-endorphins charging around in his bloodstream to have all Manhattan singing for a month—has a different vision.

What he sees in the Eco-Challenge is a vast world of incredible beauty fraught with hidden dangers, a limitless choice of pathways and solutions, a goal that seems clear and grows fuzzy as one proceeds but is nevertheless attainable by a tight group of people working together, relying on one another. In this world, the kind of leadership that leads somewhere is less pushy and totalitarian, the teamwork that works is more inclusive and free-form. In this vision, winning isn't high-fives and victory struts and mindless machismo, but something more interior, private: people can win without finishing, or lose even when they cross the line first.

Words have different weight. *Fun* and *nice* are not weaknesses—the stuff of wimps, the uncool—but strengths. Like *joy* and *adventure*, they harbor a deep seriousness and a delightful imprecision, poised in delicate balance, deliciously pure. It is the Eco-Challenge, and it's a lot like life.

Tom Mueller, a writer based in Italy, is completing a novel about the building and rebuilding of St. Peter's Basilica, and the mystery of St. Peter's tomb.

STEPHANIE SPEAKMAN

In Hot Pursuit

She headed into the hills to round up wild horses.

BRUMBY RUNNING! DOES THE PHRASE QUICKEN YOUR HEARTBEAT in anticipation of high adventure at breakneck speed? Are we talking river rapids or wild horses? If you have read the great Australian ballad *The Man from Snowy River*, by A. B. (Banjo) Paterson (or seen the movie with Kirk Douglas), you probably know exactly what brumby running means: chasing and roping wild horses in the high country of southeastern Australia.

But did you know you could still do it today?

Although brumbies are scattered in various pockets of the country and are plentiful enough to be considered a nuisance in the Northern Territory where, competing with sheep and cattle for pasture, they are hunted and shot from helicopters, they are relatively unbothered in the southern state of Victoria. The local people occasionally catch brumbies—they are smaller and weedier that standard horses—and break them in to sell as children's ponies or to breed to stock horses, producing useful trail mounts.

The first brumby herds are said to have formed in the mid-nineteenth century, when the O'Rourkes, early settlers, pulled up stakes and abandoned their livestock. The name may derive from a Major James Brumby, a turn-of-the-century soldier who, when transferred to Tasmania, left his cavalry mounts behind to fend for themselves. Brumby catching has been a side occupation for mountain cattlemen, who lease the high-country grazing rights, ever since. In the past, when the demand for horses was great, traps disguised as corrals were constructed, the remains of which can be seen today. Now, brumby runners generally head off with a couple of dogs to locate the herds, a few days' provisions, catching ropes, and halters.

Chris Stoney, a 32-year-old fifth-generation farmer who grew up mustering cattle on his grandfather's mountain lease, was our guide. Although he had never caught a brumby or even ridden through the country we were going to, Chris is an accomplished horseman, having repeatedly won the Cattlemen's Cup and the Great Mountain Race, annual and very demanding cross-country races for stockhorses in Australia. Chris's family owns Stoney's Bluff and Beyond Trail Rides, an outfit that specializes in taking small groups through the mountains of Victoria. My sister Margaretta and I had gone adventuring with Chris before:

*I*n the mountain ranges, which are inhospitable or inaccessible to cattle, virtually all damage done to native flora and fauna can be attributed to feral horses.

The horses are having a traumatic effect on precisely those remote and inaccessible areas that hikers and nature lovers so prize for their pristine habitats and native animals,. The horses consume remote mountain water holes and despoil others with their dung. Because rivers and creeks rarely have running water in them, they seldom get seldom get flushed and are therefore easily polluted. The horses also deplete food and destroy cover so necessary to native wildlife.... It's not just that these are among the most beautiful landscapes in the Northern Territory, but also that these are the last refuges of threatened and endangered native species.

◆

—Richard Symanski,
Outback Rambling

to a three-day race meet in the bush, to an Outback pub and to a mysterious hidden lake called Tali Karng.

This time we were going to northeastern Victoria in search of brumbies, and Chris had done considerable research—organizing local guides, reconnoitering campsites and obtaining permits. We would use four-wheel backup to obviate the need for pack horses. Chris had also asked Dean Bachman to meet us in the Limestone Country to show us how it was done. Dean, at about thirty, has probably caught more brumbies than anyone else in Victoria today, on one occasion bringing seventeen out, all tied head to tail.

Eighteen of us left from Stockyard Creek, the Stoney summer camp on the Howqua River, just above the town of Mansfield, in mid-February. There were six Americans (all women), six Australians, and another half-dozen staff, some to ride and some to drive. We took three spare horses, which would run loose after a day or so; saddlebags were stuffed with shoeing gear, radio equipment and medical supplies. Everything else for sixteen days went in two vehicles: a conventional, if somewhat battered, Isuzu Trooper and a specialty truck designed for these sorts of adventures—hot water and refrigeration were among its luxuries; both had winches and chains.

The terrain of northeastern Victoria is varied and can be formidable, rising from lush, riverbank country with huge tree ferns, banksia, and rampant blackberry through towering hardwood stands of mountain ash and woollybutt—enough eucalyptus to cure the common cold—to remote alpine regions. Here ghostly snowgums spread their gnarly branches over rich summer pasture. Delicate trigger plants snap up unwary insects amid clumps of snow-daisies and everlastings in a profusion of purple, white, and yellow. Still higher, the shale-covered mountain ranges shade off in hazy blue ridges that corrugate into knobs and bumps on the horizon with names like Buffalo, Buller, Cobbler, Feathertop, and the Crosscut Saw.

Our route would take us some 200 miles in a northeasterly direction right up to Mount Kosciusko, Australia's highest peak, and the Indi River, which becomes the mighty Murray and forms the border with New South Wales. From previous long rides, Margaretta and I knew to expect the unexpected. We had eaten bogong moths and found them delicious. We knew there would be poisonous snakes and this time we would learn to marinate and cook them. We looked forward to meeting a few old friends along the mainly deserted track, cattlemen like Froggy McMahon, wise and bush savvy, who told his tales, oblivious to the flies that wandered across his leathery face to drink from the corners of his eyes.

The first five or six days were familiar to those of us who had spent time in these mountains. We camped by rivers—the water is all drinkable—swam, fished, and rode long hours over Magdala and the Howitt High Plains, through the Wonnangatta Valley, past the gold-mining ghost towns of Grant and Talbotville to the pub at Dargo and across those high plains to the Bogong Country. Horses and riders became lean and fit.

We settled into a much-loved routine: rising at dawn to the cries of the kookaburras and Chris's cheerful rooster crow, pulling the billy can off the fire for hot tea, nose-bagging the horses, eating heartily ourselves—yes, Vegemite on toast was always available—and, finally, striking the tents before packing lunches and saddling up. Our mounts ran the gamut from pure Arabian to draft, stockhorse, and thoroughbred crosses. Most were small, clean legged, with cold, hard ligaments, and had stood the test of time. Generally, we averaged twenty miles a day and didn't push the pace.

We rode in groups or single file along the cliffs at whatever speed seemed appropriate. No one mollycoddled us or told us how to ride, but anyone who tried to put their horse "into a frame" or "on the bit" would get a gentle reminder that the trip was long and hard, and, as Banjo Paterson wrote in *The Man from Snowy River*, "No use to try for fancy riding now." We rode in stock saddles or military ones dating from World War I, and we examined our horses' backs closely at the end of the day as we washed them. If a saddle sore seemed to be starting, the rider would switch to a spare horse for a time.

Nearly always the vehicles had preceded us to camp. After pitching tents and rolling our sleeping bags or swags, we would lend a hand with anything that needed doing, although volunteers tended to be scarce when it came to erecting the dunny (latrine). Then it was beers chilled in a nearby river, snags (sausages) and steaks on the fire, heaps of veggies, a sweet sticky pudding (sent along by Chris's grandmother), jokes, recitations, and songs, all under the Southern Cross and a myriad of unfamiliar constellations.

Several days out we saw our first brumby at a little off-season ski resort called Dinner Plain. It was a weanling colt, lost from its band, that had followed a local trial-ride outfitter in. He had big kind eyes, a nicely sloped shoulder and a gutful of parasites, but nothing a good dose of worm medicine would not cure.

In Omeo there was a party at the Hilltop Pub to say good-bye to a few who had to leave and to welcome in some Australians, bound by their common love of foxhunting, and now, keen to chase brombies. We shouted beers (bought rounds) to one and all, danced around the jukebox to hit tunes from the '60s and rollicking bush music and, before long, met the dawn. The publican indulgently saw us off to our horses, sympathizing with the hung over as he mopped his floor. A tolerant and hardy breed!

We were ten days out now and limbered our horses up by racing them across the dried-up lake at Benambra. Dean Bachman and his friend Rusty Conolly turned up to take us into the Limestone Country and on to the Davies Plain. By the next day we were there. Brumby droppings in three-foot piles—it's part of an equine ritual—and well-licked natural salt holes were the telltale signs. At lunch Dean and Rusty briefed us, while some strapped on knee guards and others practiced roping stumps. Three things to remember: one, always follow the brumby exactly, for it knows the way across the treacherous, bottomless hidden bogs; two, if you find that you have been left alone, don't move on— someone will return for you—but the country is thick and vast, and can swallow you up; three, if you find yourself flying headlong into a tree, pull your horse's head up so that it will hit the tree before you do. Sobering!

We mounted quietly and jostled each other for the first places in the single file—those with catching ropes shifted them off their shoulders. Since stock saddles do not have horns, the idea is to find a tree as soon as a brumby is roped, tie it first to that and then change the lasso for a halter and rope that are strapped to the front of the saddle. We peered into the undergrowth: visibility was about fifty feet. Several times we stopped after seeing a flicker of motion that always turned out to be a Hereford. Then full stop, and Dean whispered, "Horses!" We moved before they did, but only those of us in front saw the flashing tails as the mob flew off through the undergrowth. Dean's solid buckskin knew his business and was off at their heels, agile as a polo pony, jumping fallen timber like a thoroughbred. In a matter of seconds we had lost him. We regrouped and waited, increasingly convinced that Dean had caught a brumby.

Forty-five minutes later we heard Dean's "cooee"— the traditional Australian bush call, with emphasis and high pitch on the second syllable. We "cooeed" back until he came into view and led us to his captive, standing quietly haltered and tied to a snowgum. It was a dark brown filly with a notched ear indicating

---

*N*ear Eucla, on the shores of the Great Australian Bight at the border between Western Australia and South Australia, an unusually high wire-netting fence spears out across the plain toward the northern horizon. At a point about fifty miles from the coast, it turns east to run parallel with the Transcontinental Railway. Then it turns to follow a tortuous northeasterly path for many miles across dusty plains, dry riverbeds, rocky hills, desert sand dunes, tracts of napunyah, lignum, and mulga scrub, to end on a flowing river draining rich green hills....

Called officially the Dingo-proof Barrier Fence, it is generally referred to by bushmen as "the dog fence," and it was installed to protect the sheeplands of southern South Australia, New South Wales, and central Queensland from dingoes.

◆

—Jeff Carter, *People of the Inland*

previous capture. Dean gently released her after a few minutes, explaining that he intended to keep only yearling colts. Their future is dim in the wild since they are ousted from the group upon sexual maturity and spend the rest of their lives scrapping with other young stallions or fighting older band leaders, even to the death. Mature males are definitely to be avoided, said Dean, describing how one had charged his horse and reared up inches from his own face before sinking its teeth into his shoulder.

We rode on for a couple of hours, without seeing anything, the chase having cleared the area. Then, almost into camp, we came across a little group of brumbies standing right on the four-wheel-drive track, and we set off as fast as our horses could run. Suddenly, we were off the road into the rough stuff, and things became very untidy. The wild horses were among us and behind us, close enough to touch as they raced by. Chris had managed to rope his own horse's front legs and it stopped abruptly; one guest's saddle had slipped under his horse's belly, leaving him slightly bloody on the ground, and Dean had disappeared again. Eventually, we sorted ourselves out. No one was hurt, and we found Dean just over the rise, with a big-bellied gray mare he was tying to a tree. We waited for her breathing to settle and then brought her on to our camp. Wild horses won't be led, but they will go along in front of a ridden horse, restrained by the rope and halter.

We stayed right on the bank of the Indi that night and made an electric-tape corral for our horses there, too, since there was no pasture. The brumby we tied just outside the corral's perimeter.

It had been a big day and we were in tents early, almost asleep, when the sounds of wild snorting and hoofs clattering in the river awoke a few of us. Dean and Chris were just scrambling from their swags (bedrolls), Dean pulling on his boots and spurs automatically until someone reminded him that his strides (trousers) were missing. Dean's plight, revealed by the full moon, lightened the serious situation for a moment. The brumby stallion had come for his mare, frenzying our horses into breaking the corral tape. The majority had gone bush and crossed the Indi into New South Wales.

We quickly filled nose bags. Chris and Dean saddled two straggler horses and shot off across the river. Half our group slept quietly while the rest of us cordoned off the track above the camp to prevent the horses from going on by if and when they were found. It took the better part of the night, and tremendous good luck, but the horses were rounded up in the end—a saga reminiscent of Banjo Paterson's verse. We built up the campfire, drank rum to keep out the chilly and listened to brumby-running stories for hours, knowing we had been privy to a little bit of the Snowy River legend.

At dawn, the brumby mare had a suckling foal; the stallion stood defiantly on the escarpment above, and we released them to him.

We caught five more brumbies over the next two days, and Dean kept one colt. Chris roped a mare after a long and tiring gallop and brought her back to cheers and toasts honoring his achievement. We encountered danger frequently on the cliffs and in the flat-out pursuit; one of our horses barreled into a tree, carried half of it away, but, remarkably, only fractured its nose. We were grateful for the earlier briefing, for a rider would not have survived such a blow.

We ended up at Tom Groggin, the famous old cattle station, nestled in mountains and frequently cut off from the world by snows and floods. We caught large yabbies (crayfish) in the Indi and boiled them for tea. The station manager brought his tow-headed family down to our campsite on the river, and we shared the evening. Cocooned in a life unchanged by time, with only slow-moving satellites crossing the night sky to remind us of the other world, we reveled in the fact that for now, and for us, this was the real world. Tomorrow we would ride out down the river as it gathered creeks and streams to become the Murray. We would pass Jack Riley's grave where, in 1914, a likely inspiration for *The Man from Snowy River* had died of a fever before he could reach help. And, as Chris finished reciting the poem by firelight, we promised ourselves that we would return the next year to share the rigors, the beauty, the mateship and the uncluttered life of the Australian cattlemen.

And down by Kosciuski, where the pine-clad ridges raise
Their torn and rugged battlements on high,
Where the air is clear as crystal, and the white stars fairly
    blaze
At midnight in the cold and frosty sky,
And where around the Overflow the reed-beds sweep
    and sway
To the breezes, and the rolling plains are wide,
The man from Snowy River is a household word today,
And the stockmen tell the story of his ride.

*Stephanie Speakman and her husband Bill live near Kennett Square,
Pennsylvania where she is actively involved with steeplechase and foxhunting
horses. A frequent traveler to Australia, she and her partner, Maria Wray,
own a restaurant in Lakes Entrance, Victoria, which specializes in Mexican
cuisine. She also has shot a documentary film, with her friend Chris Stoney,
covering an eighteen-day horse trek across the Victorian High Country from
Mansfield to the Snowy River.*

A Wild Ride in Arnhem Land

A visitor gets a glimpse of a world few get to see.

IT WAS THE TRANSITION TIME BETWEEN DRY AND WET SEASONS. The sun was hot, the air humid, the bush green, bursting with new life. Flies buzzed around us. A hundred birds sent up a greeting: a barrage of squawks, whistles, and caws from red-collared lorikeets, red-winged parrots, blue-winged kookaburras. We were walking through the bush along the Western Arnhem Land Escarpment, a sandstone outcropping that juts abruptly from the floodplain in this isolated land on Australia's northern coast east of Darwin.

Max Davidson, former farmer, longtime bushman, buffalo hunter, and now our guide, led us around boulders and under sandstone arches to a spot in the shade of a river red gum. There, under huge stone overhangs that sheltered two areas that could easily accommodate a dozen people, spread paintings in red and yellow ocher of animals, spiritual beings, and rough line art that would be impressive in any museum.

"I found these sites in 1988," Max said, not boasting, just filling in some history. "The traditional owners said there was no art out here. No one's been living here for about forty years. I was hunting buffalo with a German. We'd been out all day and were heading back. I decided to go a way I hadn't gone before, just to look

around, and we walked down through these stones and found this.
I'd guess only about three or four hundred people alive today have
ever seen it."

I just sat and stared for the longest time when Max said some
of this art was 20,000 years old.

I'd met Max when I'd flown in that morning from Jabiru, a settlement in the middle of Kakadu National Park a mere fifteen-
minute flight away. He was as broad as he was tall, with a blondish-
white beard trimmed close, and similar hair poking from beneath
his hat.

Arnhem Land is off-limits to non-Aboriginal people. Permits
for visitors can be obtained, but only if you come in with one of
the few safari camp operators. Fines are high if caught without a
permit, and solo travelers will not be welcomed by local people,
who prefer to be left alone. Max was invited to set up camp in the
area near Mount Borradaile by his longtime friend, Charlie
Munguda, with whom he'd hunted buffalo for years.

We'd headed out by jeep on a track that soon disappeared and
bumped along past gum trees and over any plants smaller than the
vehicle. Flies swarmed around our faces and I donned a fly net, an
essential piece of equipment for softies like me. Max, of course,
hardly noticed them.

We parked the jeep and set out on foot, with Max stopping to
describe features of the bush. Stringybarks and woollybutts, two
common trees, are the most common used to make didgeridoos; a
billygoat plum, a native tree with small fruit, has 50 percent more
vitamin C than an orange. Green ants are lemon flavored (I know,
because Max offered me one to sample and I could hardly say no),
and Aboriginals take the whole nest, scrunch it up, mix it in water,
and drink to treat colds. They eat the bloodwood nut, and use the
flaky bark from the paperbark tree to build ground ovens for cooking almost anything. They start with hot rocks in a hole, add a layer
of paperbark leaves, some water, more layers of leaves, then fish,
wallaby, buffalo, whatever is the day's meal, and cover with paperbark layers. Termite mounds, conical eruptions of the red earth
that sometimes reach over six feet tall, are used for medicinal pur-

poses. The pitaradia acts as a decongestant; there's a grasshopper here that eats this plant and nothing else.

Paperbark is a mellelucca, the family that provides tea tree oil, and the bark grows in dozens of thin layers to become several inches thick. Early whites who came to Australia did paintings on paperbark, but the Aboriginals didn't. They used stringybark trees instead.

We tasted this and sampled that, learning a little about how to survive on "bush tucker," food the locals have been eating for millennia.

We descended from the scrubby grassland to shady gum forests and walked toward the floodplain, a vast sweep of lush green grass, water, and birds by the hundreds of thousands. Flocks of egrets hung out in distant trees, white specks against deep green; huge flocks of magpie geese fed in the wetlands or filled the sky; iridescent kingfishers flitted here

> *S*ome kind of eucalypt, with leaves gleaming in the sky is bound to be remembered: a great sufficient red gum of the plains or river flats; or a patient coolibah with faith in the dry creek bed; or a mountain ash, taut and monumental of trunk in the company of giants; these are all Australian symbols. Many an expatriate has burnt a few aromatic gum leaves from his homeland, and discovered a compound sensory delight. The carolling of the magpie that "overflows like bubbling water," the blue haze of the ranges, perhaps the texture of broad slabs of sun-warmed granite...the smoke of gum leaves may be redolent of any of a thousand memories.
>
> ◆
>
> —John Mayston Béchervaise, *Australia: World of Difference*

and there; white-breasted sea eagles (*marawudis*) swept the sky for a distant perch.

Soon we came upon the art sites, where we sat in awe. Conversation was subdued because the presence of so many generations represented by that art made us seem small beyond description. How many years do we have? Seventy-five? Eighty? A few more if we're lucky, considerably fewer if we're not? This work had been here for at least 20,000 years. It was impossible to wrap my mind around that.

Max has an outdoorsman's respect for the land and an anthropologist's respect for Aboriginal culture. "When an Aboriginal dies," Max said, "the clan gets together and has a 'sorry' where they spend four days with the body. They cut themselves, and talk, to show they're sorry that he's gone. Then they place the body on a tree platform for two years, and afterwards out of respect they collect and clean the bones, wrap them in paperbark, and inter the bones in the rocks. Every time they touch the body they have a ceremony. When someone dies they believe the spirit is gone, back to the ground, to the mother.

"Everything in Aboriginal society is shared," he continued. "If I've got money, you've got money. Nothing is kept personally. If Charlie comes to me and says he needs money, I have to give it to him because I'm his brother. When he sees his friends and he's got money, he gives it to them. It's just the way it is."

Max refuses to speculate beyond what's really known about the

---

*T*hen, as today, it was important to Aboriginal people that every stranger who stayed for any period of time in their community be given a "skin name" and assigned a kinship position. This action does not denote "initiation," as some recipients of such titles have claimed; it is simply a means by which Aborigines indicate how close or distant they feel toward a newcomer. At Yirrkala in northeastern Arnhem Land, I became known as "wife" to the late Mawalan, ceremonial leader of the Rirratjingu clan; in the Gunbalanya region, I was designated "daughter" to Bobby Bardjarai Nganjmirra of the Kunwinjku.

◆

—Dorothy Bennett, "Collecting Stories of the Dreamtime," *Kunwinjku Art from Injalak* art here because anything else would be fooling yourself. "Lots of people who didn't know much about the art here are now experts. Most of it they make up because the only people who know what these paintings mean are the artists who did them. There's no need to tell lies about this, only what we know. There's plenty to look at here."

It is generally accepted that Aboriginal rock art is a continuous tradition dating back at least 35,000 years which chronicles traditional culture. Max pointed out faint red lines on the rock that indicated the oldest example of this art, when long blades of grass were dipped in ocher and slapped against the walls. A later example was hand prints, where the artists covered their hands with ocher and pressed them against the wall. Later still, they mixed ocher with saliva, held their hands against the wall and blew the color around it to form stencil patterns.

Simple stick figures and ancestral creation figures appeared around 10,000 years ago. At the same time active human figures began to appear, people in dynamic motion. Yam figures date to about 7,000 years ago as a staple in the diet, and around the same time began the X-ray style, renditions of animals with their internal organs visible.

In all cases, the paintings reflect the external world surrounding the people who lived here, and the internal spiritual world that tracks their journeys from the Dreamtime, the time of creation. The galleries display thousands of images, and if one could look deeper into the rock it would be thousands upon thousands because generation after generation the paintings were painted over, not erased but covered with new work. The colors are still vibrant, the detail refined, because the ochers bond chemically with the rock. As long as the rock is there the art will be there.

In time we walked on through a labyrinth of sandstone channels that in some places were narrow and dark and in others opened up like courtyards to the sky above. We were actually about fifteen feet below the ground with daylight streaming in amidst a jumble of huge roots from the gum trees above. The roots were as big as tree trunks and shot down from above like pillars, then snaked along the ground looking for soft spots in the rock to reach the aquifers below.

Thunder pealed in the distance, and a moment later the sky darkened, the wind came up, rain began to fall. Max took us into a dark cavern where he asked us not to take pictures. Roots reached down from above and the dark floor was covered with human bones—skulls, femurs, pelvises, you name it.

"This was a burial site," Max said, "but the bones have fallen through the ceiling. The site was up above."

This scattering of old bones in the dark dirt of a sandstone cavern felt natural, dignified. Thunder rolled again, a deep, wondrous sound. Nature speaking. Saying hello, who's next? In the context of antiquity here, all of us, to be sure, were passing like raindrops into the thirsty earth.

When the rain let up we headed back, the sky breaking into tumbling thunderheads and brilliant patches of blue. Crows and corellas yelled at each other like neighbors bickering over the back fence, and the light was a rich gold.

Later we headed out to explore the billabong by airboat. Max fired up the engine and it sounded like the wrath of God, the giant fan blasting air at anything behind it. Max suddenly got a boyish grin on his face and told us to climb aboard. His helpers shoved us into the water and it lapped around our ankles. Whoa, we were sinking. The stern was heading down. But Max saw it, revved the engine and the boat righted itself. We did a 360 and headed upstream, or at least what looked like upstream to me, but on a billabong there's no such thing as upstream.

We headed into a narrow channel overhung with trees. The evening light was angular, a rich golden hue, lighting up the trees and the lilies and the grasses in iridescent green. The roar of the engine was deafening, vibrations ran through the aluminum hull, through our handholds and into our arms, like being jolted by lightning. The cacophony of birds was gone, lost in the shriek of machinery. It was the strangest wilderness experience I've ever had, making our way through a pristine landscape where little has changed in thousands of years on a machine as loud as an aircraft. But it was also deeply exhilarating.

You don't really have too much choice in these regions when it comes to exploring the billabong. You have to go out in a sturdy boat with a motor. Try a canoe or kayak and you're likely to experience an early end—as crocodile chow. The saltwater crocodiles up here are huge and abundant, and they will eat anything silly enough to present itself.

Max guided us through the increasingly narrow channel until it was barely wider than the boat. Slowly now, nudging against both sides, the dark, loamy earth grabbing at us. Water surged up on the banks, pushed ahead of us by the boat, but soon we were stuck, or so it seemed. Max revved the engine to screaming and the boat shuddered through, only to get hung up again. We were all in on the act now, pushing against the trees to keep the bow in the channel, jumping onto the bank to push the boat back in the water, the mud sucking at our feet. Pushing like mad, the engine shrieking like a banshee, engine wind ripping through the trees, water flying, and I looked up at Max and he sat there high on his perch, broad arms gunning the engine, trying to force that thing through, wearing a huge grin.

We got through that bind and ran into another. Max got into the water up to his knees to free the boat, and eventually we broke out into deeper, wider water. A moment later we saw a crocodile, and I realized that not once in our effort to get the boat through did I think about the danger. Was there danger, really? It sure seemed like it. There were crocodiles everywhere, why not where we got stuck? We could have stepped on one and only realized it when he let us know.

But now we were free and cruising the billabong. Crocodiles dove with one swipe of their powerful tails as we surprised them. Waterbirds took flight as we approached. A darter dropped from a tree fruitlessly trying to catch air before he hit the water like a bomb, then ran ahead on the surface till he got airborne and out

of our way. Trees lining the channel whipped by, and we broke
out onto the floodplain into that glorious, golden light. Huge
clouds tumbled along the horizon glowing white and yellow in
the evening sun. For as far as we could see the landscape was silvery water and brilliant green vegetation, a fertile, primeval soup
as close to the origins of life as I'll ever get. Flocks of magpie
geese fed in the thousands all around us. Thousands more took flight as we passed, fill-ing the sky with their grace-ful forms. Ibises and egrets hung out in the trees, jabirus watched from the distance.

We raced across the bill-abong, the airboat blasting over lilies floating on the sur-face. Each time we bore down on another patch I was sure we'd slam into earth and go flying into the water where the hungry crocodiles waited. Max staunchly kept the throttle forward and we flew on, bumping over the matted growth, free of obsta-cles, free of restrictions, cruis-ing the floodplain.

Later, clouds darkened the sky and rain fell in a torrent. We put on rain jackets but within minutes were soaked to the skin. Max pulled up under a dense canopy of mangroves and said, "Do you want to hold up for a while?"

---

*T*he world's rain forests are thought to have begun around present-day Melbourne some 120 million years ago, when Australia was part of the granddaddy of continents, Godwanaland. Twenty million years later, all of Australia was covered by rain forests. But sixty-five million years ago, when Oceania broke off from the continental mega-merger and became islands, the dry look began to replace tropical condi-tions. The rain forest retreated to an area less than 1 percent of the continent. Logging in the last 200 years has reduced the forest total to .3 percent. Moves are currently afoot to try to bring several other forest parcels on the Cape threatened by develop-ment under federal protection.

◆

—Tony Perrottet, "Going Off the Deep End," *Escape*

"Why?" I laughed. "Makes no difference to me."

"Can't get wetter than we are," he said, and off we went, Max's poncho blowing in the wind like a shroud.

It was like flying through a thunderstorm in an open plane. The air was water and we could hardly see. Forward, faster. Birds scattered, and the boat raced over the water into the storm.

Gradually the rain let up and eventually stopped. Now we had a chance to look at the land, illuminated in soft, heavenly light. Max edged the boat aground so we could get out and rest awhile. Soaked as we were, it was nice to be on land, even though it was boggy.

Max began digging in the earth with his bare hands to collect some bush tucker, legumes from the roots of grass, busting up the knotted earth. Clumps of grass flew this way, clots of soil flew that way. He dug, and dug, fingering the roots, rejecting them as too scrawny. He kept at it, oblivious of my calls to stop. "It's O.K., Max, we don't need to taste them."

He seemed obsessed, as if starved, and I began to think he deposited us here just so he could get some of this bush food. He was grinning, glowing, completely consumed by this communion with the Earth. And then he found them. He pulled up some skinny bulbs, knocked the dust off, put them in his mouth and chewed. He smiled, then looked at me.

"This one'll be sweet," he said, handing me a dusty clod. It wasn't. It was dry and starchy, something I wouldn't choose to eat but could live on if I had to. But to Max it was pure heaven, God's own repast, and he waited only an instant to make sure I approved before he dug for more.

After he'd eaten his fill, we wandered up past land that looked as if it had been rooted to death by wild pigs. We sat on the rocks and talked about life out here, the almost overwhelming serenity of it all, and Max began to get wistful about the old hunting days.

"There'd be forty buffalo over there, sixty over here. Now, naturalists consider the buffalo a pest that destroys the integrity of the billabong because it's not an indigenous animal. But they're beautiful animals. They've been in the area for a couple hundred years, and it can't hurt to have them around in small numbers. It's a shame to try to take out an entire species, especially when they provide a source of food and income for the Aboriginals."

Then he began to tell stories, rolling them off his tongue like sweet water, one after another of his days in the bush with Charlie Munguda, and Big Bill Nadji, the traditional owner of Kakadu, and sundry other characters. He talked on and on, re-counting tales full of love for the land, for his wild way of life, for the Aboriginal people.

Suddenly a wave of melancholy swept over me. Looking around at this extraordinary land of billabong and floodplain, I felt a deep emptiness, a loneliness rooted in my sense of having no connec-tion to the land. Where was I from? What did I know of ancestry and earth? Was this just a malady of my own, or symbolic of a malaise shared by all First Worlders? The kind of connection I lacked you can only get from working the earth, coming from it, knowing it as part of your spirit. The Aboriginals had it. Max had it. But looking at that amazing green land carved in squiggly pat-terns by rivers and streams and buffalo channels, I knew it was something I would never have, unless I changed my life com-pletely. And maybe even that wouldn't be enough.

The light was failing, dropping in pinks and purples. The sky was going dark, and we headed back. We took it slowly, enjoying the flight of magpie geese, the purple reflections of clouds on the water, the calm after the storm. Suddenly a huge splash erupted to our left and Max stopped the boat immediately. Waves two feet high coursed toward us from the single flick of a crocodile's tail, and the boat rocked as if crossing a wake. There wasn't a sound on the billabong until Max uttered, "Now that was a big crocodile."

The image of that crocodile we didn't see stayed with me. The power of that creature, so ominous, so primeval, so bent on satis-fying its hunger and nothing more, reflected the frightening beauty of these wild places. There are things here we cannot fathom, powers that make a mockery of our civilized concerns, hidden creatures with clear meanings. We are at the top of the food chain, yes, but only by a thread.

Larry Habegger, executive editor of Travelers' Tales, has been writing about travel since 1980. In the early '80s he co-authored mystery serials for the San Francisco Examiner *with James O'Reilly, and since 1985 their syndicated column "World Travel Watch," has appeared in five countries and on WorldTravelWatch.com. He regularly teaches the craft of travel writing at workshops and writers conferences, and he lives with his family on Telegraph Hill in San Francisco.*

DIANE CHRISTIANSEN

An Island to Ourselves

Be careful what you wish for.

BEING STRANDED ON A DESERTED TROPICAL ISLAND WITH YOUR
lover is a fantasy many, including Hollywood, have dredged up
over the years as a solution for what ails us. My husband Jeff and I
were ripe for turning such a fantasy into reality. After all, we hadn't
come all the way from California to Australia's Great Barrier Reef
to hang out with crowds of other tourists. We definitely needed a
change—and soon!

On the morning of the seventh day I was up early for one of
my island strolls when I found myself in the company of one
worn and weathered local, Captain Brian. He was the owner of
an eighteen-foot trimaran which he had used to motor visitors
around the reef for the past twenty years.

I told him that my husband and I were getting tired of all the
tourists, and he responded with an exciting proposition: for a
small fee he could take Jeff and me to a "very primitive" island,
twenty-eight miles south of Dunk and return in two weeks time
to take us back to the mainland. Like its owner, the boat wasn't
in great shape but, what the heck, the deal sounded affordable
and almost too good to be true—a tropical vacation fantasy in
the flesh. Enthused and proud of myself for swinging such an

adventurous deal, I went back to share our latest good fortune with Jeff.

We spent about $100 stocking up on supplies. I thought it would be fun to finally learn how to fish, so we stuffed some line and hooks into our packs. We bought all our favorite treats. We pictured ourselves lying back and reading for hours, snacking away the days and enjoying intimate moments on our own, personal fantasy island.

It took us a leisurely two and a half days just to reach Hinchinbrook Island, camping on tiny islands that dot the area, some no bigger than a spit of sand and a palm tree. Jeff and I swam and snorkeled along the way, with Captain Brian sailing beside and behind us. Huge sea turtles joined us from the sea grass depths; schools of electric fish darted by; sea eagles soared and dove for fish around us.

One morning, chilled after a two-mile swim, we stood in knee deep water on a twenty-five- to thirty-foot-tall coral bommie, letting the warm sun toast our backs. The water was green and deep around

*D*unk was the final resting place of E. J. Banfield, who contributed as much to the world's image of paradise as Gauguin in Tahiti or Robert Louis Stevenson in Samoa.

In 1897, at the age of 45, this unassuming British-Australian newspaperman was told by doctors that he had perhaps only three months to live. Immediately, he quit his job, packed up, and moved with his wife to the unsettled shores of Dunk. Most of E. J.'s friends considered him deranged to be consigning himself to a lonely, wretched death. If the wild Djuru natives didn't get him, the heat, bugs, and tropical fevers would. But twenty-five years later Banfield and his wife were thriving in their private idyll, and he was famous throughout the English-speaking world: his first memoir, *Confessions of a Beachcomber,* peppered with acute and lyrical observations of his natural refuge, was an international best-seller. A string of sequels was consumed with equal hunger.

◆

—Tony Perrottet, "Always Go North," *Islands*

our small platform of coral. Suddenly, a seven-foot reef shark shot out at us from below, pulling up short when it was close enough for us to see its tiny eyes. I stopped breathing—adrenaline surged. It suddenly occurred to me that my bright new phosphorescent Nikes looked very much like the parrot fish in these waters. Parrot fish are prey to these sharks. More adrenaline. The shark began circling.

Jeff and I, masks in the water, rear ends high in the air, rotated around and around as we jostled each other to stay on the tiny surface area of our bommie while keeping our eyes on the shark. It circled an agonizing three times before disappearing as abruptly as it had appeared. We left a wake in our hurry to swim back to the boat—snorkeling was definitely over for the day.

We reached our destination not long afterward, and it took three trips in a dinghy through small breaking surf to unload all our food and equipment. I had made a tracing of Captain Brian's chart, which showed the outline of the island, including drainages with intermittent freshwater streams, and an X marking the spot where Captain Brian said he was "pretty sure" there was an "exclusive resort." By my reckoning, finding the resort would involve a twenty-one-mile trek through a dense rain forest if a real emergency arose.

There really was no need for worrying though. After all, we could expect Captain Brian in two weeks, when he would arrive to spend a few days with us on the island before boating us back to the mainland. We gave him money for his time and some extra funds to purchase the needed supplies we would require for the extra few days on the island once he returned. As Captain Brian sailed off, we waved good-bye and then headed down the beach to find the perfect campsite.

What mattered most during our first few island days was that we were finally alone! We had fun setting up an elaborate "Swiss Family Robinson" camp, and exploring. It was winter in the northeast tropics of Australia. The days were warm and the nights were delightfully cool. We didn't wear any clothing, unless we were hiking, and Jeff made himself a great palm frond hat to keep the burns to a minimum.

Days were as you would imagine, filled with reading, eating, collecting shells, bodysurfing, exploring freshwater streams and waterfalls, and hiking to the ends of our mile-long white sand beach. We discovered tracks of Australia's giant five-foot-long goanna lizards and watched the cockatoos, bright and wild against the dark green rain forest. We also talked for long hours and days, about our pasts, our families, and how we wanted our future together to be.

We sat under our tarps and watched how the sea changed with the coming of each warm afternoon squall. We noticed how the waves would come in bigger and faster, and how the water would get cloudy before each squall hit. We were absolutely alone and loving it.

After Day 9 on the island we joked about the possibility of actually becoming stranded on this island—kind of a Robinson Crusoe situation for real. Although we both knew that kind of event only happened in movies, we started planning for a worst-case scenario. We took stock of our supplies and discovered that we were already a bit low. We decided we'd better start rationing and try our luck at fishing. We stowed away a couple of cans of food for the hike out, just in case.

We started fishing. I got frustrated easily. Jeff was patient. He caught tasty fish from our lagoon right away. It was good to know that if we really had to, we could catch fish.

We also found about five good coconuts that the bush rats hadn't found first. They tasted great. Another good food, should we really need it.

By Day 14, our supplies were nearly depleted. I was losing weight and for the first time in my life not enjoying it. Fishing started consuming most of our waking interest and time although this incessant practice, for me, did not improve my skill.

Two days later, sitting by a deep tide pool, I caught a lobster quite by accident. It put up an amazing fight to survive. I struggled with the "beast" until Jeff arrived, to find me hunched over and beating the hell out of a crustacean—he actually had to pull me off it to get me to stop. The situation was beginning to feel serious, and still there was no sign of Captain Brian.

After the lobster episode I stopped trying to fish altogether. I discovered oysters and spent my days gathering. It is a feeling I will never forget: waking up in the early morning, hunger gnawing at my insides, and hiking off to the oyster beds to gather as many oysters as possible before high tide. We ate an estimated ten kilos of oysters in all. There was no more time or energy for reading, lolling, and exploring; we were focused on the basics. While I gathered, Jeff hunted—both of us with our eyes searching the horizon for Captain Brian.

On Day 21 Jeff sliced his toe on a rock. We knew that infections in the tropics set in fast, so we decided to try to reach the "pretty sure it was there" resort. We had given up on Captain Brian's return.

The next morning, we checked my tracing of Captain Brian's chart. Finding freshwater was a question in our minds and from earlier explorations we knew that the shoreline was extremely rocky, so it would be slow going. After pondering the map for a while we thought we could save maybe seven to ten miles off the estimated twenty-one if we took a shortcut through the rain forest estuary, rather than follow the coastline all the way around to the north end of the island. Jeff and I were experienced hikers and could handle any terrain, or so we thought.

It was a particularly hot day, and feeling weakened by weight loss and by our overloaded backpacks we pushed our way inland for almost four hours. We were moving as fast as possible because we were unsure of just about everything; where we were headed, when we would find freshwater again, and how long it was going to take to get to the "resort." Adding to our misery were the razor-sharp palm vines we had to contend with.

I was sweating profusely and exhausted when I slid down an embankment and was suddenly jerked to a stop by a complicated mesh of "lawyer vines" (so called because they will grab at you and keep you all tangled up for ages). Hanging there suspended, I felt like a bug in an immense spider web. I made some joke about finally getting to use the saw blade on my Swiss Army knife. It was an absurd (but typical) attempt to keep our spirits up, and Jeff probably could have done without the cheerleader routine.

Before I tell you what happened next, I'd like to share with you some relevant tidbits regarding Australia's *insecta*—in particular, green ants. They are the size of black carpenter ants, with transparent green abdomens, and are so aggressive that the presence of larger mammals passing near a branch on which they are crawling triggers a jump and attack response. Their bite is so tenacious that brushing against their bodies causes their heads to be left imbedded in the flesh.

So, there I was, laughing uproariously for good effect and sawing away, shaking the entire rain forest around me. It was then that the unbelievable happened: a nest of angry, swarming green ants fell on my neck.

I screamed and screamed, all the while ripping and tearing myself free of the vines. Jeff tore off my pack and shirt and slapped at the ants while I tried to keep them from crawling into my eyes, nose, ears and mouth. Jeff's horrified look didn't help calm me any, but time passed in some unreal way and finally, at last, the biting stopped.

Though green ants are not poisonous and the pain of their bite didn't last long (only the memory), the episode was the last straw. We gave up on the shortcut and turned back to the coast. We would now face the grueling miles of rocky cliffs.

On the third morning of our foot journey—twenty-four days after our arrival on the island—we discovered a trail leading up from the beach. And, there, before our eyes and most definitely not an apparition was a man approaching, obviously well fed and relaxed. This was it! We were saved!

We could hardly wait to greet the man, tell him what had happened, capture him with the essence of our arduous saga and watch his eyes bug out in disbelief. We eagerly approached him and began spilling our story. He took his time looking us over. He listened awhile. Then, he turned away, uttering in apparent disgust just one word: "Yanks."

The resort was down the trail a little ways. We had to hike over the airstrip to get to the palm-lined swimming pools and cool drinks. Sure, we didn't look much like exclusive resort guests—

tired, sweaty, dirty, and schlepping packs—but the resort treated us well, even if our initial encounter wasn't brimming with friendship. After recounting our story, much to the disbelief of our hosts, we were told that the estuary we had initially planned to cross (before the ants turned us back) was brimming with saltwater crocodiles. Terrific.

What ever happened to Captain Brian? We never knew. He could have been lost at sea or in a good drunken stupor somewhere. He could have just ripped us off. All in all, though, we wish him well.

I still fantasize about my personal island paradise. Maybe someday I'll go back. I imagine Jeff would head off to an island paradise again too, but this time with crates of food, nearby room service and a guaranteed trip off the island.

Diane Christiansen began her adventurous lifestyle at the age of twenty. Her first adventure with her husband Jeff was walking 1,600 miles, the length of California. After graduating from college with a degree in environmental sciences and planning, she "followed her bliss" and went to work as a professional naturalist, river guide, and backpacking, climbing, and sea kayaking instructor.

Sand Sailing

*The Henley-on-Todd Regatta gives new meaning
to the phrase, "down a lazy river."*

THE THREE-HOUR FLIGHT FROM SYDNEY TO ALICE MAKES MY
earlier journey seem as tortured and slow as a drunken weave
home from the pub. But just as flying shrinks all sense of distance,
so too does it sharpen contrast. Before, the center of Australia
seemed no more remarkable—or unremarkable—than the
bleached and barren scrub I had hitchhiked through to get there.
This time, climbing out of Sydney smog and easing down through
the cloudless blue of an Outback afternoon, the center seems as
light and crisp as the celery in my Bloody Mary. I stare out the
window at the squiggly ridges of sand, swimming like minnows
across the surface of the desert, and feel as I did so many months
ago, when I flew over Australia for the first time and imagined that
I was descending onto an alien planet.

I have arrived during the early heats of the Henley-on-Todd,
a bush parody of the annual regatta on the Thames in England.
Parody begins with the Todd River, a dried-up channel of sand
snaking through the heart of Alice. Then there are the "sailors":
teenagers mostly, in sneakers with their legs poking out from underneath bottomless boats. Standing inside the hollow crafts,
holding the sides at waist height, they wait for an "admiral" to fire

the starting gun, then sprint down the riverbed, around two oil drums, and back to the finish line, canvas sails flapping in the windless desert air. A thin stream of spilled beer is the only moisture in sight.

"Some fine sailing there!" the admiral shouts as two boats butt each other and capsize, like toddlers wrestling in a sandbox. "But I'm afraid both ships have been disqualified. The judges are waiting to see which one brings in the biggest bribe."

It has the look of Page-One stuff to this reporter's eyes. Better get some background information. At the beer tent I meet the regatta's founder, a laconic, gray-bearded man in a sailor's cap named Reg Smith. He dreamed up the regatta twenty-five years ago, while working in the weather tower at the Alice airport. The job was undemanding: Alice skies are almost always clear, and in those days there was only one airplane arrival each day. So Smith sat there, staring into space, until he was struck by one of those thunderbolts of Outback inspiration—the same kind of vision, say, that spawned the first bush bank or Darwin's Beer Can Regatta.

"Racing boats down a dry river just seemed like the logical, sensible thing to do out here," Smith explains. Behind him, the sailors rest while two rowboat crews paddle through the Todd with sand shovels. "Of course when we started, the race was a little more primitive than now."

So primitive that yachts snagged their sails on overhanging gum trees, or foundered on sandbars in the Todd. Then one year the riverbed had the temerity to fill up after a rare burst of rain; water had to be channeled off so the boats could "sail" undisturbed. The trees and sand have since been tamed, and the race sponsors now have an insurance policy against the Todd ever flowing again at race time.

But a certain primitive spirit has remained unevolved. The day's final contest pits two boats, mounted atop four-wheel drives, in a gladiatorial duel to the death. In one corner a three-masted pirate ship called the HMAS *Nauteus*, and in the other a boat called *Bite Ya Bum*, which claims as its insignia a huge middle finger raised defiantly on the stern.

The crew members look like riot police on R and R. Wearing gas masks and crash helmets, they are heavily armed with water cannons, gravel, paint, flour bombs, water bombs, smoke bombs, and anything else that makes a mess and is easy to throw.

The battle is no more of a spectator sport than the America's Cup. A huge cloud of dust and smoke envelops the duel, and the crowd waits expectantly, trying to judge from the groans which ship has the upper hand. Then a broadside of water and paint clears the dust for a moment. There is a glimpse of the *Nauteus* crew clambering over the gunnels of *Bite Ya Bum* for hand-to-hand combat, and the battle is quickly done.

The victorious crew heads straight to the beer tent to sink a few more schooners. "We stole most of their ammo before the race," the *Nauteus* skipper says, pulling back his gas mask to swallow a beer.

And down in the Todd, a group of Aborigines reclaim the polluted riverbed, bemused by this strange white fellas' Water Dreaming.

Tony Horwitz has been a correspondent for The Wall Street Journal *and a staff writer for* The New Yorker. *He won a Pulitzer Prize for national reporting in 1995 and is the author of several books, including* The Devil May Care: Fifty Intrepid Americans and Their Quest for the Unknown, Blue Latitudes: Boldly Going Where Captain Cook has Gone Before, Confederates in the Attic, *and* One for the Road: Hitchhiking through the Australian Outback, *from which this story was excerpted.*

DAVID YEADON

* * *

The Peacock's Tail

*Alone in southern Tasmania, the author discovers
a thing or two about leeches—and himself.*

THANKFULLY THERE WERE NO "HARD BITS" FOR THE FIRST FEW
miles. I felt as if I were walking on soft clouds across the bouncy
buttongrass path that headed southeast from Melaleuca toward
Cox Bight, my first destination on this six- or seven-day odyssey.

It was a couple of hours before the silence began to creep in
and I realized that seven days of solitude suddenly seemed like a
hell of a long time. On most of my long-distance hikes I've usually had company for at least part of the journey. But on this one,
I had no one and no real prospect of hearing a human voice for a
week or more unless I met someone coming the other way. What
should I do with all that time? Dictate some short stories into my
tape recorder? Start my autobiography? Compose a few songs?
Compress all my meager world-wanderer wisdoms into a few
pungent anagrams? Or merely go mad, howling at this desolate
unpeopled place like a hyped-up hyena?

Goethe got it right, as he usually did: "In every parting there is
a latent germ of madness." Or Father Navarette: "It is no small
contradiction to human nature to leave one's home." Well—home
was a long way off, just about as far as it could be on any part of
the globe. But I'd found a temporary home of sorts in Deny's little

fiefdom, populated by Bob and Steve and the Willsons. Was I crazy
to have left there? Should I have stayed and learned more about
Bob's thirty years in the bush, or Steve's love for the orange-bel-
lied parrot, or the tenacity of the Willsons' hard lives?

The balance will come, I told myself. It always does. In any situation, a benign reality usually composes itself out of the oddest of
circumstances. Just let it come in its own time. Let the journey take
on its own rhythm and pace and flow. And just flow with it....

The path stuck to the
plain, which narrowed gradually between the misty
New Harbour and Bathurst
ranges. Mount Counsel with
its quartzite flanks glowered
down. My map showed
an enticing place—Hidden
Valley—high on its upper
flanks and normally I'd be
tempted to take such a diver-
sion. But the land discour-
aged such fancies. I knew this
kind of country well from my
days among the Pennine bogs
of Yorkshire. I knew how the

A vast area of Tasmanian
wilderness has been
designated a "World Heritage
Area" by UNESCO, including
South West National Park, a
place of unpredictable weather,
rough terrain, and deep isolation.
Only experienced bush walkers
should set off to explore it.

♦

—LH

seductively soft surface of the heath could give way without warning to pernicious mud holes that sucked and gurgled at unsus-
pecting limbs and devoured boots with malicious glee, leaving
walkers in goo-laden stockings while their footwear was absorbed
forever into the acidic mulch of the mire. The hardy walkers who
ignore trails across such territory are known as "bog-trotters," as
they leap like oversized, overweight ballet dancers from tussock to
tussock. Some are lucky and escape the embarrassing boot-losing
predicaments. Many do not and end up being half carried, half
dragged off the stagnant plateaus by their grinning colleagues, to
the warmth and nurture of valley inns.

I hadn't brought a spare pair of boots, only some soft sneakers for evenings by my campfires. If I lost my boots I wondered what I'd do—or, more precisely, what the trail would do—to my feet. Not to mention the leeches....

Here it starts, I thought. The old mind-yammer. The silly fantasy-plagued "what if" scenarios that can wear a buoyant spirit down to a morose depression in a few unchecked reveries. None of those on this trip, please. All I have is me this time. No company, no helping hands, no jolly singsongs in the evening chills, no one to set perspectives straight, no one to calm fears and chase away fickle thoughts that appear—unexpected and uninvited—out of the miasma of the singular mind.

I tried to lift my confidence with memories of other solo journeys: that trek through Panama's Darién, those days on the deserted beaches of Barbuda, my unsuccessful climb up the Ruwenzori. They all began this way—a little wobbly at first as the spirit finds the fine line between freewheeling fantasy and the darker deeps of the mind, and then on into the days of balance and balm when the experience becomes pure, clean adventure.

Dawn was promising enough: a crystal-clean light pushing the night clouds out to sea and touching the land with gold. No rain, no winds. A fine day for walking. The surly Ironbounds rose up in front of me; gilded peaks with jagged summits, flecks of ice and snow on the ridges. An ancient bulwark of Precambrian metamorphic rocks. Very impressive.

A majestic bird flew overhead as I collapsed the tent and loaded the backpack. The large white head was hawklike and its white belly sparkled as it soared the updrafts with a broad wingspan of five feet or more. I learned later I'd seen a sea eagle, a voracious eater of reptiles, other birds, and, when available, even penguins. Not a very pleasant creature—but on that sparkling morning it seemed an omen of better days ahead.

The path climbed steadily up open sedgeland onto a broad subalpine zone. Pockets of King Billy pine clustered in gullies and sheltered places, their deeply furrowed trunks and branches contorted, juniper-fashion. Small white daisies with golden centers glowed in the wind-scoured scrub; compact clusters of dainty red Christmas bells rose among the grasses.

In spite of their ominous name, the Ironbounds peak at little more than 3,000 feet, and while the climbing was tough going, it was made easier by the benign weather and ever-broadening vistas of mountains and bays. The wind increased as I approached the summit and I spotted places where previous walkers had camped huddled in the low bushes. I considered calling an early halt to the day and hunkering down to enjoy the views, but my legs kept on moving and I followed the contours around the northern rim of the massif, humming happy songs and wondering how to prepare a celebratory feast of my one solitary steak (another gift from Bob) for dinner that night.

I saw new patterns of vegetation from these heights, patterns that were invisible at lower elevations—brilliant green swatches of sphagnum moss invading the small ponds and pools that lay scattered across the mosaics of darker green and bronze cushion-plant plains. The patterns were jigsawlike, thousands of microenvironments from the sedge grasses to the mosses to the lichen-blotched rocks and strata. Patches of pink mountain rocket and cheeseberry bushes adorned with bright red berries gave a rich resonance to the more muted tones of the buttongrass plateaus.

On a dull day the colors would doubtless be leeched out to an army-tent khaki, but today the sun revealed the land's true richness: a brilliant panoply of tones and textures that made me wish for canvas, palette, and brushes; a magnificent display of the subtleties, the intricate, juxtapositions and meldings of plant colonies set beside the milky whorls and snakelike doodlings of sand patterns beneath the blue-green waters of the bays. And yet, despite all these delights, I could sense the restless riot of the land itself: towering broken cliffs; spars of brittle basalt; fjordlike incisions where the warmer, higher post-ice-age waters had penetrated deep into once-forested valleys; bold bluffs and phallic intrusions of dolerite into the spuming surf; the bleedings of frost-shattered ridges and razored escarpments in the form of peat-brown streams pouring from the hills; the bleached bones of ancient bedrocks protruding through the sloozy-oozy mud; the wind-torn trunks of trees, blasted of bark, blanched and twisted by a tempestuous climate that just never lets up—scratching and scraping the land down to its ultimate peneplain in the hollow howling vastness that is South-West Tasmania.

I had a sudden flash of the neat little hedge-rimmed fields, ordered orchards, and Ireland-green, sheep-studded vales that awaited me way to the east around Hobart, far beyond these tumultuous ranges. I thought of the curling country roads, the pie shops smelling of fresh-baked pastry, the rowdy smoke-filled pubs, and the demure tin-roofed bungalows adorned with red and white trim and set in gardens of privet, hollyhocks, and geraniums.

I would be there soon, I promised myself—showered, deloused, primed up on Foster's ale, choosing dinner from menus with frilly borders, sleeping on soft mattresses, dry and warm, and savoring all the wonders of a world that, up here, seemed very far away.

But enough of such hedonistic imaginings! I was less than halfway to such bucolic destinations, with a lot of tough hiking ahead and challenges to be overcome.

And the challenges came fast. Actually a mere hour or so after my contemplations on the Ironbound ridge, as I left the heights and began my descent toward the long beach on Prion Bay, everything changed. The bare, wind-tossed tops gave way to some of the thickest, most tangled and tortured rain forest it has ever been my misfortune to encounter. Out of the bright light and into a gray-green gloom of a nefarious netherworld.

Now, rain forests have their fascinations. Even that eerie dwarf forest I'd discovered at Cox Bight possessed, in daylight, a certain rampant, raging charm. But this was altogether different—a far more intense, menacing place where there seemed to be little in the way of order or subtleties. The forest just flared up and thrust me into it, following a trail that had the remarkable ability of vanishing in the difficult places, leaving me scrambling through mud and slime and decaying moss beds without any sense of direction—except down.

And down and down, deeper into the sticky gloom of ancient

Gondwanaland species—more tall King Billy pines, eucalyptus, myrtles, celery-top pine, and a tangled understory of laurel, whitey wood, waratah, dwarf beech, and ferns, all competing for scarce light and root space—oh, and mosses too, in strange and exotic forms: pillars, mattresses, balls, bouquets, and furry smotherings of trunks and branches. Had the mood been more conducive I might have dallied here and undertaken a photographic essay of these myriad species, possibly even bagged a few samples for later identification. But the mood was definitely not conducive to anything except survival and eventual extrication on the beaches of Prion Bay, far, far below.

And then I noticed the leeches.

Well, not so much noticed. I merely sensed something peculiar on my left arm under layers of damp clothing. Something moving very slowly. Almost like an involuntary muscle spasm except it was happening in three distinct places simultaneously.

I looked down. I'd forgotten to fasten the Velcro cuff of my parka, Either that or it had been ripped open in my frequent fights with vines and branches. And so there it was, dangling loose, allowing whatever it was easy access to the soft flesh of my lower arm.

Actually, I knew what I would see even before I pulled back the layers. Once before, during my adventures in the marshlands of the Caspian, I had experienced the stomach-wrenching sight of slimy black creatures growing bigger by the second as they sucked the blood from my legs and shins.

And, oh, yes, there they were. Three big ones this time, happily slurping away on my precious life fluid, oblivious to the discomfort they were causing in the pit of my stomach....

Think back. How did my friends tell me to get rid of them in Iran? Something hot. A cigarette tip, a match—burn their tails and off they drop. But I remembered that method had not been too successful. In their haste to remove their blood-gorged, balloon-like bodies from my flesh they forgot to coagulate their incisions and left oozing wounds in their abandoned snacking spots. But what the hell? Anything was better than watching these miniature monsters have their way with me. So out with the lighter: flick…another flick…and another…and nothing. Not even a spark. Certainly nothing like a flame. Useless damned things, these lighters. A bit of damp and they seize up like oil-starved engines.

Okay. Next solution? Salt. That's it. A scattering of salt on the tail and off they come. But I didn't have any salt. All the dehydrated fare I carried in little aluminum pouches was already presalted. I had a tiny bottle of soy sauce I always carried with me to perk up bland restaurant meals, but…aha! I did have one possible resource. Bob's bag of "emergency goodies." I'd already found his antihistamines for the bites of jumping ants. But what other delights had he shoved into the left-side pocket of my backpack?

With amazing grace and delicacy, I removed my backpack and used my right hand to burrow into the pocket. His gift was larger and more varied than I'd realized—mosquito repellent, high-energy health bars, Band-Aids, a large bandage, iodine, hydrogen peroxide, and—voilà—a small cylindrical container of common table salt. A message was scrawled on the outside. "So they got you too! Best. Bob!" Yes, very amusing, my friend. Quite droll, really. You knew the damned creatures would find a way in somewhere. Well—you were right. And thank you for your gift of salt.

It worked. I tested the fattest one first. A few sprinkles on its lower regions and the thing tightened into a ball like a frightened snail, slowly released its suckers, and fell off with a sickening thump onto the wet moss of the path. This time it had thoughtfully sealed the tiny wound (maybe hoping for a comeback) and nothing except a little trickle of blood escaped. The other two behaved equally politely, so I resisted the temptation to stomp them into a gooey pulp and let them digest their stolen snack undisturbed by a quick belt from my boot. I cleaned the bluish wounds with peroxide, rolled down my shirtsleeve, and zipped the parka, fastening the Velcro catches as tight as a tourniquet.

But I was still curious about these evil black things. I hadn't seen any sign of them higher up. Maybe I'd been too concerned with keeping to the almost-invisible trail. Now I began to investigate the vegetation more closely and, lo!—there they were, camouflaged among the leaves and ferns in thready black shadows, nothing like the bloated horrors still digesting their meal on the mossy path.

I vowed to be more cautious, more aware. I also vowed to get out of this foul place as fast as my legs and spirit would carry me.

I arrived a few hours later at the graceful arc of Deadman's Bay enclosing yet another soft white sand beach. Most of the rain forest lay behind me but exuberant flurries of vegetation encroached on the shore and clustered thickly along either bank of Deadman's Creek. I was tempted to camp for the night but as dusk was a way off and the sky still contained slivers of blue, I decided to continue on around Menzies Bluff to the four-mile linear strand of Prion Beach.

New vistas awaited me here. Behind the dwarf forest on the ancient dunes lay the large inland New River Lagoon and, towering over the landscape, the white mass of Precipitous Bluff. Tall eucalyptus forests clung to its lower slopes and rising out of this luxuriant green mass were striated dolerite crags whipped by clouds and sparkling in patches of sunshine. To camp beneath such crags would be fitting relief from a long, weary day.

But as I walked the seemingly endless strand, a dark sense of loneliness and utter

Tasmania. Even the name sounds remote, although in fact it's just another state in Australia. From the rivers and ancient temperate rain forests of the southwest coast to the mountains of north-central Tasmania, nearly a third of the state is given over to parks, mostly dedicated to wilderness preservation.

Regardless of its beauty, Australians on the mainland tend to forget about it. They sometimes leave it off the map altogether. When I applied for a visa at the consulate in New York, the Australian-born clerk told me it wasn't valid in Tasmania. "That's a separate country," she said. "It's nothing to do with Australia." That sounded remote enough for me.

◆

—Ann Jones, "Soaking It All In," *Women's Sports & Fitness*

isolation descended on me. The place looked so empty. So untouched. Somehow its drama and beauty exaggerated the intensity
of my strange mood. Surely I shouldn't feel depressed in the midst
of such magnificent scenery. I should feel elated, full of a sense of
achievement. After all I was now well over halfway. Only another
three days at most before the cozy comforts of Cockle Creek.

But the mood wouldn't lift. The beach seemed to go on forever. No footprints. No signs of campsites. Nothing—except me
and this enormous awesome space.

Something felt to be banging against the edges of my mind. I
remembered a quote from James Hillman: "The way through the
world is more difficult to find than the way beyond it." I sensed I
had reached an impasse of sorts. My expectations of this experience did not correspond with the actuality. And what made it so
odd was that, as soon as that impasse occurred, I began hunting in
my head for a rationale, a definition of my "problem"—my unexpected depression. What's happening? my mind called out. This is
not the way it's supposed to be. But something on the other side,
a whisper, a mere breath of thought, came through: There's no
"meant to be," there's only "is." And a memory. A memory of lines
from Thomas Moore's splendid book *Care of the Soul* (I found the
quotation later):

> Modern psychology…is often seen as a way of being
> saved from the very messes that most deeply mark human
> life as human. We want to sidestep negative moods and
> emotion, bad life choices and unhealthy habits. But if our
> purpose is first to observe the soul as it is, then we may
> have to discard the salvational wish and find deeper
> respect for what is actually there. By trying to avoid
> human mistakes and failures, we move beyond the reach
> of the soul.

And later—at the end of Moore's magic book:

> We know soul is being cared for when our pleasures [in
> my case the opposite, but the point's the same] feel deeper

than usual, when we can let go of the need to be free of
complexity and confusion, and when compassion takes
the place of distrust and fear.

It is the "letting go" that is the key. The releasing of expectations and predigested experiences and the acceptance of "what
is"—good, bad, elating, depressing, hurtful, ecstatic—all the myriad range of emotions and feelings and insights that have always
been and always will be part of our complex human fabric.

Only then, according to Moore, does soul coalesce "into the
mysterious philosopher's stone, that rich, solid core of personality
the alchemists sought, or it opens into the peacock's tail—a revelation of the soul's colors and a display of its dappled brilliance."

Moore's image of the peacock's tail had endured in my mind
and it came at just the right moment. Something was happening.
As I slowly began to accept the strange mood that had abruptly
swept over me, it no longer seemed to be a problem but merely
another nuance, another facet, of the journey's multifaceted se-
quence. It didn't really matter much whether I felt sadness or
gladness; the mood was irrelevant to the process—the learning,
the insights, the new ways of seeing that were now somehow en-
compassing the depression and leading me on to another level of
perception.

Something definitely was happening. Something I remembered from a Tom Robbins novel (I forget which) that suggested
the difference between an adventure and a suicide is that the adventurer leaves himself a margin of escape, and the narrower the
margin, the greater the adventure. Well, I certainly hadn't come all
this way for a lonely suicide in this desolate land; I'd come on an
adventure, to narrow the margins, follow the escape routes, and
see where they led.

And this one was leading to somewhere rather wonderful, a
place an Aborigine had tried to explain to me a few weeks previously during my journeys in the wilds of Western Australia. He
talked of a web, a web of song (songlines) and legends that en-
veloped the world, a web in which time was irrelevant. Everything

that is and ever was is part of that web—everything in constant interaction—everything in kinship within the web—all humans, all
creatures, all mountains, rivers and streams, trees, even individual
rocks, all animate and interrelated within an all-enveloping web.

My walk was no longer a morose, bad-mood-bound plod. In
fact, I was now unaware of actually walking on this immense sandy
strand. I was becoming part of it; the still silent place was buzzing
with "presence"; the web was forming. The sheafs of dune grass,
the fuzzy huddle of dwarf forest on the lee side of the dunes, the
soft slitheriness of trillions of sand grains, the tiny marks and footprints etched in the grains, the hiss and suck of the surf, the breezes
swirling among the marram grass, the slowly undulating movements of the clouds, the fractured complexities of the distant dolerite crags—even the silence itself both in the land and, growing
more each minute, in my mind...all part of the eternal web.
Another reality, where things are not fractured, fragmented,
labeled, separated, but rather bound together in an inevitable totality that melts the barriers of insight, merges the boundaries between things, and lets the incredible wholeness and completeness
of everything come roaring through into a previously blinkered
and now suddenly unlocked perception.

All the clever doodads of the mind—rationales, expectations,
critical faculties, intellectual framings, prejudices, fears, measure-
ments, discretions, manners (you know all the rest)—seemed to
drown in a deluge from some subconscious force that had lain
dormant for too long and was now released with such vigor and
clarity that "moods" seemed to be easily breachable barriers—
even welcome doors—into the miracle of the *now*, the infinitely
intricate web of a reality without time and without boundaries.

The inner self becomes turned inside out. It no longer resides
with the head but transforms into a transparent funnel linking
mind and this newfound actuality. I've experienced similar fleeting
sensations before, particularly in spaces whose immensity seems to
threaten the stability of the rational mind. It occurred when I was
crossing the Sahara with the "Blue People" of Morocco, the Tuareg
tribesmen. Left for hours above the infinities of sand on a camel's

back, I found my mind at first desperately rushing around within itself trying to maintain the edges, the flimsy superstructure, of sanity. It was only when I learned to let go and become part of the rhythm and flow of the journey itself, to enter into its timelessness, that the antics of my overcharged brain no longer seemed relevant to the larger patterns of perception emerging out of the apparent nothingness.

And in other places too—on the plains of Venezuela's Los Llanos, in the vastness of the Inner Mongolian grasslands, across the white infinities of India's Rann of Kutch, and even in the intense head-blasting riot of stimuli that is Nepal's Kathmandu—all places where nothing makes any sense until you stop trying to make sense and let the incredibly rich totality of each place deluge and envelop you in its own overwhelming web.

And so back to my Tasmanian beach, my seemingly endless strand of soft sand, where my bad mood was no longer even a memory and I gave myself up, for the first time on the journey, to the wholeness and wonder of the place itself. And my soul slowly became a peacock's tail....

David Yeadon is an illustrator, journalist, photographer, and the author of many books, including The Way of the Wanderer, Seasons in Basilicata, National Geographic Guide to the World's Secret Places, *and* Lost Worlds: Exploring the World's Remote Places, *from which this story was excerpted. He lives in New York's Hudson Valley and occasionally in Japan with his wife, Anne.*

PART FOUR

IN THE SHADOWS

ROFF MARTIN SMITH

Thirst

Deprivation stretches the limits of civility.

THESE DESERTS NEVER SEEM TO END: THE KIMBERLEY, THE GREAT Sandy, the parched rimrock of the Pilbara. I've come 300 miles south of Port Hedland, and every bloody one of them grinding down one abandoned stretch of highway after another, the tedium of earth and sky relieved only by occasional columns of dust hundreds of feet high swirling in the distance. Willy-willies, the Aborigines call them, and they can flip over a car.

Worst of all are the flies, thousands of them, all seeking moisture in my eyes, nose, ears, at the corners of my mouth. They're so bad that it's better to ride through the heat than stop and have their loathsome little feet all over my face. Sometimes my panniers are so thick with flies they look as if they've got black lace doilies draped over them.

I wish I could say I filled these miles with ennobling introspection, but the Outback has long since beaten that out of me. I pass the time trying to remember the lyrics to songs—from heavy metal to Cole Porter—reciting dialogue from movies, or listing state capitals, presidents, the starting lineup of the '69 Cubs. One game I like to play is making up a guest list of six people—anybody, past or present—I'd like to invite to lunch. Anything to escape the here and now, the thirst, wind, and loneliness. And yet, strangely enough, part of me likes this duel. We meet at dawn, the desert and I, to see who'll come out on top by the end of the day.

As the hours pass, I find myself thinking more and more about my native New England, images of cool green villages, pretty back roads canopied with leaves, the brook that runs past my family's old farmhouse in New Hampshire. My thoughts always seem to circle back to water. Cold sweet water. In a tall glass beaded with moisture. The reality here is grimy water bottles cooked by the sun until the liquid inside is as warm as stale tea and tastes nauseatingly of soft, heated plastic. Even so I suck it in greedily, up to a quart every ten miles. I buy distance with water. By ten in the morning the heat is usually so intense that it's poor economics to keep pedaling. I curl up in whatever scraggly bit of shade I can find and stay still, rationing my sweat.

Today, though, I pressed on an extra couple of hours in the hope of making the Nanutarra Roadhouse—and its air-conditioned diner. I'd already come seventy miles, and the temperature in the sun must have been crowding 140 degrees. The last of my five-gallon water supply ran out three miles shy of the roadhouse, and I stumbled in a lifetime later, crazed with thirst. I slumped into a chair, set up twenty-four dollars' worth of bottled water and sports drinks in front of me (that's about one and a half gallons of liquid), and returned the stare of the road-train driver at the next table. He spoke: "Mate, you know there's a cyclone coming?

"Tropical Cyclone Ophelia," he said, cutting a corner off his steak.

"A Cat Three storm coming in fast off Christmas Island. Expected to hit the coast near Karratha sometime tomorrow. Hope you're heading south. I gotta drop a load off in Hedland tonight, but then I'm turning around as fast as I can and hauling ass out of there. A storm can cut the highway for weeks. Christmas is coming, and I really want to be with my family. Know what I mean?"

Yes, I know what he means, Ophelia be damned. I'll rest here a bit longer, watch the cricket match on the TV by the "truckers only" table, then push on. I feel like a punch-drunk boxer answering the bell for round sixteen.

It's been cooler today, no more than 95 degrees, thanks to a high, thin veil of cloud that crept over the sky early this morning as stealthily as a cat on a mantelpiece. The winds slacked off too. I rode hard and made good time. The first thunderheads didn't catch me until about thirty miles ago, and I arrived at Minilya under a drenching storm, the first rain I've seen since Kununurra. I've come 130 miles, and my legs are so tired I can hardly stand.

Now I hear on the radio that my heroics were for nothing. Ophelia broke up. Modest squalls are all we'll get. The rain has freshened things up, and I ought to make hay while the sun doesn't shine. They say a hot front's moving in tomorrow. When I groaned about the constant head winds, a road train driver laughed: "Mate, they're going to get a lot worse around Geraldton. You'll have winds every inch of the way. It's bad enough in a rig. You must be mad to tackle this on a bike."

Seven hundred miles to Perth.

These past twenty-four hours have shown me the best and worst of the Outback. It started yesterday at the Wooramel Roadhouse, when I rode up around noon, baking in the 113-degree heat. I circled the building, wondering if it was open. There were no cars, no people, just the hum of a diesel generator. I tested the door. It slid open, and I walked into the dim coolness of a diner. A woman stood behind the counter, arms crossed, glaring at me with a face as hard as a coin. I ordered a meat pie and a Coke and asked where I could fill my water bottles.

"We sell water here," she snapped, pointing to a fridge: "Four dollars a bottle."

This was a first. It was about fifty miles to the next roadhouse, so I sat down to estimate how cheaply I could get there in this heat. The woman stared at me some more. A lean, sour-faced man stepped out of the kitchen. While the two of them were glaring at me, a woman with two small kids drove up in a steaming Holden.

"Can you please help me?" she asked. "My car's overheated and I need—"

"We sell water here."

She couldn't afford their water, and because she wasn't buying anything else, they asked her to leave. She and the children waited outside in the heat until another motorist gave her water. More cars pulled up outside. There was a sudden flurry of activity in the diner. While the woman jotted down lunch orders, the surly manager glanced in my direction.

"What are you looking at?"

"I'm not looking, I'm staring." Suddenly I felt too far from home. He ambled over to my table with a false smile, like a hangman sizing me up for the drop. "Yeah? Guess what? I don't want you around. Get out."

"Why so unfriendly?"

"That your bike out front? I'm going to smash it."

I followed him out the door. He looked over his shoulder and ducked out of sight. I saddled up and rode.

I hadn't gone two miles when a four-wheel-drive vehicle pulled up beside me. It was Dave Steadman who with his wife Margot owns Wooramel Station, a 400,000-acre sheep station nearby. "I'm awfully sorry about that back there," he said when he heard of my departure. "I wouldn't want you to get the wrong impression of us out here just because of him. I'd like it if you'd stop by and spend the night with us. What do you say?"

Roff Martin Smith also contributed "Down a Lazy River" in Part One.

MICHELLE SNIDER

✦ ✦ ✦

The Persistence of Rain

A fantasy farm stay gets washed away.

IT HAD SEEMED PROMISING ENOUGH THAT EARLY MORNING AFTER finally leaving the unforgettably bleak roadside motel. The day was already brilliantly sunny with that bleached edge found in ozone-deprived Australia. Walking out of the generic orange and brown room which smelled of rarely being occupied, the first thing I noticed in the empty parking lot was a supernaturally large dead beetle, legs in the air on the already simmering pavement. Why was everything in Australia always so big? It wasn't a question one could ever truly answer, so I stepped out into the sun and trudged down the driveway, my thirty-five-pound pack sealed to my back like a cocoon, to stand in the road to catch the bus to the train. Although I had already spent a couple of days taking a plane and multiple buses and trains from Sydney, by the time I reached my destination in far North Queensland, it had taken yet another day.

It was one of many things about Australia that I didn't sense at all until I got there. On the map, the country looks about the size of United States; in fact it is about 80 percent as large as the United States. But whereas the U.S. is crisscrossed relentlessly with highways and freeways, Australia is stunningly unpaved. Nearly every-place in the States feels easily accessible, but there is a hard-earned

joy that one feels in Australia when you actually arrive at the place
you want to go. Still, my journey to the farm was nearly seamless;
all the segments of my trip worked out and I found myself being
greeted at the station by my host, her young female guest, and a
male friend who I never saw again after that evening. I was ready
and eager to begin a new adventure.

Then I noticed the ants. In the car. All over the car and all over
me. I smelled the smoke. All three of them, puffing away around
me, this woman from distant Northern California, where smoking
without a care was a thing of the past. They talked among themselves in thick Queensland accents which I had only begun to understand. It was a joke among my Sydney friends (including one
who was from Queensland) that Queensland was the most backward of the Australian states, the most "hick" or "redneck" as we
would call it in the U.S. After all, they reminded me, Queensland
was the home state of Parliament's most-hated and most hateful
member, Pauline Hanson, who could be generously described as
making Jesse Helms look liberal. Sitting in the back seat of that car,
I suddenly had one of those remarkable moments of clarity, where
I stepped out of the romanticism of travel and realized how far I
was from home. There I sat, a small spot of desert orange on the
huge world map that hangs on my kitchen wall, in a remote part
of Australia, where I didn't know a soul, not even the people who
were driving the car.

It had seemed promising when I read about it. And when I
talked about it, it sounded downright adventurous. The plan was
to work on this farm for several hours a day in exchange for room
and board and a chance to meet the locals, get off the beaten path
and work up an honest sweat. For a young woman who was sick
of hostels and cheap beer, it was an opportunity to see the "real"
Australia. Although I had friends in Melbourne as well as Sydney,
here was a chance to head up north, far away from any city and
any accent that sounded familiar. And so my organic farm fantasy
began with me in that miserable car.

It still seemed promising when I arrived at the farm after
passing down a road with a prominent sign announcing "Emu

crossing!" It was just what I wanted it to be: tropical, funky, and remote. The house was at least a mile from the "main" road and down a dirt road that had seen numerous downpours and too many heavy cars in recent months. It was the wet season in far North Queensland, and even the tourists stayed home during these sloppy months up north. I didn't know that. I just took one look around the small house surrounded by the thick smell of green and smiled.

The house was small and open to the world outside with netting for windows and a wide tin roof. The netting held back the breeze just enough to keep it from feeling invasive and the sound of insects and birds hung in the air as a constant buzz. I felt as though I could breathe fresh air like this forever. A hammock hung in one of the windows and it was there that I first wrote in my journal about this new place, "I'm in a space where I feel inclined to take a long hard look at myself." After all, I was in this vast country with the ulterior motive of uncovering what my life's work was meant to be.

The whole experience stopped feeling quite as promising when I learned where I would be sleeping: on the floor of the kitchen, between where the garbage can (cockroaches) and food shelves (spiders) were. Basically, it was a mat on the cement floor. My host explained to me that she usually had a bed for her workers, but since she had a guest in town I had to make do with the floor. I am not afraid of dirt or most bugs, but this was Australia, where the bugs are not friendly. And working my butt off most of the day only to plop down on a cement floor next to old cigarette butts and dead ants was not part of my fantasy. As I later wrote, "There's a sense of safety and space in this house, but also a knowledge that almost everything out there could find its way in here." Nevertheless, I was open to the experience, so I pulled out my sleeping bag and made do. It was actually almost homey, surrounded by tall shelves and hidden among big bags of rice. And, after a bunch of people showed up and we all laughed over the sound of the tropical rain, it did feel like it was going to be okay.

But, of course, that is when the drama really started. As we sat around on couches, chairs, and the floor, a story started to unfold from my host. It was your typical story of love gone wrong, but mixed with an extra dose of jealousy and betrayal and revolving around a self-centered, angry ex-boyfriend who seemed to make a habit of coming to the house uninvited to mouth off and defend his actions. And, unfortunately, my host always seemed to give him an audience and sometimes even a spot in her bed. Still, she spoke for what seemed like hours, rehashing all of the ways he had treated her badly. Of course, if she had been an old friend instead of a new acquaintance, I would have told her honestly that she was letting him treat her this way. I did sense that the whole situation had something to do with the fact that she was in the middle of nowhere and terribly lonely, and there weren't many men to choose from. Sitting in that room and listening to her go on and on, I remembered how, when I told my friends that I was going to Australia for two months, a typical reaction was to tell me about what backward, sexist louts Australian men were. Well, my experience with them

The he sexism of English society was brought to Australia and then amplified by penal conditions. A convict woman needed unusual strength of character not to be crushed by its assumptions. Language itself confirmed her degradation, and some sense of this may be gleaned from the slang and cant words applied to women in Georgian times—a brusque, stinging argot of appropriation and dismissal.

A woman was a *bat*, a *crack*, a *bunter*, a *case fro, cattle*, a *mort*, a *burick*, or a *convenient*. If she had a regular man, she was his *natural* or *peculiar*. If married, she was an *autem mott*; if blonde, a *bleached mott*; if a very young prostitute, almost a child, a *kinchin mott*; if beautiful, a *rum blowen*, a *ewe*, a *flash piece of mutton*. If she had gonorrhea, she was a *queer mort*.

◆

—Robert Hughes,
*The Fatal Shore: The Epic of
Australia's Founding*

had been pretty similar to my experiences with American men, and some of them had been completely charming, but it seemed I was finally going to meet one of these stereotypical Aussie men. And, knowing that my train south wouldn't arrive for four days, there was no escape from whatever was to come.

The next day began at six, with a quick breakfast as we suited up for the morning of work. I of course brought all the wrong clothes for farm work. However, my hiking boots were deemed adequate for the wet day that loomed ahead. As it turned out, I had never experienced a wet day like a far North Queensland wet day. After about five minutes of water pouring down on me, it became useless to try to shelter myself in any way at all. There I stood in a pile of mud, with water running off me as if I were standing under a high-powered shower. Luckily, I was surrounded by Australians, who do seem to have an unusual ability to just deal with a situation.

The bulk of the farm was on the crest of a hill and consisted of about a hundred fruit trees. My job was essentially to tear out some of the most massive weeds I had ever seen, a job that entailed lengthy stabbing at the ground with relatively ineffectual tools until finally came the satisfying pull of a loosened weed. The rain turned on and off, washing the sweat off my face along with a torrent of mosquito repellant.

Yet, I was working hard and actually loved the tough, physical labor and the feeling that came with being able to clearly see what I had accomplished in a day. Although, of course, that was just the first day. That was before the boyfriend showed up.

The screaming started on the second night. I had just started to drift off to sleep when I heard wheels on the drive and the opening of the screen door. I knew instinctually that it was him, and the buildup from my host over the past days had us all on edge for a confrontation. From my spot in the kitchen I could only make out some of the words, even though there was no door between that room and the living space. The rain on the roof only made it possible to hear what was said loudly, but soon that turned out to be most of the conversation. Within an hour of listening, I felt more physically threatened by this man than I have ever felt in my life.

He came into the house as if he owned it and dominated the space with his blinding self-absorption and radiating anger. I wanted nothing more than to just get away from the situation, but there were no options. There was no privacy in the house at all and to go outside in that weather at that hour was impossible. I was stuck until he finally left in the early morning.

My host felt so guilty about keeping me on edge most of the night that she decided to give me the next day off. The rain let up and we jumped in her car so she could show me around the area. I was finally out of the house and the stifling rain, but again felt trapped because of her incessant complaining and nonstop smoking. I didn't feel I could ask her not to smoke around me because I was dependent on her for everything, including getting the hell out of there and back to the train station. There were no taxis or buses to catch, and the depot was ten miles away. My closest friend was hundreds of miles away and the telephone only worked when you could hear over the rain. There was no way out, not for two more days when my train would finally come. Only two days, but it felt like forever.

He came again the following night, but this time I remembered my earplugs. Although they still didn't block out all the sound, they did work with the rain to make it more tolerable. I kept waiting for an outburst of physical violence, because it seemed that his anger was spinning out of control. I could hear both my host and her guest pleading and reasoning with him, and I wished with all my heart that they would tell him he needed to shut up and get out. Of course, with the net windows and nonlocking doors, it wasn't much of a threat. So it was another sleepless night and a sweet relief to hear that I would be the only one in the fields that morning. The promise of peace and solitude recharged my spirits as I headed out alone and the others went into town.

I started working high on the hill, near the road that sloped and dropped into puddles and mud slides every few feet. The rain was light, but my clothes and shoes were still wet anyway, and it felt like a gift to be out in the open air by myself. For the first few hours, I was productive. The work felt like meditation. The rain increased as the air got warmer, but then it abruptly cooled and started to pour. I was determined to put in my day of work, so I stayed out there until it became nearly impossible to see and the road began to resemble a river. My host had been gone for nearly four hours and I had no idea when she might return. Yet, she was my way back to the house. Finally, I realized that I wouldn't even be able to get back if I waited much longer as the road was disappearing before my eyes and the rain only came down harder. I picked up my tools and headed through the flood to find shelter, warmth, and protection.

The roof was roaring in protest as I came in the porch to strip off my clothes. The nets blew in toward the center of the house and the air chilled me to the bone. After a short, blissful shower I made myself some food, but when I sat down to eat and read I realized I couldn't even hear myself think. The wind was blowing through my wet hair and pushing the pages of my book against my fingers, resisting my attempts to calm them. It felt like I was being pounded on all sides. I shoved the book aside and put on a CD and then another and another, but I couldn't hear the words no matter how high I turned up the volume. I tried to write in my journal, but the words couldn't reach the page from all the drumming that clogged my skull. Finally, I got down on my mat and crawled into my sleeping bag and plugged up my ears, but still the rain pounded relentlessly, never letting up for even a second. There was an insanity to this noise that can only be experienced to be understood. All I know is that, for the first time in my life, I truly felt as if I was going to lose it. I huddled deeper and deeper into my sleeping bag until that too became a prison that shut me out from the rest of the world and made me feel that I was suffocating. I stood up in the middle of that oppressive place and just cried and cried. Sobbed, really, feeling the deepest isolation I have ever known.

At that exact moment, the phone rang. I ran to grab it and could barely make out the sound of my best friend calling from California. I poured out my story to him, not knowing if we were still connected because I could only hear more and more rain. I told him I thought I was going crazy, that I didn't think I could deal with the overwhelming claustrophobia of this whole situation any longer. It seemed like I was going to be stuck in that house forever, that my host was never going to come back and that the rain would never stop. I can't imagine how much I must have worried him, but he stayed calm and shouted, just loud enough for me to barely hear, "It's going to be all right. You can get through it. I love you, Michelle!" That was all I could hear. But it was enough. I felt as if I was being sucked into a dark hole, but he reached down to me over thousands of miles and pulled me out.

The next morning I was all smiles as I left for the train station. My pack was in the back as I sat next to the window and watched the deep green pass by. To this day, I have never been so glad to leave a place, especially to leave the countryside and head back to the city. Who would have guessed that in a country so open I could have felt so confined? The clear sky looked innocently down at me as I closed my eyes and breathed.

Michelle Snider is a freelance writer based in Oakland, California. She has been published in San Francisco Bay Area newspapers and dreams of one day writing a column dedicated to sharing diverse ideas for traveling cheaply and responsibly in places all over the world.

VAL PLUMWOOD

Being Prey

She looks into the jaws of Infinity.

IN THE EARLY WET SEASON, KAKADU'S PAPERBARK WETLANDS ARE especially stunning, as the water lilies weave white, pink, and blue patterns of dreamlike beauty over the shining towers of thundercloud reflected in their still waters. Yesterday, the water lilies and the wonderful bird life had enticed me into a joyous afternoon's idyll as I ventured onto the East Alligator Lagoon for the first time in a canoe lent by the park service. "You can play about on the backwaters," the ranger had said, "but don't go onto the main river channel. The current's too swift, and if you get into trouble, there are the crocodiles. Lots of them along the river!" I followed his advice carefully and glutted myself on the magical beauty and bird life of the lily lagoons, untroubled by crocodiles.

Today, I was tempted to repeat that wonderful experience despite the light drizzle beginning to fall as I made my way to the canoe launch site. I set off on a day trip in search of an Aboriginal rock art site across the lagoon and up a side channel. The drizzle turned to rain within a few hours, and the magic was lost. At thirty-five degrees Celsius, the wet season rains could be experienced as comfortable and welcome: they were late this year, and the parched land and all of its inhabitants eagerly awaited their

303

relief. Today in the rain, though, the birds were invisible, the water lilies were sparser, and the lagoon seemed even a little menacing. I noticed now how low the fourteen-foot Canadian canoe sat in the water, just a few inches of fiberglass between me and the great saurians, close relatives of the ancient dinosaurs. Not long ago, saltwater crocodiles were considered endangered, as virtually all mature animals were shot out of the rivers and lakes of Australia's north by commercial hunting. After a decade and more of protection, their numbers are beginning to burgeon. They are now the most plentiful of the large animals of Kakadu National Park, which preserved a major area of their breeding habitat. I was actively involved in the struggle to keep such places, and for me, the crocodile was a patent symbol of the power and integrity of this place and the incredible richness of it aquatic habitats.

After hours of searching the maze of shallow channels in the swamp, I was unable to locate the clear channel leading to the rock art site, as shown on the ranger's sketch map. When I pulled my canoe over in driving rain to a rock outcrop rising out of the swamp for a hasty, sodden lunch, I experienced the unfamiliar sensation of being watched. Having never been one for timidity, in philosophy or in life, I decided, rather than return defeated to my sticky caravan, to explore a clear, deep channel closer to the river I had traveled along the previous day.

The rain squalls and wind were growing more severe, and several times I had to pull my canoe over to tip the rainwater out of it. The channel soon developed steep mud banks and snags, and the going was slow. Farther on, the channel opened up, eventually petering out, blocked by a large sandy bar. I pushed the canoe toward the bank, looking around carefully before getting out in the shallows and pulling the canoe up. I would be safe from crocodiles in the canoe—I had been told—but swimming, and standing or wading at the water's edge were dangerous. Edges are one of the crocodile's favorite food-capturing places. I saw nothing, but the feeling of unease that had been with me all day intensified.

The rain eased temporarily, and I picked my way across a sandbar covered with scattered scrub to see what there was of this puzzling place. As I crested the gently sloping dune, I was shocked to glimpse the muddy brown waters of the East Alligator River gliding silently only a hundred yards ahead of me. The channel I followed had evidently been an anabranch and had led me back to the main river. Nothing stirred along the riverbank, but a great tumble of escarpment cliffs up on the other side of the river caught my attention. One especially striking rock formation—a single large rock balanced precariously on a much smaller one—held my gaze. As I looked, my whispering sense of unease turned into a shout of danger. The strange formation put me sharply in mind of two things: the indigenous Gagadgu owners of Kakadu, whose advice about coming here I had not sought, and of the precariousness of my own life, of human lives. As a solitary specimen of a major prey species of the saltwater crocodile, I was standing in one of the most dangerous places on the face of the earth.

I turned decisively to go back the way I had come, with a feeling of relief. I had not found the rock paintings, I rationalized, but it was too late to look for them now. The strange rock formation presented itself instead as a telos of the day. I had come here, I had seen something interesting, now I could go, home to caravan comfort.

As I pulled the canoe out into the main current, the torrential rain and wind started up again; the swelling stream would carry me home the quicker, I thought. I had not gone more that five or ten minutes back down the channel when, rounding a bend, I saw ahead of me in midstream what looked like a floating stick—one I did not recall passing on my way up. As the current moved me toward it, the stick appeared to develop eyes. A crocodile! It is hard to estimate size from the small nose and eye protrusions the crocodile leaves, in cryptic mode, above the waterline, but it did not look like a large one. I was close to it now but was not especially afraid; an encounter would add interest to the day.

Although I was paddling to miss the crocodile, our paths were strangely convergent. I knew it was going to be close but was to-

tally unprepared for the great blow that came against the side of
the canoe. Again it came, again and again, now from behind, shuddering the flimsy craft. I paddled furiously, but the blows continued. The unheard of was happening, the canoe was under attack,
the crocodile in full pursuit! For the first time, it came to me fully
that I was prey. I realized I had to get out of the canoe or risk being
capsized or pulled into the deeper water of midchannel.

The bank now presented a high, steep face of slippery mud, difficult to scale. There was only one obvious avenue of escape, a paperbark tree with many low branches near the muddy bank wall.
I made the split-second decision to try to leap into the lower
branches and climb to safety. I steered the canoe over to the bank
by the paperbark and stood up ready to jump. At the same instant,
the crocodile rushed up alongside the canoe, and its beautiful,
flecked golden eyes looked straight into mine. Perhaps I could bluff
it, drive it away, as I had read of British tiger hunters doing. I waved
my arms and shouted, "Go away!" (We're British here.) The golden
eyes glinted with interest. I tensed for the jump and leapt. Before
my foot even tripped the first branch, I had a blurred, incredulous
vision of great toothed jaws bursting from the water. Then I was
seized between the legs in a red-hot pincer grip and whirled into
the suffocating wet darkness below.

The course and intensity of terminal thought patterns in near-
death experiences can tell us much about our frameworks of sub-
jectivity. A subjectively centered framework capable of sustaining
action and purpose must, I think, view the world "from the inside," structured to sustain the concept of a continuing, narrative
self; we remake the world in that way as our own, investing it with
meaning, reconceiving it as sane, survivable, amenable to hope and
resolution. The lack of fit between this subject-centered version
and reality comes into play in extreme moments. In its final, frantic attempts to protect itself from the knowledge that threatens the
narrative framework, the mind can instantaneously fabricate terminal doubt of extravagant, Cartesian proportions: *This is not really
happening. This is a nightmare from which I will soon awake.* This desperate delusion split apart as I hit the water. In that flash, when my

consciousness had to know the bitter certainty of its end, I glimpsed the world for the first time "from the outside," as a world no longer my own, an unrecognizable bleak landscape composed of raw necessity, that would go on without me, indifferent to my will and struggle, to my life or death.

Few of those who have experienced the crocodile's death roll have lived to describe it. It is, essentially, an experience beyond words of total terror, total helplessness, total certainty, experienced with undivided mind and body, of a terrible death in the swirling depths. The crocodile's breathing and heart metabolism is not suited to prolonged struggle, so the roll is an intense initial burst of power designed to overcome the surprised victim's resistance quickly. Then it is merely a question of holding the now feebly struggling prey under the water a while for an easy finish to the drowning job. The roll was a centrifuge of whirling, boiling blackness, which seemed about to tear my limbs from my body, driving water into my bursting lungs. It lasted for an eternity, beyond endurance, but when I seemed all but finished, the rolling suddenly stopped. My feet touched bottom, my head broke the surface, and spluttering, coughing, I sucked at air, amazed to find myself still alive. The crocodile still had me in its pincer grip between the legs, and the water came just up to my chest. As we rested together, I had just begun to weep for the prospects of my mangled body, when the crocodile pitched me suddenly into a second death roll.

When the tearing, whirling terror stopped again (this time perhaps it had not lasted quite so long), I surfaced again, still in the crocodile's grip, next to the stout branch of a large sandpaper fig growing in the water. I reached out and held onto the branch with all my strength, vowing to let the crocodile tear me apart rather than throw me again into that spinning, suffocating hell. For the first time I became aware of a low growling sound issuing from the crocodile's throat, as if it were angry. I braced myself against the branch ready for another roll, but after a short time the crocodile's jaws simply relaxed, I was free. With all of my power, I used my grip on the branch to pull away, dodging around the back of the fig tree to avoid the forbidding mud bank, and tried once more the only apparent avenue of escape, to climb into the paperbark tree.

As in the repetition of a nightmare, when the dreamer is stuck fast in some monstrous pattern of destruction impervious to will or endeavor, the horror of my first escape attempt was exactly repeated. As I leapt into the same branch, the crocodile again propelled itself from the water, seizing me once more, this time around the upper left thigh. I briefly felt a hot sensation before being again submerged in the terror of the third death roll. Like the others, it stopped eventually, and we came up in the same place as before, next to the sandpaper fig branch. I was growing weaker, but I could see the crocodile taking a long time to kill me this way. It seemed to be intent on tearing me apart slowly, playing with me like a huge growling cat with a torn mouse. I did not imagine that I would survive, so great seemed its anger and its power compared to mine. I prayed for a quick finish and decided to provoke it by attacking it with my free hands. Feeling back behind me along the head, which still held my body in its jaws, I encountered two lumps. Thinking I had the eye sockets, I jabbed my thumbs into them with all my might. They slid into warm, unresisting holes (which may have been the ears or perhaps the nostrils), and the crocodile did not so much as flinch. In despair, I resumed my grasp on the branch, dreading death by slow torture. Once again, after a time, I felt the crocodile jaws relax, and I pulled free.

I knew now that I must break the pattern. *Not* back into the paperbark. Up the impossible, slippery mud bank was the only way. I threw myself at it with all of my failing strength, scrabbling with my hands for a grip, failing, sliding, falling back to the bottom, to the waiting jaws of the crocodile. I tried a second time and almost made it before sliding back, braking my slide two-thirds of the way down by grabbing a tuft of grass. I hung there, exhausted, defeated, *I can't make it, I thought. It'll just have to come and get me.* It seemed a shame, somehow, after all I had been through. The grass tuft began to give way. Flailing wildly to stop myself from sliding farther, I found my fingers jamming into the soft mud, and that supported me. This was the clue I needed to survive. With the last of my strength, I climbed up the bank, pushing my fingers into the mud to hold my weight, reached the top, and stood up, incredulous. I was alive!

Escaping the crocodile was not by any means the end of my struggle to survive. I was alone, severely injured, and many miles from help. During the struggle, I was so focused on survival that the pain from the injuries had not registered. As I took my first urgent steps away from the vicinity of the crocodile, I knew something was wrong with my leg. *The bastard's broken my knee.* I did not wait to inspect the damage, but took off away from the crocodile in the direction of the ranger station.

After putting more distance between myself and the crocodile, I felt a bit safer and stopped to find out what was wrong with my leg. Now I was aware for the first time of how serious my wounds were. I did not remove my clothing to see the damage to the groin area inflicted by the first hold. What I could see was bad enough. The left thigh hung open, with bits of fat, tendon and muscle showing, and a sick, numb feeling suffused my entire body. I tore up some of my clothing to try and bind the wounds up and made a tourniquet for the thigh to stanch the bleeding, then staggered on, thinking only of getting back to the ranger station. Still elated from my escape, I imagined myself, spattered with blood and mud, lurching sensationally into the station. I went some distance before realizing with a sinking heart that I had crossed the swamp above the station in the canoe and that without it I could not get back to the station under my own steam. Perhaps I would die out here after all.

I would have to rely on being found by a search party, but I could maximize my chances by moving downstream toward the swamp edge, about three kilometers away. Still exhilarated by my escape, perhaps now I had a chance of survival. I had recently been reading Robert Graves' memoir of soldiers in the First World War who had been able to walk long distances with severe injuries and survived. Walking was still possible, and there was nothing better to do. Whenever I lay down to rest, the pain seemed even worse. I struggled on, through driving rain, shouting for mercy from the sky, apologizing to the angry crocodile, calling out my repentance to this place for the fault of my intrusion. I came to a flooded tributary and had to make a large upstream detour to find a place where I could cross it in my weakened state.

My considerable bush experience stood me in good stead, keeping me on course (navigating was second nature), and practiced endurance stopped me from losing heart. As I neared the swamp above the ranger station after a journey of several hours, I began to black out and had to crawl the final distance to its edge. I could do no more for myself; I selected an open spot near the swamp edge, and lay there in the gathering dusk to await what would come. I did not expect a search party until the following day, and I doubted I could possibly last the night.

The heavy rain and wind stopped with the onset of darkness, and it grew perfectly still. Dingoes howled, and clouds of mosquitoes whined around by body. I hoped to pass out soon, but consciousness persisted. There were loud swirling noises in the water, and I knew I was easy meat for another crocodile. After what seemed like a long time, I heard the distant sound of a motor and saw a light moving across the other side of the swamp. Thinking it was a boat crossing the swamp to rescue me, I had enough strength to rise up on my elbow and call out for help. I thought I heard a very faint reply, but then the motor grew fainter and the lights went away. Thinking I had imagined the voice, I was as devastated as any castaway who signals desperately to a passing ship and is not seen.

It was not from a boat that the lights had come. Passing my caravan, the ranger noticed there was no light. He had come down to the canoe launch site in a motorized trike to check and, realizing that I had not returned, stopped his motor to listen. He had heard my faint call for help across the dark water, and after some time, a rescue craft appeared. As they lifted me into the boat that was to begin my thirteen-hour journey to Darwin Hospital, my rescuers discussed the need to go upriver the next day and shoot a crocodile. I spoke strongly against this plan: I was the intruder on crocodile territory, and no good purpose could be served by random revenge. The area was full of crocodiles in the water just around the spot I was lying. That spot was under six feet of water the next morning, flooded by the rains signaling the onset of the wet season.

In the end I was found in time and survived against many odds, thanks to the ranger's diligence, my own perseverance, and great good fortune. A similar combination of good fortune and human care enabled me to overcome an infection in the leg that threatened an amputation or worse. I probably have Paddy Pallin's incredibly tough walking shorts to thank for the fact that the groin injuries were not as severe as the leg injuries. I am very lucky that I can still walk well and have lost few of my previous capacities. Lady Luck shows here, as usual, her inscrutable face: was I lucky to survive or unlucky to have been attacked in the first place? The wonder of being alive after being held—quite literally—in the jaws of death has never entirely left me. For the first year, the experience of existence as an unexpected blessing cast a golden glow over my life, despite the injuries and the pain. The glow has slowly faded, but some of the gratitude for life it left will always be there, even if I remain unsure whom I should thank. The gift of gratitude came from the searing flash of near-death knowledge, a glimpse "from the outside" of the alien, incomprehensible world in which the narrative of self has ended.

There remain many mysteries about the reasons for the attack on the canoe itself, which are unusual in crocodile lore. One issue on which there has been much speculation is the size of the crocodile. It has always been difficult for me to estimate its size because for most of the attack, it was either only partly visible or had ahold of me from behind. The press estimate of fourteen feet—which they arrived at somehow and published widely some five days before I made any sort of statement on the subject—was, I think, certainly an overestimate. One glimpse of the partly submerged crocodile next to the fourteen-foot canoe suggested that it was not as long as the canoe. If the press had an interest in exaggerating the size of the crocodile, the park service, which feared legal liability, had an interest in minimizing it; neither group seemed interested in my views on the matter.

> *E*qually at home in the fresh or salt water, salties thrive in Kakadu's floodplains, billabongs and tidal rivers. Mature males can attain a length of eighteen feet. Though mostly feeding on large fish and birds, bulls have been known to attack full-grown water buffalos. Signs posted the warning: "Danger. Large crocodiles frequent this area. Do not enter water. Keep children and dogs away from waters edge." Yet whether basking on the muddy banks or propelling themselves sinuously through the water, the salties we encountered seemed largely unfazed by a boatful of excited gawkers scuttling about for a good view.
>
> ◆
>
> —Paul Prince "Off in the Wild Down Under," *Travel Holiday*

The park service speculated that the crocodile may have been a young male evicted from breeding territory and perhaps embattled by other crocodiles. Their theory is that the crocodile attacked my canoe after a collision by mistaking it for one of these older aggressive crocodiles. From my perspective, however, there are some problems with this account. It is very unlikely that I accidentally struck it with the canoe, as the story assumes and as some press reports claimed. Crocodiles are masters of water, and this one was expecting me and saw me coming. The crocodile most likely observed the passing of my canoe on the way up the channel only a short time before, as it did seem to *intercept* the canoe. Why should a small crocodile of less that ten feet aggressively attack a much larger, fourteen-foot-canoe "crocodile" unless we assume that it was bent on suicide? The smaller the crocodile, the more implausible such an attack story becomes. Because crocodiles become sexually mature at around ten feet, the park service's minimization story of a "self-defense" attack by a "small" evicted crocodile is not even internally consistent. My personal estimate is that it was probably a medium crocodile in the range of eight to twelve feet.

Possible explanations for the anomalous attack are almost limitless. Perhaps the crocodile's motives were political, against a species-enemy, human beings are a threat to crocodiles, of a more dire kind than crocodiles are to human beings, through the elimination of habitat. The crocodile may have thought that any human being who ventured alone into these waters in those conditions was offering itself as a sacrifice to crocodile kind. The extreme weather events may have played a role. The crocodile is an exploiter of the great planetary dualism of land and water. As Papua New Guinea writer Vincent Eri suggests in his novel, *The Crocodile*, the creature is a sort of magician: its technique is to steal the Other, the creature of the land, away into its own world of water where it has complete mastery over it. Water is the key to the crocodile's power, and even large crocodiles rarely attack in its absence.

The crocodile is then a boundary inhabitant and may take a person in a canoe as either of the land or of the water. If a crocodile perceives such a person as *outside* its medium of mastery, the person may not be seen as prey and may be safe from attack. If a person in a canoe is perceived as potentially of the water, as he or she might easily be in an early wet-season day of torrential rain when the boundaries of the crocodile empire are exploding, the person may be much less that safe. Clearly, we must question the assumption, common up until the time of my attack, that canoes are as safe as larger craft because they are perceived similarly as outside the crocodile's medium.

The most puzzling question of all, of course, is why the crocodile let me go. I think there are several factors here. Because it was not a large crocodile that can kill with little effort, perhaps I was marginal prey. The depth of the water and the way it had ahold of my body made it hard for it to keep me under, and it may have let me go the first time to try to get a better grip higher up on my body. Its failure to keep me submerged suggests that it could have underestimated my size, seeing me sitting in the canoe, or overestimated the depth of the rapidly rising water. Maybe it was a stray or a newcomer to the area who did not know the terrain well and was not familiar with the good drowning spots in the shallower back channels. My friend the sandpaper fig allowed me to retain a determined grip on my own medium and contributed essentially to my survival, In another encounter in the territory a few years earlier, an adult man was saved from a fourteen-foot crocodile dragging him off in shallow water by the grasp of a ten-year old girl pulling the opposite way.

Perhaps, too, the crocodile let go its hold because it was tiring; I experienced the crocodile through the roll as immensely powerful, but that intense burst of energy cannot be sustained long, and must accomplish its purpose of drowning fairly quickly. I have no doubt that had the crocodile been able to keep me submerged after the first roll, there would have been no need for a second. My advice for others similarly placed is the same as that of Vincent Eri, who used the crocodile as a metaphor for the relationship between colonized indigenous culture and colonizing Western culture. If the crocodile-magician-colonizer can drag you completely into its medium, you have little chance; if you can somehow manage to retain a hold on your own medium, you may survive.

Val Plumwood survived this incident in February 1985. She has been a visiting professor at North Carolina State University and at the University of Montana, Missoula, and a research fellow at the University of Sydney. Her most recent book is Environmental Culture: The Ecological Crisis of Reason.

ALLEN NOREN

A Plague of Mice

There are many strange happenings
in the Australian night.

IT SEEMED AS IF THE OUTBACK WOULD NEVER END, THAT NO matter how far we drove there would always be this dry, red landscape and limitless sky. From it the most extraordinary things materialized: emus and kangaroos, dingoes and wild horses, flocks of galahs, their pink breasts like mirages against the sky. Once, a monitor lizard at least four feet long eyed us and tasted the air with its tongue as we passed.

The thought of the Outback never ending was just fine with Suzanne and me. We had been driving across it for two months in a temperamental old van we'd bought back in Sydney. We'd covered over 3,000 miles and, depending on which way we decided to head next, still had at least twice that far to go. At the end of each day we unfolded our map, guessed where we were, and became giddy with the thought of all those miles before us. Each one felt like a hundred dollars in the bank.

The evenings were our favorite time. The heat, which peaked above 120 degrees most days, moved west like the tide follows the moon. The interminable black flies, so thick during the day that we had to wrap our faces in scarves to keep them out of our mouths and eyes and ears and noses, settled somewhere for the night, though we never discovered where.

Suzanne and I made a ceremony out of stopping the van. We sat for a moment with the engine idling, looked at each other, and then turned the key off. The sound of all that nothing washed over us, and as it did we felt the deep contentment of desolation.

We felt like astronauts as we scouted around collecting bits of scrub for a fire. Several times I went so far that I lost sight of the van and realized how easy it would be to get lost in all that sameness. People vanished out there all the time. They wandered over a rise, turned around, and recognized nothing. They'd wander until the cold night air and then the heat of day did them in. Just a few months earlier a man had been found a few hundred feet from his car. He died of thirst even though there were several gallons of water behind the driver's seat. As I was out there I realized it could happen as easily as getting swept into the ocean by a freak wave. Far overhead there was almost always the contrail of a jet, like a rope that was just out of reach.

The world took on form as the sun set. Rocks that had been flattened by the heat rose from the earth and became angular and rich with color. Tiny leathery leaves appeared on the scrub where there had been none before. Animals stirred. A rush of cold air came with the quickening darkness and our small fire became the center of the universe.

At the end of one of these evenings we spread our blankets out in the back of our van and settled down to sleep. I was almost dreaming when Suzanne jerked beside me as if she was having a dream. She did it again and screamed.

It wasn't a small scream, one that suggested surprise or fright. It was a scream of terror. My first thought was that a snake had slipped into the van, one of those notorious Australian snakes whose bite can kill a full-grown man in minutes.

"Did you feel it?" Suzanne shrieked. I turned on the flashlight and saw that Suzanne was crouched on top of our blankets now, her eyes wide with fright as she stared at the place where her feet had been.

"What is it?" I asked and carefully pulled the blankets back, ready to smash whatever was there with our heavy flashlight.

"I don't know. Something against my leg."

We carefully went through all our bedding and found nothing. We looked around our water bottles and in our boxes of food and clothes. Nothing.

"Just a dream," I said hopefully.

"No," she said. "There's something in here."

I lay back down and tried to be an example by closing my eyes and pretending to sleep. Suzanne remained sitting upright, pushed her body against mine, and scanned the inside of the van with the beam of the flashlight. Finally, she turned it off and lay down next to me. The silence of the night returned like a blanket.

I was almost asleep again when we heard a rustling toward the front of our van.

"Hear that?" Suzanne said.

"Sounds like a mouse," I said.

"Oh," she said, relieved that it wasn't a snake. "You think we should put him out?"

"Let him eat a little something," I said, feeling at peace with the world.

We ignored the mouse for a while, but his constant chewing and rustling were as loud as someone sawing boards.

"Allen," Suzanne said. "Allen? I think he's got a friend."

We listened.

"There's one in the bed!" she screamed. "It crawled over my face!"

At the same time I felt the soft body of a mouse run the length of my thigh as it sought a place to hide.

Suzanne flicked on the flashlight again and scanned the van. "Oh, my God!" she whispered in horror. "They're all over!"

I followed the beam of the flash, and I too was horrified. Mice scurried over everything—the floor, our clothes, our box of food, on the backs of the seats, and over our bedding. Suzanne screamed again and began slapping herself. The beam of the flashlight cut across the inside of the van as she flailed. "They're on me!" she screamed, and I could feel them on me too.

I got the flashlight out of her hands and brushed mice off our skin. I pulled one from her hair and threw it toward the front of the van.

"Get them out," she whimpered. "Please, Allen. Get them out."

I got up to open the sliding door on the side of the van and felt a soft body give beneath my bare foot. I slid the door open but had to tug. I looked down with the flashlight and saw that several mice had become caught in the mechanism and were crushed there.

Suzanne screamed again and I turned the flashlight on her. Mice covered her skin like flies.

I became enraged. Beginning at the back of the van I turned over everything and began beating mice with my fists. Their small bodies broke open beneath it and my fists became covered with blood and a viscous mess of intestines. I made a safe corner for Suzanne and put her there, whimpering and shaking, as I worked toward the front of the van, turning over every box and book and bit of clothing and smashing anything that moved as I went.

Our box of food was infested with mice and I threw all of it out the door. I watched in horrified fascination as a loaf of bread was jerked here and there, as if I'd thrown it into a lake full of starving fish.

The ground moved. It was covered with a tide of frantic mice. I wondered if we'd be eaten alive.

I yelled and bellowed as I smashed mice, crushed them in my hands, and threw them out the open door. I found where they were coming through, a hole beneath the passenger's seat as big as my ring finger, which I plugged with a piece of wood. I went through the van three times until I had killed them all.

Nothing moved. Not even Suzanne. But then she said, "I can hear them. They're coming for us."

I heard them too. They were all over the underside of the van,

chewing the tires and running along the frame and wiring, searching for a way in.

I climbed into the driver's seat and prayed that the engine
would start. It did and I began driving. I drove all night, blood
caked on my hands, to escape the plague of mice.

*Allen Noren has been traveling throughout the world for the past twenty
years. He now lives in Northern California. "A Plague of Mice" is an
expanded excerpt from his book,* Storm: A Motorcycle Journey
Around the Baltic Sea, *published by Travelers' Tales.*

＊ ＊ ＊

Storm Warning

*The annual Sydney-to-Hobart yacht race is usually
a test of sailors and boats, but in 1998 it was
a challenge beyond comprehension.*

THE ENTRANCE TO SYDNEY HARBOUR IS BARELY 1,500 YARDS wide, flanked by high basalt cliffs. Shaking free its lesser brethren, *Sayonara* was the first to burst through the gap, followed immediately by George Snow's streaking *Brindabella*. As the yachts wheeled to the south, surging by the crowds baking on Sydney's famed Bondi Beach, a strong northeasterly wind billowed their sails. Aboard *Sayonara*, Larry Ellison ordered the spinnaker hoisted, and set a course due south. A spreading host of smaller boats helmed by well-known Aussie captains soon followed, led by Martin James's *Team Jaguar*, Rob Kothe's *Sword of Orion*, the mammoth seventy-footer *Wild Thing*, and the Queensland yacht *B-52*. Thanks to the strong winds, by midafternoon much of the fleet was on a record pace—with the gentlemen's boats, such as Richard Winning's striking *Winston Churchill* and Tony Mowbray's beloved *Solo Globe Challenger*, in the rear.

Few in the fleet were alarmed by Peter Dunda's storm warning, which was broadcast at 3 P.M. by the *Young Endeavour*, an Australian Navy brigantine whose radio was staffed by race volunteers. Sailing off Australia means an occasional blow of fifty knots or more, especially in Bass Strait, and few in the race expected to finish without encountering such winds. "The warning on Saturday didn't say anything more than what you could expect in any Hobart," recalls Rod Hunter, navigator on the Adelaide yacht *VC Offshore Stand Aside*. "It was for the forties and fifties, a southerly buster. We sail in forties and fifties all the time. It's normal. It's just a fact of life." Recalls Larry Ellison, "There was a sense of 'Storm? Piece of cake!' Of course, no one said anything about a hurricane."

Back in the pack, the nine veteran Tasmanian sailors aboard *Business Post Naiad* greeted news of the storm warning with hearty laughter. Almost all had been sailing Bass Strait since they were boys, and they were accustomed to fighting the strait's steep, choppy waves and fifty- and sixty-knot winds. The skipper, Bruce Guy, speculated that the coming blow might actually give them an advantage the next day. "The guys from behind, who haven't been in Bass Strait before, they're going to get a bit of a dustup," observed Rob Matthews, housing inspector.

The powerful wind at their backs, Ellison would later say, should have been a warning. It was "explosive, gusty," he notes, and it quickly began to take a toll on *Sayonara*. By late afternoon, as *Sayonara* and *Brindabella* left the rest of the fleet miles behind, the gusts had blown out three different spinnaker sails aboard Ellison's boat and had snapped the brass fitting of one of the spinnaker poles, damage Ellison had never seen, before. But the boat was simply going too fast for this to worry anyone. That afternoon *Sayonara* hit a boat record, 26.1 knots, and was already on pace to break *Morning Glory*'s 1996 record time.

As darkness fell around nine, the wind swung around, as predicted, and began blowing hard out of the south. Raindrops pelted *Sayonara* as the boat crossed the incoming front, and the crew of twenty-three slipped into their bright-red heavy-weather gear. By 11, *Sayonara* was plowing into a forty-knot head wind. Waves grew to fifteen, then twenty feet, and almost everyone on board began to experience seasickness. "Anyone that said he didn't get sick out there is lying," recalls Ellison. "We had guys who've sailed the Whitbread [round-the-world race] puking their guts out, like five times in the first twelve hours. We were on the Jenny Craig plan—a great weight-loss experience."

By the time *Sayonara* entered Bass Strait after midnight, Ellison was having difficulty driving the boat. Heavy, dark clouds hung down, obscuring the horizon, and the flying spume and rain stung his face. A small rip developed in the mainsail, and when crewmen went to fix it they found the giant sail was tearing out the metal track that fastened it to the mast. Around three Ellison realized he couldn't take it anymore.

"You take over," he yelled to Brad Butterworth, a veteran New Zealand sailor standing to his side in the cockpit. "Get me outta here!"

Ellison went below decks to check the weather forecasts with his navigator, Mark Rudiger. Just as he walked up to the navigation, Ellison saw a new satellite photo—downloading onto one of Rudiger's laptops. Stunned, both men looked for several seconds at the ominous doughnut of white clouds forming above Bass Strait.

"Mark," Ellison finally said, "have you ever seen anything like that before?"

Rudiger slowly shook his head. "Well, I have," Ellison said. "It was on the Weather Channel. And it was called a hurricane. What the fuck is that thing doing out here?"...

2:30 P.M. Sunday

Simon Clark sat on the starboard bow of *Stand Aside* and dangled his legs into the booming waves. Clark, a 28-year-old who had sailed since he was a boy, and three friends had joined up with Adelaide businessman James Hallion's eight-man crew, and Clark thought Hallion had driven a bit conservatively early in the race. Nevertheless, they had busted down the coast at an average speed of fifteen knots, even hitting eighteen and nineteen at times.

Around noon, as winds continued to pick up, they had taken down the mainsail and put up a storm jib, expecting heavy weather. Clark wasn't too worried, nor was anyone on board. By two, winds were hitting just thirty-five or forty knots, while Clark had seen only one "green wave"—that was what he called it—a rogue wall of water that looked as if it had risen straight from the mossy bottom of Bass Strait.

Suddenly he saw another. As the wave rose up before him, Clark thought it looked like a tennis court standing on end.

"Bear away!" he shouted.

Hallion was unable to steer down the wave. The boat rode high on the wave and slithered to the left. Just then the wave crested and crashed onto the deck, rolling the boat hard to port. As *Stand Aside* fell down the face of the wave, its roll continued. For a fleeting second it felt as if they were airborne. Then they landed, upside down.

Slammed facedown into the roiling ocean, Clark felt a terrific pain in his left knee; his anterior cruciate ligament had snapped like a rubber band. Underwater, he unhooked his safety harness and floated to the surface just as the boat righted itself. Pulling himself back on board, Clark was stunned to see a seven-foot gash in the cabin; the mast lay draped over the side, broken. His crewmates were no better off. His friend Mike Marshman had somehow lost a chunk of his finger. Another man had broken ribs, still another a nasty cut across his forehead. Within minutes *Stand Aside* began sending out the first of what would be many Maydays that afternoon.

3 P.M.

As the storm system intensified, the first to encounter the full force of its lashing winds was a group of a half-dozen yachts led by *Sword of Orion*, which was running seventh overall as the afternoon began. Like so many others, Rob Kothe, the boat's 52-year-old skipper, had shrugged off the storm warnings, but as he staggered down the companionway to call in *Sword*'s position at the 2:05 radio check, he realized conditions were growing far worse than anything they had been warned of. Now about 100 miles south of the sleepy port of Eden, Kothe's boat began to experience winds above ninety miles an hour. The sharp, spiking green waves towered forty and fifty feet over the boat, crashing into the cockpit, churning his crew's bodies like laundry and stretching their safety lines to the breaking point.

In a race, weather data is a jealously guarded secret, something boats rarely share. As Kothe sat at his radio console belowdecks wiping seawater from his face, he tuned his HF dial to the race frequency and listened as boat after boat, going in alphabetical order, radioed in its position and nothing more. When it came to the Ss, Kothe listened to *Sayonara's* position report, then made a decision that probably saved many lives: he gave a weather report. "The forecast is for forty to fifty-five knots [of wind]," Kothe announced to the fleet. "We are experiencing between sixty-five and eighty-two. The weather is much stronger than forecast."

Kothe listened as the radio operator aboard *Young Endeavour,* obviously struck by the news of winds approaching 100 miles an hour, repeated the warning to the fleet. Back in the pack, about two dozen boats, including the Queensland yacht *Midnight Special,* decided to quit the race and head for the port of Eden....

3:35 P.M.

After finishing his impromptu weather report, Rob Kothe emerged onto the deck of *Sword of Orion* to find that the winds had suddenly fallen to fifty knots—"a walk in the park," as he later put it. Had the storm passed? Or were they merely in its eye? At 3:35—he looked at his watch—Kothe got his answer. As if a door had swung open, the winds slammed back hard, spiking up above eighty miles an hour. Kothe gave orders for everyone but two crewmen, a young bowman named Darren Senogles and the 33-year-old Olympic yacht racer Glyn Charles, to remain below. Kothe ran down the companionway, then radioed the *Young Endeavour* that *Sword of Orion* was quitting the race and heading back north, toward Eden.

Sword's decision to turn north, however, sent it back into the strongest winds wrapped around the eye of the storm. "The storm," Kothe later observed, "didn't give a rat's ass whether we were still racing or heading to port." After fifteen minutes, as Kothe hunched over the radio, he felt the boat rising up an especially steep wave. Suddenly *Sword* rolled upside down and they were airborne, falling down the face of the wave for a full two seconds, until Kothe felt his boat hit the ocean with a sickening crack. Seconds later the boat rolled back over, righting itself, and he found himself facedown on the floor of the cabin, bound up with ropes and shattered equipment as if he were a broken marionette. As Kothe struggled to regain his footing, he heard Darren Senogles's waterlogged screams from above deck: "Man overboard! Man overboard! Man overboard!"

It was Glyn Charles. When the wave hit, Charles had been at the helm, attempting to muscle the seven-foot-wide wheel through oncoming waves. The force of the wave apparently swung the boom around like a baseball bat into a fastball; it struck Charles in the midsection, driving him against the spokes of the wheel and snapping his safety harness. As everyone else scrambled up onto the broken deck, Charles could be seen in the water about thirty yards away.

"Swim! Swim!" people began shouting as Senogles frantically wrapped himself in a long rope and prepared to dive in after his friend. Charles, obviously stunned, raised a single arm, as if the other was injured. Someone threw a life ring toward him, but Charles was upwind, and the ring sailed helplessly back onto the deck.

Just then another huge wave broke and boiled onto the deck, knocking people and equipment about. By the time Kothe regained his feet, Charles was 150 yards off. The roll had actually torn the deck loose from the cabin below, and the men on deck, crouching unsteadily, were powerless to retrieve the struggling Brit. In the roiling seas Charles could be seen only when he crested a wave. Everyone watched in agony for a seemingly endless five minutes as he floated farther and farther from the boat. And then he was gone.

Kothe had already raced to the radio and began sending out an urgent Mayday. But the boat's mainmast lay broken in five places and had lost its aerial. Kothe broadcast Maydays for a solid two hours. But no one in a position to help Glyn Charles heard a word Kothe said....

5:30 P.M.

"Mayday! Mayday! Mayday! Here is *Winston Churchill, Winston*

Churchill. We are taking water rapidly! We can't get the motor started to start the pumps! We are getting the life rafts on deck!"

His mast and long-range aerials still intact, Richard Winning broadcast a furious Mayday even as seawater lapped onto the deck and the rest of the crew dropped the boat's life rafts over the side. Winning had been at the helm a half-hour before when a sneering green wave had slapped the old wooden yacht, knocking it flat on its side. Below, John Stanley, a taciturn 51-year-old Sydney marina manager, had been thrown into a wall as the three starboard windows imploded and foamy saltwater sprayed across the cabin. When the boat righted itself, Stanley noted with horror that a full six feet of *Churchill's* inner bulwarks was gone. "Must've sprung a plank!" Stanley yelled to Winning.

They were going down fast. As seawater began sloshing across the deck, Winning and his eight crewmates, ranging from a Sydney merchant banker to a friend's 19-year-old son, scrambled into the life rafts—Winning, the boy, and two others in one, Stanley and four friends in the other. The inflatable black rubber rafts were both topped with bright-orange canopies, which could be tied shut, though seawater still poured in, forcing the men to bail constantly. As *Churchill* sank, Winning managed to tie the two life-rafts together, but the waves tore them apart barely ten minutes later. The two boats, climbing, then falling down the faces of fifty-foot waves, lost sight of each other soon after. Winning could only hope his Mayday would be answered....

7 P.M.

Peter Joubert, a wry 74-year-old engineering professor at the University of Melbourne, had quickly grown tired of fighting the waves in this, his twenty-seventh Hobart. The spume blasting his forty-three-foot *Kingurra* felt like a pitchfork jabbing into his face; the only way he could steer was to wear goggles. Around six he curled up in a bunk and fell into a deep sleep, leaving the driving to the group of younger men who had the energy to fight the waves.

At seven Joubert woke with a start to the sound of a "horrific crash like none I'd ever heard before." The boat pitched hard to port, and he felt a massive pain spread across his chest; a slumbering crewman in another bunk had flown across the cabin, slamming into his ribs, breaking several and rupturing his spleen, Joubert later learned. As seawater gushed into the cabin, he lurched out of the bunk and crawled to the nav station, where his 22-year-old grandson helped him flip on the pumps. Glancing up the companionway, he saw three crewmen, including his friend Peter Meikle, lifting an American named John Campbell, 32, back on deck. Just then Joubert heard someone cry, "Man overboard!" It was Campbell. Halfway back onto the boat, he had slipped out of his jacket and safety harness and slid back into the ocean, wearing nothing but long underwear.

Joubert grabbed the radio. "Mayday! Mayday! Mayday! We have a man overboard!" he shouted.

As Joubert began to go into shock, Campbell floated swiftly away from the boat. *Kingurra*'s motor wouldn't start; the storm jib was shredded. There was no way to retrieve him.

"Mayday! Mayday!," Joubert repeated. "We need a helicopter!"

About 7:20 P.M.

Barry Barclay, the 37-year-old winch operator on a Dauphin SA 365 helicopter operated by the Victoria Police air wing, had just finished refueling at his base in Melbourne when the call came in that racers were in trouble. Scrambling east over the mountains known as the Great Dividing Range, Barclay and his two crewmates stopped to refuel once again, at the dirt airstrip in Mallacoota, before heading out into the howling winds in Bass Strait. First ordered by the Maritime Safety Authority's war room to rescue sailors off *Stand Aside*, Barclay's crew detoured en route when word came of a man overboard off *Kingurra*. Cutting through the swirling clouds at speeds topping 200 miles an hour, the helicopter reached *Kingurra*'s last reported position in ten minutes—only to find nothing there. "I think we've overshot them!" pilot Daryl Jones shouted. "I'm heading back!"

Just then Barclay hailed the boat on his radio. In a shaky voice Joubert told him Campbell had last been seen about 300 yards off the port bow. Jones wheeled the copter around as Barclay scanned the seas below. It was almost impossible to see. Even at an altitude of 300 feet, the waves seemed to be reaching for them, trying to suck them into the sea.

"Got something!" yelled Dave Key, another crew member. Barclay hung out of the copter's left-hand door and saw a white life ring winking among the waves; he thought he saw someone waving from inside it. But as they neared its position, the ring shot high in the air and flew off, tumbling crazily over the wave tops. There was no one inside.

Just then, out of the corner of his eye, Barclay caught a flash of movement. Peering down through the spume, he could just make out a man in the water, clad in blue long johns, waving. It was Campbell.

"I've got him! I've got him!'" Barclay shouted.

Hovering above him, Barclay played out a hundred feet of wire cable and slowly lowered Key into the ocean. Three times he raised and lowered Key, like a tea bag, as the waves engulfed him and drove him under. When Key finally reached Campbell he was limp, at the edge of consciousness, and unable to help as the paramedic tried to slip the strop over his head. Eventually Key got him into the strop and Barclay began winching them toward the helicopter.

Just as the two men were about to reach the open doorway, the winch froze. Barclay hurriedly cycled through a series of switches, trying to unlock it. It was no use. Campbell and Key hung two feet below the doorway, Campbell too exhausted to pull himself into the copter. Finally, giving up on the winch, Barclay reached down, grabbed Campbell by his underwear, and yanked him into the aircraft. Key soon followed. Campbell lay on his back, saying over and over, "Thank you thank you thank you thank you."…

11 P.M.

When Rob Matthews emerged from belowdecks to take his turn behind the wheel of *Business Post Naiad*, the Tasmanian boat was a wreck. The splintered mast lay roped to the deck. Below, the contents of the refrigerator had spilled out and were sloshing about in eight inches of water along with shattered plates and cups; the stove had broken free of its mounting and was careening about with every wave. Bruce Guy, the boat's owner, flipped on the pumps, but they jammed with debris within minutes and failed. Reluctantly, the crew had activated an EPIRB and, after rigging a new aerial, had radioed in a request for helicopter evacuation.

As Matthews took the helm, flying spume sandblasted his face. Phil Skeggs, the easygoing locksmith and the boat's least-experienced sailor, stood beside him in the cockpit, shouting out compass readings, as Matthews attempted to ram the boat through waves he could barely see. At one point the moon broke through the clouds, giving Matthews a view of the enormous waves just as they crashed onto the deck. He decided he liked it better in the dark.

Just past eleven, after the moon disappeared, leaving them once more wrapped in darkness, Matthews felt the familiar sensation as they began to creep up the face of what seemed like an especially large wave. Then, suddenly, the boat, was on it port side and they were airborne once again, falling down the face of the wave. In midair the boat overturned, landing upside down in the trough. Plunged underwater, tangled in a morass of ropes and broken equipment, Matthews held his breath. He tried to remain clam as he waited for the boat to stabilize, as it had before. When it didn't, he attempted to shed his safety harness so he could swim out from beneath the boat. But he couldn't unfasten the hook. Just as he was running out of breath, a wave tossed the boat to one side, allowing a shaft of air into the cockpit, then slammed the boat down on his head yet again.

Coughing and sputtering, Matthews was driven underwater once more. The cockpit walls jackhammered his head and shoulders. Now convinced that the boat would not right itself, he struggled again to get out of the safety harness. Finally managing to undo it, he kicked free of the boat and surfaced at the stern, where he grabbed a mass of floating ropes, "hanging on like grim death," as he later put it. There was no sign of Skeggs. "Phil! Phil!" he began shouting.

The scene belowdecks was bedlam. Water began gushing into the cabin from the companionway as the six men, trapped upside down, struggled to find their footing on the ceiling. The only light came from headlamps two of the crew had thought to grab, which now, as they lurched about, filled the cabin with a crazy, strobe-like effect. Bruce Guy and Steve Walker, fearful the boat was sinking, rushed to clear the companionway of debris, then kicked out two boards that blocked their exit to the sea below. In a minute the water level stabilized as the trapped air prevented more seawater from entering, leaving the men up to their waists in water. Guy began trying to muscle one of the black life rafts out the companionway.

"Bruce, wait," Walker said. "We're not taking on any more water. You're going to get another wave shortly. I reckon it'll flip us back over." Just then, the sound of a waterfall, the next giant wave, filled their ears. "We're goin' over!" someone shouted.

The boat flipped once more, sending everyone in the cabin toppling. As the boat righted itself, seawater began cascading over the cockpit into the cabin. Now Walker was certain they were about to sink. As others leapt by him to wade up on deck, Guy suddenly slumped into the water. Walker grabbed him before he went under. He held his friend's head and watched as his eyes rolled back, then shut. Guy, Walker realized, was having a massive heart attack; before he could do anything, Bruce Guy died in his arms. Walker dragged him to a bunk, where he cradled his head and attempted to clear his mouth, but it was too late.

Meanwhile, in the moments before *Business Post Naiad* righted itself, Rob Matthews had clung to the side of the boat, sitting on the broken mast in neck-deep water. As the waves tore at him, he saw he would need to raise himself onto the keel or risk being sucked into the sea. Exhausted, he was just about to set his feet on the submerged mast when the boat began to right itself. To his dismay, the mast beneath him shot upward, flipping him into the air like a flapjack. Matthews landed with a crunch in the cockpit just as the boat finished rolling over. He looked down and saw Phil Skeggs's motionless body, wrapped in a spaghetti of ropes on the

floor of the cockpit. As his crewmates hustled up the companionway and administered CPR, Matthews was too exhausted to do
anything but watch. Their efforts were in vain. Skeggs, the gentle
locksmith, had drowned.

About 4 A.M. Monday

The orange-canopied life raft holding John Stanley and his
four friends from *Winston Churchill* began to disintegrate sometime after three that morning. By then everyone aboard was fighting hypothermia and injuries. An outgoing Sydney attorney, John
Gibson—"Gibbo" to his mates—had cut two of his fingers down
to the bone trying to manhandle a rope during their rushed exit
from *Churchill* twelve hours before. Stanley had broken his ankle
and torn a net of ligaments in his hip when a wave had tumbled
the raft, wildly throwing the five men together. There was no
first-aid kit, nor, aside from the biscuit Stanley had stashed in his
jacket, any food.

The real problems had arisen after midnight. An unusually large
wave—Stanley could often identify the big ones because they
sounded like freight trains—had tossed the raft upside down, leaving all five men up to their necks in the water, their feet resting on
the submerged canopy, the bottom of the raft inches above their
heads. It was impossible to right the raft from inside. Someone
would have to swim out through the submerged canopy opening,
with no lifeline, and try to pull them upright. Jimmy Lawler, the
Australian representative for the American Bureau of Shipping,
said it wasn't possible. He couldn't get through the opening wearing a life vest, and wasn't willing to shed his vest.

In twenty minutes they began to run out of air. Stanley found
himself gasping for breath. To get air, they agreed Lawler would
use his knife to cut a four-inch hole in the bottom of the raft. He
did so, and for a time they were actually comfortable. But then it
happened: another wave flipped the raft upright again. Suddenly
the five men found themselves sitting in a life raft with a constantly
growing tear in its bottom. The weight of their bodies gradually
ripped apart the underpinnings of the raft. In a half hour they were

forced back into the water, this time clinging to the insides of their now doughnut-shaped raft. They tried to maintain their spirits, but it was difficult. Other than Gibson, who kept up a steady patter of jokes, the men were too tired to talk much.

In the darkness before dawn no one heard the black wave that finally got them. One moment they were inside the raft, shoulder to shoulder, breathing hard. The next they were airborne, hurtling down the face of the gigantic unseen wave. Stanley was driven deep beneath the raft, but somehow managed to keep his hold on it. Fighting to the surface, he looked all around and saw nothing but blackness. "Is everyone here?" he shouted.

"Yeah!" he heard a sputtering voice answer to one side. It was Gibson, the only one of the five who had worn a safety harness he had clipped to the raft.

Stanley craned his head, looking for the others. His heart sank: about 300 yards back he could see two of the three men. He was never sure whom he missed: Lawler, John Dean, a Sydney attorney, or Mike Bannister. All three men were gone.

"We can't do anything for them," Stanley said. "It's impossible."

"Just hang on," Gibson said. "For ourselves."…

All down the east coast of New South Wales and out past Gabo Island, the rescues continued in the first hours after dawn. The remaining sailors aboard *Sword of Orion* scrambled aboard a hovering Seahawk, while a medevac out of Canberra winched the seven survivors off *Business Post Naiad*, leaving the bodies of Phil Skeggs and Bruce Guy to be picked up later. *B-52* struggled under its own power into Eden harbor just after lunchtime. In the hour before dawn the yacht's port-side window had imploded, sending gushers of seawater below; the crew had somehow managed to nail wooden planks over the windows and had spent the rest of the morning bailing with buckets. Tony Mowbray's *Solo Globe Challenge* would be one of the last to reach port, limping into Eden on Wednesday morning.

Late Monday afternoon the lifeboat carrying Richard Winning and three other survivors from *Winston Churchill* was spotted, and everyone was winched aboard a waiting helicopter. Like those aboard *Churchill's* other raft, Winning's group had capsized twice during the night. Unlike the occupants of the other raft, however, Winning had bravely swum outside and forcibly righted the rubber inflatable, which had then survived the night intact....

9 P.M.

Night began to fall with no sign of *Churchill's* second life raft. At the rescue center in Canberra, hope was dwindling that the men would be found. At Merimbula the civilian aircraft—those without any night-rescue capabilities—began landing, one by one. None had seen anything that looked remotely like a life raft. Then, just after 9, a P3C Orion on its way back to Merimbula saw a light flashing in the darkening ocean below. Descending to 500 feet, the pilot spied two men clinging to a shredded orange life raft. It was John Stanley and "Gibbo" Gibson, still alive after twenty-eight hours in the water.

"Gibbo!" Stanley rasped, swinging a handheld strobe. "I think they've seen us!"

Within minutes, during which the sun set, Lieutenant Commander Rick Neville had his navy Seahawk hovering seventy feet above Stanley and Gibson. Petty Officer Shane Pashley winched down a wire into the waves below and, as Neville fought to maintain position in the gusting winds, managed to get a rescue strop around Gibson. As the two men were lifted skyward, a terrific gust blew the Seahawk sideways, dumping the pair back into the waves. Neville swung the chopper around once more, and this time the two waterlogged men were successfully winched aboard.

It was too much for Neville. His Radalt auto-hover system was being overtaxed by the winds, and he was unwilling to send Pashley back into the ocean. Stanley, he decided, would have to make it into the rescue strop on his own. As Neville maneuvered the Seahawk back over the raft, Pashley dangled the strop down into the sea, and Stanley somehow grabbed it and hoisted his upper body into it. The winch lifted him into the air, but when he was twenty feet above the waves, Stanley felt a weight around his ankles and realized, to his dismay, that he was still hooked to his life raft, which was sagging in midair below him. Reluctantly he shrugged himself out of the strop and dropped like a stone back into the sea, where he managed to unhook the raft. Once again the strop was dangled to him, and once again he got into it. This time everything worked. After more than a day in the ocean, Stanley and Gibson were on their way home.

8 A.M. Tuesday

As *Sayonara* tacked the last mile up the Derwent River toward the Hobart docks, a small launch with a bagpiper aboard swung alongside. It was the most stunning sunrise Ellison had ever seen, splashed of rose and pink and five different hues of blue, and as the pipes played a mournful tune, the enormity of what the fleet had endured hit all twenty-three men aboard the winning yacht. *Sayonara*'s sideband radio had shorted out, and it hadn't been until late Monday afternoon that the crew learned of the tragedies in their wake. As they reached the dock and piled out to hug their loved ones, Ellison was overwhelmed. "It was an incredible moment of clarity, the beauty and fragility of life, the preciousness of it all; that's when people appreciated what we had been through," he recalls. "Having said that, if I live to be a thousand years old, I'll never do it again. Never."

Amid all-too predictable recriminations, Hugo van Kretschmar, commodore of the Cruising Yacht Club of Australia, stoutly defended the club's decision to continue the race despite warnings of bad weather. Even as he announced an internal investigation, van Kretschmar pointed out, correctly, that the decision whether to race is traditionally left up to the skipper of each boat. Yacht-club officials, after all, had the same forecasts that every skipper had. As a result, few of the sailors who survived the race were willing to attack the organizers. One exception was Peter Joubert of *Kingurra*, who emerged from several weeks in the hospital sharply critical of race management. "The race organizers weren't properly in touch with what was going on out there—they just didn't know enough," Joubert says. "It's only a yacht race. It's not a race to the death." Outside Australia, the judgment was just as harsh. "They should have waited; there is ample precedent for waiting," notes Gary Jobson, the ESPN sailing analyst. "But race officials were under a lot of pressure. Live TV, all these people, a major holiday."

Three days after *Sayonara* crossed the finish line more than 5,000 people gathered on Hobart's Constitution Dock for the memorial service for the six men who died in the race. The funerals of Bruce Guy, Phil Skeggs, James Lawler, and Mike Bannister were to follow shortly; the bodies of John Dean and Glyn Charles have never been found. "We will miss you always; we will remember you always; we will learn from the tragic circumstances of your passing," van Kretschmar said as the muted bells of St. David's Cathedral rang out. "May the everlasting voyage you have now embarked on be blessed with calm seas and gentle breezes. May you never have to reef or change a headsail in the night. May your bunk always be warm and dry."

Bryan Burrough, a special correspondent for Vanity Fair, *is the author of four books, including the #1* New York Times *bestseller* Barbarians at the Gate *and* Public Enemies: America's Greatest Crime Wave and the Birth of the FBI, 1933–34. *Burrough lives in New Jersey with his wife and two sons.*

WILLIAM T. VOLLMANN

$\star^{\star}\star$

The Street of Stares

Racial tensions have a human face.

No, no, I did not go all the way to Blacktown (and in Launceston a disgusted cab driver said: Have you heard the latest? In your country the schoolchildren have to sing Baa, baa, green sheep in order to avoid offending the niggers. Next thing you know some do-gooder will say the name "Blacktown's" not good enough for them!); I did not go all the way to Blacktown, because Redfern was closer, and because a waiter had proudly related: I took a girl to Redfern and she went white as a sheet! She didn't know we had neighborhoods like that in Australia.—Being already as white as a sheet myself, in part due to birth, in part to illness, I figured that no red fern or black town or green sheep could make me seem any whiter. The NEXT TRAIN sign said BLACKTOWN but I did not go there; I rode between the grim-grimed pillars and arches with steel on top, was carried out past bulldozers gnawing gravel and then in again. NO THOROUGHFARE. TRESPASSERS WILL BE PROSECUTED. That was what you saw if you tried to exit the wrong way at Redfern Station. The wide-graveled channels of railway beds beset me with brick walls. The train went on to Blacktown, and a man with a pole came and slammed Blacktown away to bring up another destination.

Under the sign, another man stood drinking V.B. He held the can very tightly in his hand. He did not quite reek as some drunks do but he was beery enough. He looked into my face. They called him black and that was what he sometimes called himself, but actually his skin was more reddish, almost Venetian red like that of the brown-haired Aboriginal girl on the train who'd looked at me with such big searching brown eyes, working her plump, kissable lips as if to say something that she'd never said; this man opened his mouth and said: Buy me another, mate? How 'bout it?—Then he fell down. That was Redfern Station.

Outside there was a street, and across the street was a wall with a giant snake painted on it in Aboriginal style, with the words 40,000 YEARS IS A LONG TIME...40,000 YEARS STILL ON MY MIND. Turning the corner of this street, at the Redfern Aboriginal Cooperative, I found myself looking down a narrow street where right away a fat woman with a beer in her hand said: Excuse me. Could you spare a smoke? and the wall went on down that street, muraled with silhouettes who had white-dotted skeletons; and I saw grimy rainbows and dot-painted flowers and then the street narrowed further, sloping down into shady house-walls where people sat on their porches listening to radios, drinking, smoking and staring out. This was the Street of Stares. I had the feeling of coming into a place where I did not belong. White shoes and socks glowed on dark and shaded bodies, all lining the way and watching me. Second storeys gaped doorlessly like the bomb-burned flats I'd seen in Sarajevo; sky shone through one such hole; the others were dank and dirty and graffiti'd, coolly unfriendly like the eyes of the watchers, or so it seemed to me as I went on, remembering times when I'd come into certain black neighborhoods in my own country and found myself immediately hated, but then a man nodded back at me and said: G'day, mate! and I was comfortable again, which might have been stupid, because Snake, who that day became my wise uncle, told me: I'm not allowed to go out at night. My woman don't let me. Lotsa fights. I tell you now, don't walk around here.—That was Snake, and his woman was Sadie, and then there were Ruthie and Rob, all of whom lived together farther down that narrow street which smelled in places like air-plane glue, not as far as the very end where thick gratings and brick mirrors greeted the next highway, across which lay the stink-ing pub where I bought the case of Victoria Bitters so that Rob would like me and take me in to Ruthie, Sadie and Snake behind that wall built less of grimy brick than of stares.

Originally we was from up the bush, Snake said, opening the first V.B. North coast. We came just visiting here. Then we stayed.

Tell you something about Redfern, the younger man cut in. They got a different attitude here. A bad attitude.

So why did you come vis-iting then? I asked.

Well, really there wasn't nothing up there, said Snake. Not enough to do. More opportunity in the city than in the country. That's why we're here.

Yeah, look at him talk, laughed Rob as he took out a beer. What kinda *opportu-nity* have you found, Snake? What kinda *opportunity's* any-body got in this town?

A lot of people playin' the numbers just to pass the time, Snake admitted. Really can't go anywhere. I'm only just visitin'. Wanna go back, huntin' and fishin'. And my woman, she's from the snow country, the table lands.

"The government, they use words, too. They plenty good at using words just like they used to be plenty good at using guns. They stopped using guns on us black people now. Now they use words on us. They come here to Mowanjum, they have a talk-talk-talk with us. Lotsa times they come. Lotsa talk-talk-talk. Plenty meetings, meetings, meetings. They tell us they gonna do this and they gonna do that. They tell us they gonna give Mitchell Plateau back to us so we can go and live there.

"They tell us when they're through diggin' holes for all the aluminum we can have the land back. Oh, no, not all the land, just a little piece of the land. Just the size of a matchbox."

◆

—Harvey Arden,
Dreamkeepers: A Spirit-Journey into Aboriginal Australia

I miss the trees, the mountains, the grass, agreed Sadie wearily, sipping at her V.B.

All we need up there was a tent, said Snake. Like, you could go to the river and get everything. I can kill anything with a stone that big. I could take two men out. I done it before.

Maybe someday I'll go somewhere, said Ruthie. Because they always stare. If I was sittin' on a train, I look out the window so they don't bother me. Some people don't have no respect. Oh, how they stare!

Shall we speak of stares? I myself seldom fail to gaze into other faces as they come to me. Looking is a natural act, and if Ruthie had come to my notice on a bus I would have looked at her because she was beautiful, but Ruthie would not have known that I was looking at her for that reason. That afternoon she said to me: When you get in a bus, the first thing people do is look you up and down, see if you're black.—I guess that was how it was for me, that first time I came into Redfern. They were all gazing at me— all of them!—and I was not their color. Maybe each gazed at me for his own reasons, but because they all gazed I had to assume a single reason, the same one that Ruthie assumed in her bitter anger. So perhaps the way to discover people's lusts and angers is not to fish behind their peering eyes but to read what they write on the walls of their public toilets. In a men's room at the Sydney airport I came across this profundity:

KILL ALL ABO'S I HATE COONS HA HA FUCKEM

which another soul had seconded as follows:

ABO'S WILL RUIN AUSSIE LAND

—a remarkable reversal of fact which took my breath away so that I almost did not appreciate the remarks of the third sage who had weighed and balanced and urinated and concluded: GOOKS ARE WORSE.—What exactly does it mean for land to become Aussiefied? Let me introduce a retired farmer I met in Tasmania, where the exterminations of the last century enjoyed great success: there are no full-blooded Tasmanian Aborigines anymore. Horses bowed in the whitish and yellowish grass where this farmer had lived his years out, and huge cylindrical bales stood upon the fields like gateposts for the low blue sea-wave of mountains to the west. Age parted him from his farm, but his heart lived there yet; I think he was homesick for his peppermint gum trees.—The wildlife around here is a tremendous problem, he told me. You clear a field here and the animals will come from miles around, just strip it, clean it out, particularly kangaroos and wallabies.—He was the son of pioneers whose hard work had justified them to themselves. The land belonged to them. The kangaroos had no right to it. I requested his views on those strange, dark, barrel-shaped marsupials called Tasmanian devils, and he said: People in fat lamb areas could have experienced a lot more problems with them than I did. On my 250 acres, while I did see them, they were never in sufficient numbers to cause a problem.—Their foreseeable extinction could not grieve him. Maybe he was even glad. I was even glad. It is not for me to hold him blameworthy. He paid allegiance to the laws he believed in, and lived quietly. If some native plant or animal caused "trouble" or a "problem" then he resolutely defended his interests; otherwise he kept neutral. He didn't kill venomous snakes, for instance, unless he found them close to the house. This philosophy, so conveniently practical with its tiny cabinets of self sameness, had come with a drawer to fit native people in also.—The whites have just about had enough of free handouts to the blacks, he explained. A few educated Aboriginals tend to cause a bit of trouble. The uneducated black, he don't expect so much.

Snake, Sadie, Ruthie and Rob did not expect very much, I guess, maybe because they knew that Redfern was Aussie land.— This used to be a white community, Snake said, opening another V.B. Before the blackfellas moved in. The whitefellas want it back. They want to put a carpark in.

William T. Vollmann's books include Rising Up and Rising Down, You Bright and Risen Angels, The Rainbow Stories, *and* The Atlas, *from which this story was excerpted. He is the recipient of a Whiting Foundation Award, and he lives in California.*

PART FIVE

THE LAST WORD

TONY HORWITZ

Noodling

*Traveling through the Outback is risky
and serendipitous, like life.*

THERE'S ONLY ONE THING I DREAD MORE THAN SETTING UP CAMP at night in the Great Outdoors, and that's breaking camp at morning in the Great Outdoors. At least in the dark you can just curl up in your bag and be done with it—if there are no cyclones lurking about. But mornings are pure hell. I like to wake slowly, over a cup of coffee and the sports page, not scramble around in the dawn chill for socks and shoes, then hike off for a "dingo's breakfast"—a pee and a good look around. That's my idea of a lousy way to start the day.

Weathering a hurricane has one advantage. Since I've got my entire wardrobe on already, all I have to do is shed a few layers into my pack and hike out to the road. The night breeze has died down, from cyclone to mere gale-force winds, so I'm reasonably cozy, propped against my pack with a blanket around my shoulders.

If I only had some food. It is part of my poor camping technique to never have victuals on hand when I'm a million miles from nowhere. And there's still no sign of a proprietor at the roadhouse. Maybe he's asleep, as any sensible person would be at this hour. Maybe I should wake him up. Maybe he's awake already, cooking me two dozen flapjacks with six fried eggs smiling on top, and coffee strong enough to kick–start a cadaver. Then again, maybe he's off shopping in Alice.

I try to distract myself by reciting "The Love Song of J. Alfred Prufrock." I memorized the first few stanzas between Sydney and Alice, but now, in the middle of the poem, I keep getting stuck on the same two lines: "I have measured out my life in coffee spoons" and "Would it have been worth it, after all, after the cups, the marmalade, the tea." The whole poem's about breakfast if you read it right.

My imaginary marmalade and tea is interrupted by a very un-poetic roar down the road. bbbbbbrrrrrr. BBBBBrrrrrrrr! I squint at the horizon. It looks as if the night wind has blown away all the trees, hills and scrub. The landscape is so flat and bare that I feel as if I might be able to see all the way to Alice. But all I can pick out is a tiny speck, coming toward me, going bbbbrrrr, BBBBBrrrrr! It is moving at a pained, slow crawl, like me before my morning coffee. A few minutes later, the ute [Americans would say pickup truck] limps to a halt beside me. There are four Aboriginal men staring sullenly out from the cab and a dozen jerry cans of petrol vibrating in the back. Judging from the noise, there's some kind of prehistoric beast with pins stuck in its nose stuffed under the bonnet.

"Where ya headed?" I shout at the driver, a very black man with a massive bush of hair. He looks at me blandly. I point at the southern horizon and bob my head up and down.

"Pedy," he mumbles. I point at the back of the truck, then at myself and bob my head again.

"Hey, mate. Okay," he mumbles. I scramble into the back and squeeze myself between two petrol drums, like a stowaway on an oil tanker. We rumble off at twelve miles an hour and the hideous noise starts again. BBBRRRRRRRRRRR! I have gone from the eye of a hurricane to the belly of a sick, screaming whale. BBBBB-BBRRRRRRRRRRRRRR! I toss the blanket over my head again and the noise goes down a decibel or two. BBBbbbbbrrrrrrr. It's beginning to look like another underwear job.

It's also beginning to look like a very slow drive to Coober Pedy. Ten minutes down the road, the driver stops and feeds the monster a drum of petrol. Then he rolls the empty barrel into the scrub and hops in beside me, letting someone else take the wheel. I offer the three words of Pitjantjatjara I picked up at Ayers Rock—*Uluru, paya* (thank you), and *rama-rama* (crazy). He offers his sum total of English—okay, hey, mate, yes. We shout our three words in every possible combination, then smile and nod at each other for 125 miles.

Actually, it's hard not to nod when you're swerving and bumping over a road that's like gravel laid over choppy surf. Only the oil drums keep me from going overboard. And there's nothing to look at except a cloud of dust shooting out behind the truck, with glimpses to either side of baked and empty desert. By midmorning, the heat becomes staggering; even in the windblown rear of the ute, I can feel the sun burning every inch of exposed flesh. Nothing to do but huddle beneath my blanket, wedge some of it under my bum as a shock absorber, and tough it out.

A few hours later my companion squeezes up front again with his mates. Then something strange happens. The ute veers off the main road (such as it is) and onto what looks like a dingo trail. I clutch the side of the truck as we bounce between bushes and churn through deep sand. I have a hitchhiker's distrust of detours, particularly when the main road is itself a detour from any habitable territory.

I bang on the back window and get no response; apparently, there's some kind of domestic squabble going on up front. The ute lurches to a halt behind a clump of mulga and the four men pile out, talking loudly in Pitjantjatjara and gesturing at me. All I know is that something ugly is about to happen, and whatever it is, I'm along for the ride.

One thing's for sure; I'm not going to talk my way out of this one, whatever it is. All I can do is listen to their chatter and let my paranoia run riot in translation. ("How much money do you think he has?" "Do we kill him or just leave him here to bake?") Nor can I sort of mosey off into the scrub—"Some other time, fellas"—and run for it. Not here, at the center of the bottomless dustbowl that is Outback South Australia. I'd make it three hours at the most before collapsing of heat exhaustion, dehydration, or worse.

"Hey, mate!" It is the driver speaking. He is walking toward me, sweating nervously, with one hand clutching something in his pocket.

"Hey, mate!" He pulls his hand out and thrusts it toward me. I freeze. Then his fist uncurls to reveal a pile of crumpled two-dollar notes.

"Okay, yes!" he shouts.

I look at him blankly. Yes, what? He's exhausted his English and his body language isn't helping. Nor does my extensive Pitjantjatjara vocabulary seem appropriate. *Rama-rama? Uluru?*

"Grog, mate," says one of his companions. "Black fellas can't buy us grog."

We move to dust language now and he draws a map headed back the way we came. South of the spot where we turned off, he sketches a square, and what looks like a bottle. "Black fellas can't buy us grog," he repeats, handing me the money and the key to the ute. "Two, mate."

Slowly I get the picture. They want me to take their money, and their truck, and drive to the roadhouse to buy two cases of beer. For some reason—a racist publican, I assume—they can't buy it themselves. They'll wait here until I return.

The request says a lot about their trust and my lack of it. All I have done to win their confidence is utter three words of pidgin Pitjantjatjara. All they have done to lose my trust is talk loudly in a language I don't understand. Paranoia took care of the rest.

My first reaction is relief that nothing sinister is afoot and that I can atone for my suspicions by helping them out. For the first time on my journey, I feel as if I've violated the unwritten contract of trust between hitchhiker and hitchhikee. But they don't know that, and anyway, I can make up for it by buying a few beers.

But as I dodge sand traps on my way back to the main road, another dilemma surfaces. I am not by nature an interventionist on the matter of personal habit. Live and let live; drink and let them get drunk. That's the reckless half of my hitchhiker's valor. The discreet hitchhiker in me is screaming caution. We are still 200 miles of rough empty road from Coober Pedy. With a case or two of beer on board, it could be a long, even futile journey.

Or is this prejudice again, welling up in the background as it threatened to do a moment ago, when I began hearing the racist chorus of Territory voices I've managed to ignore until now?..."Don't turn your back on a black fella..." "An Abo will cut your throat faster than you can say boomerang..." "Whatever you do, mate, don't take a ride with boongs."

My contact with Aborigines has consistently contradicted these dire warnings. From Cunnamulla to Tennant Creek to Ayers Rock, I've been treated by blacks with an openness and generosity not always evident among whites. This last incident is further proof of Aboriginal goodwill. How many white drivers would entrust a scruffy hitchhiker with their piggy bank and sole means of transportation?

That's what makes me nervous; there is a whiff of desperation about the request. But the real problem is, I have no way of knowing if this will lead to a blowout, and no way of coping if it does. North of Alice, there was the occasional roadhouse at which to abandon ship. Here, nothing, we haven't even seen another car in four hours. The barrier between us isn't racial, it's linguistic. If things get sloppy, which they easily can after two cases of beer, we'll need more than dust drawings to sort the situation out.

As the roadhouse comes into view, I am leaning toward a compromise. My instinct is confirmed by a huge sign above the bar, which announces that it's illegal to buy alcohol before heading into Aboriginal territory. Two cases of beer might make me conspicuous. Two six-packs won't, and it also won't be enough to leave me on a walkabout in the South Australian desert.

The publican is the only person in the pub and he doesn't ask any questions. So I load up the beer, and fill my tucker box with stale bread and overpriced cheese. Then, just for security, I order a meat pie as well. After hours with no food, the microwaved chunks of meat go down like coq au vin. Picky eaters don't survive a day of roadhouse cuisine.

My companions appear unsurprised when I return with most of their money unspent and only a dozen beers. And the speed with which the tinnies are drained, crushed, and tossed into the scrub quiets any qualms I had about disobeying orders.

I am about to pass around my bread and cheese when two of the men begin helping themselves. Their offhand manner makes me realize that the gesture is neither rude nor ravenous. Rather, it seems that food and drink are assumed to be public domain. Every twenty minutes or so through the morning, a waterbag and a lit cigarette were passed to me in the back of the truck. This was my ration, my right as an occupant of the ute. It would be inappropriate—even insulting—to suggest that my food was anything but part of the collective. We eat a few slices each, share the waterbag and cigarette pack, and climb aboard for the long drive to Coober Pedy.

This time my companion in the back is Joe, he of the "black fellas can't buy us grog." His English is good enough for a halting dialogue interspersed with sign language and sketches on the dusty side of an oil drum. As far as I can make out, the men are traveling from their home on a reserve in the Northern Territory to spend a few weeks "noodling" for opal around Coober Pedy. Noodling, as Joe describes it, is a leisurely sort of look-see through the piles of rubble left by white miners and white machines.

"White fellas always go, go go," Joe says, pantomiming men driving drills and pickaxes into the ground. "They miss so much riches that way." Noodling, it seems, is not a bad metaphor for the difference between our cultures.

Indeed, Joe doesn't miss a beat along the sixty miles of unsealed road we travel after stopping for beer. Every ten minutes or so he touches me on the arm and points off toward an empty horizon. Each time there is an emu or kangaroo, almost invisible to me, but obvious as a skyscraper to Joe. The foreground is clear enough, though; long lines of abandoned automobiles stretching beside both sides of the road, like parallel queues to a scrapyard just over the horizon. Burnt cars, stripped cars, overturned cars. The place looks like a training camp for terrorist car bombers.

"Black fellas bad with cars," Joe explains. "No buy fixing out here." At least there are plenty of dead cows to keep the car bodies company. But otherwise, nothing. It is as bare and bleak a landscape as I've ever clapped eyes on.

For several thousand miles, I've been struggling for un-superlatives to communicate the un-ness of Outback scenery. The towns and people are easy enough; they have faces, buildings, features. But what can you say about a landscape that is utterly featureless? A landscape whose most distinguishing quality is that it has no distinguishing qualities whatsoever? Flat, bare, dry. Bleak, empty, arid. Barren, wretched, bleached. You can reshuffle the adjectives but the total is still the sum of its parts. And the total is still zero. Zot. Nought. Ayers Rock has a lot of blank space to answer for.

To the early explorers, this arid region north of Adelaide was simply Australia's "Ghastly Blank." Charles Sturt set off into the desert east of here in 1844 to find the inland sea, and so sure was he of success that his party included two sailors and a boat (as well as 11 horses, 200 sheep, 30 bullocks, and 4 drays.) "I shall envy that man who shall first place the flag of our native country in the center of our adopted land," he declared. But after staggering for some months through the desert, Sturt reached neither sea nor center—just the dry expanse of Lake Torrens. "The desolate barrenness, the dreary monotony, the denuded aspect of this spot is beyond description," he wrote in his journal, having described it rather well. Daniel Brock, a member of Sturt's party added, "This scene is the Climax of Desolation....Miserable! Horrible!" Not long after, Sturt launched his boat on the Darling River and then retreated to Adelaide.

Looking out the back of the ute I am amazed that Sturt made it as far as he did. Desert to the right of me, desert to the left of me, a plume of car dust shooting down the middle, I claim this spot as the landing pad for the alien probe I imagined my first day in Australia. The alien probe that drops down, declared "No life," and heads back to outer space. The probe people could sniff around her for a few hundred miles in every direction and come to the same conclusion. No life. No bloody way.

Just the sort of place you'd never want to break down in; just
the thought that comes to me as the engine coughs and goes
silent, leaving the ute half on and half off the highway. It seems
that the moaning beast under the bonnet has finally been put out
of its misery.

The four men pile out and take turns staring through the steam
rising out from under the bonnet. They study the ute's Japanese repair manual, upside down. Then they begin staring vacantly off
into space. It is the noodling school of repair. We are about to join
the long queue of automobile corpses. Looking out at the empty
desert, I don't like our chances either.

I am an automobile moron, a clod when it comes to all things
mechanical. But desperation makes for marvelous self-improve-
ment. Studying the manual, and then tangle of metal under the
bonnet, it becomes obvious to me that we no longer possess a fanbelt, if indeed we ever did. Also, whatever water the radiator once
held is now evaporating on the ground at the rate of about fifty
quarts per second.

Joe fashions a fanbelt by knotting the spare rubber flapping
around under the bonnet. But feeding our meager supply of water
to the radiator seems a little risky. If we do, and the ute still doesn't
move, we'll be fashioning straws to drink from the radiator within
a few hours.

So once again I am called into service for the purpose of liq-
uids procurement. While the four men huddle out of sight—or as
out of sight as you can in a desert, which means behind the ute—
I wait for a passing car to beg some water from. It seems that for
black fellas in this stretch of Outback, water is as difficult to come
by as beer.

The first car to pass is driven by a Romanian refugee named
Milos. He's headed north from Adelaide to "see some bush" and is
happy to give me his entire water supply, all two quarts of it. I explain to him that there's no Danube running through South
Australia and hand him his water back, along with the tourist
guide the New Zealander gave me yesterday.

A short while later, two Aborigines pull up in a battered truck. When my companions hear the familiar, accented English of fellow blacks, they pop out from behind the ute like guests at a surprise party. The six men chat away for half an hour, then conversation is followed by a pirate raid on the newcomers' water, tucker, and cigarettes. Then everyone begins chatting again. I assume that I'm witnessing a chance reunion of long-lost friends or relations. In actual fact, one of the newcomers tells me, they've met only once, on an earlier noodling expedition to Coober Pedy. The color of one's skin can be as powerful a bond in the Outback as it can be a barrier.

An hour later, the party gets around to fixing the radiator. Water doesn't revive the ute. But with the truck pushing us from behind, the engine kicks into life again, or a tubercular version of it. We cough and wheeze down the highway for a hundred yards or so—before everyone decides this is cause for further celebration. So we pile out, chat, and smoke for another half hour, then get kick-started again down the road toward Coober Pedy.

Relieved, I let out an Indian war cry—*Yihaaaa! Yihaaaaaaa-aaaaa!*—and Joe imitates me for the hour-long drive. "Do it one more," he says, as if promoting a singer to repeat a favorite refrain. "One more time, Tony." The two of us are roughly the same color from the waves of the reddish-brown dust we've been swimming through all day. So there we sit, two red-skinned Apaches, belting out war cries all the way to the opal fields of South Australia.

Late in the day we reach Coober Pedy with the fanbelt still intact, the radiator cool. I climb out of the ute, shake each man's hand…"Hey mate, okay"…"Yes"…"Okay, yes"…and hoist my pack over one shoulder. It feels like a bag full of wet fish is crawling down my back. I yank the pack off and discover that one of the cans of diesel fuel has been leaking onto it for the past ten hours or so. The frame-and-canvas pack looks and feels like a soggy spring roll, abandoned in the grease for a few days. I think of all the lit cigarettes passed between Joe and the cab during the day, directly over the diesel-soaked pack. One stray ash and my clothes would have launched to outer space.

Tony Horwitz also contributed "Sand Sailing" in Part Three. This story was excerpted from his book, One for the Road: Hitchhiking through the Australian Outback.

Recommended Reading

Arden, Harvey. *Dreamkeepers: A Spirit-Journey into Aboriginal Australia.* New York: HarperPerennial, 1994.

Béchervaise, John Mayston. *Australia: World of Difference.* Adelaide, Australia: Rigby Ltd., 1967.

Blairney, Geoffrey. *Triumph of the Nomads: A History of Aboriginal Australia.* London: MacMillan; New York: Viking Press, 1982.

Brewster, Barbara Marie. *Down Under All Over: A Love Affair with Australia.* Portland, Oreg.: Four Winds Publishing, 1991.

Bryson, Bill. *In a Sunburned Country.* New York: Broadway Books, 2001.

Cahill, Tim. *Pecked to Death by Ducks.* New York: Vintage Departures, 1993.

Carter, Jeff. *People of the Inland.* Adelaide, Australia: Rigby Ltd., 1966.

Carter, Paul. *The Road to Botany: An Exploration of Landscape and History.* New York: Random House, 1988.

Chatwin, Bruce. *The Songlines.* New York: Penguin Books, 1987.

Child, Greg. *Postcards from the Ledge: Collected Mountaineering Writings of Greg Child.* Seattle, Wash.: The Mountaineers, 1998.

Christmas, Linda. *The Ribbon and the Ragged Square: An Australian Journey.* New York: Penguin Books, 1986.

Condon, Sean. *Sean & David's Long Drive.* Hawthorne, Australia: Lonely Planet Publications, 1996.

Conway, Jill Ker. *The Road from Coorain.* New York: Vintage Departures, 1989.

Cowan, James G. *Messengers of the Gods: Tribal Elders Reveal the Ancient Wisdom of the Earth.* New York: Bell Tower, 1993.

Davidson, Robyn. *Tracks.* New York: Pantheon Books, 1980.

Davis, Jack. Mudrooroo Narogin, Stephen Muecke, and Adam Shoemaker, eds. *Paperbark: A Collection of Black Australian Writings*. Australia: University of Queensland Press, 1990.

Fuller, Elizabeth. *When You See the Emu in the Sky: My Journey of Self-Discovery in the Outback*. New York: William Morrow and Company, 1997.

Horwitz, Tony. *One for the Road: Hitchhiking through the Australian Outback*. New York: Vintage Books, 1987.

Hughes, Robert. *The Fatal Shore: The Epic of Australia's Founding*. New York: Vintage Books, 1986.

Iyer, Pico. *Falling off the Map: Some Lonely Places of the World*. New York: Borzoi Book, 1993.

Kluge, John W. *Kunwinjku Art from Injalak 1991-1992 The John W. Kluge Commission*. North Adelaide, South Australia: Museum Art International Pty. Ltd., 1994.

Morgan. Sally. *My Place*. New York: Back Bay Books, 1987.

Morris, Jan. *Sydney*. London: Penguin Books Ltd., 1992.

Smith, Roff Martin. *Australia: Journey Through a Timeless Land*. Washington: National Geographic, 2000.

Symanski, Richard. *Outback Rambling*. Tucson: The University of Arizona Press, 1990.

Theroux, Paul. *The Happy Isles of Oceania: Paddling the Pacific*. New York: G. P. Putnam's Sons, 1992.

Wright, Ronald. *Home and Away*. Toronto: Alfred A. Knopf Canada, 1993

Index

Index of Contributors

Acknowledgments

I would especially like to thank Amy Greimann Carlson, whose hard work and dedication were instrumental in bringing this book from the drawing board to completion. Many thanks also to my co-workers at Travelers' Tales, both past and present, especially James, Wenda, Sean, and Tim O'Reilly, Lisa Bach, Susan Brady, Deborah Greco, Raj Khadka, Jennifer Leo, Natanya Pearlman, Tara Austen Weaver, and Cindy Williams. Thanks also to Cynthia Lamb for her endless patience and careful, devoted attention and to Judy Johnson and Trisha Schwartz.

A special thanks to the countless people in Australia who have enhanced my travels and the work on this project, especially Scotty Boyd, Max Davidson, Malcolm Schultz, Maura Mc Cabe, Kieran Hennessy, and the good folks at the Australian Tourist Commission.

And very special thanks to Paula Mc Cabe, Alanna and Érne Habegger Mc Cabe for brightening every day.

"A Rock and a Hard Place" by Ronald Wright excerpted from *Home and Away* by Ronald Wright. Copyright © 1993 by Ronald Wright. Reprinted by permission of the author and Alfred A. Knopf, Inc. (Canada).

"Sing" by Bruce Chatwin excerpted from *The Songlines* by Bruce Chatwin. Copyright © 1987 by Bruce Chatwin. Used by permission of Viking Penguin, a division of Penguin Putnam, Inc., the legal representatives of C. B. Chatwin, and Jonathan Cape as publisher.

"Patterns in the Sand" by Robyn Davidson excerpted from *Tracks* by Robyn Davidson. Copyright © 1980 by Robyn Davidson. Reprinted by permission of Pantheon Books, a division of Random House, Inc., and Gillon Aitken Associates Ltd.

"Five Thousand Miles from Anywhere" by Pico Iyer excerpted from *Falling Off the Map: Some Lonely Places of the World* by Pico Iyer. Copyright © 1993 by Pico Iyer. Reprinted by permission of Alfred A. Knopf, Inc.

"Shearing Time" by Jill Ker Conway excerpted from *The Road from Coorain* by Jill Ker Conway. Copyright © 1989 by Jill Conway. Reprinted by permission of Alfred A. Knopf, Inc.

"Cutting Teeth in Queensland" by Robert L. Strauss published with permission from the author. Copyright © 2000 by Robert L. Strauss.

"Fraser Sand" by Tony Perrottet reprinted from the November/December 1994 issue of *Islands* magazine. Copyright © 1994 by Islands Publishing Company. Reprinted by permission.

"The Beach Comber" by Paul Theroux excerpted from *The Happy Isles of Oceania: Paddling the Pacific* by Paul Theroux. Copyright © 1992 by Paul Theroux. No changes shall be made to the above work without the express written consent of The Wylie Agency, Inc.

"The Red Centre" by Susan Storm published with permission from the author. Copyright © 2000 by Susan Storm.

"Report from Quinkan Country" by Greg Child excerpted from *Postcards from the Ledge: Collected Mountaineering Writings of Greg Child* by Greg Child. Copyright © 1998 by Greg Child. Reprinted by permission of The Mountaineers.

"A Visit to the Wandjina" by Harvey Arden excerpted from *Dreamkeepers: A Spirit-Journey into Aboriginal Australia* by Harvey Arden. Copyright © 1994 by Harvey Arden. Reprinted by permission of HarperCollins Publishers, Inc.

"Eco Trippers" by Tom Mueller reprinted from the April 1998 issue of *Hemispheres*, the magazine of United Airlines. Copyright © 1998 by Tom Mueller. Reprinted by permission of the author.

"In Hot Pursuit" by Stephanie Speakman reprinted from the March 1, 1998 issue of *The New York Times Sophisticated Traveler Magazine.* Copyright © 1998 by Stephanie Speakman. Reprinted by permission of the author.

"A Wild Ride in Arnhem Land" by Larry Habegger published with permission from the author. Copyright © 2000 by Larry Habegger.

"An Island to Ourselves" by Diane Christiansen excerpted from *No Shit! There I was…Wild Stories from Wild People* edited by Michael Hodgson. Copyright © 1998 by Michael Hodgson. Reprinted with permission of The Globe Pequot Press, Old Saybrook, CT, www.globe-pequot.com.

"Sand Sailing" and "Noodling" by Tony Horwitz excerpted from *One for the Road: Hitchhiking through the Australian Outback* by Tony Horwitz. Copyright © 1987 by Tony Horwitz. Reprinted by permission of HarperCollins Publishers Australia.

"The Peacock's Tail" by David Yeadon excerpted from *Lost Worlds: Exploring the World's Remote Places* by David Yeadon. Copyright © 1991 by David Yeadon. Reprinted by permission of the author.

"Thirst" by Roff Martin Smith reprinted from the February 1998 issue of *National Geographic.* Copyright © 1998 by Roff Martin Smith. Reprinted by permission of the National Geographic Society.

"The Persistence of Rain" by Michelle Snider published with permission from the author. Copyright © 2000 by Michelle Snider.

Selection from *Dreamkeepers: A Spirit-Journey into Aboriginal Australia* by Harvey Arden copyright © 1994 by Harvey Arden. Reprinted by permission of HarperCollins Publishers, Inc.

Selections from *The Fatal Shore: The Epic of Australia's Founding* by Robert Hughes copyright © 1986 by Robert Hughes. Reprinted by permission of Alfred A. Knopf, Inc., a division of Random House, Inc., and Harvill Press.

Selection from "From Tassie to the Top End" by Larry Habegger published with permission from the author. Copyright © 2000 by Larry Habegger.

Selections from "Going Off the Deep End" by Tony Perrottet reprinted from the March 1996 issue of *Escape* magazine. Copyright © 1996 by Tony Perrottet. Reprinted by permission of the author.

Selection from "The Language of Oz" by Daniel Burstein reprinted from the September 1990 issue of *Travel Holiday*. Copyright © 1990 by Daniel Burstein. Reprinted by permission of the author and Curtis Brown Ltd.

Selections from *Lost Worlds: Exploring the World's Remote Places* by David Yeadon copyright © 1991 by David Yeadon. Reprinted by permission of the author.

Selection from "Making Tracks in Queensland" by Robert L. Strauss published with permission from the author. Copyright © 2000 by Robert L. Strauss.

Selection from "A Matter of Perspective" by J. Kingston Pierce published with permission from the author. Copyright © 2000 by J. Kingston Pierce.

Selection from *My Place* by Sally Morgan copyright © 1987 by Sally Jane Morgan. Reprinted by permission of Henry Holt and Company, Inc. and Fremantle Arts Centre Press.

Selection from "Not-So-Wild Wildlife" by Paul Prince reprinted from the April 1989 issue of *Travel Holiday*. Copyright © 1989 by Paul Prince. Reprinted by permission of the author.

Selections from "Off in the Wild Down Under" by Paul Prince reprinted from the April 1989 issue of *Travel Holiday*. Copyright © 1989 by Paul Prince. Reprinted by permission of the author.

Selection from "Old Blokes Network" by Bernadette Doran reprinted from the September 1998 issue of *Brandweek* magazine. Copyright © 1998 by *Brandweek*. Reprinted by permission of *Brandweek*.

Selection from "Outback Overview" by Kari Bodnarchuk published with permission from the author. Copyright © 2000 by Kari Bodnarchuk.

Selection from *Outback Rambling* by Richard Symanski copyright © 1990 by Richard Symanski. Reprinted by permission of The University of Arizona Press.

Selection from "Over the Top" by Roff Martin Smith reprinted from the February 1998 issue of *National Geographic*. Copyright © 1998 by Roff Martin Smith. Reprinted by permission of the National Geographic Society.

About the Editor

Larry Habegger, executive editor of Travelers' Tales, has been writing about travel since 1980. He has visited almost fifty countries and six of the seven continents, traveling from the frozen Arctic to equatorial rain forest, the high Himalayas to the Dead Sea. In the early 1980s he co-authored mystery serials for the *San Francisco Examiner* with James O'Reilly, and since 1985 their syndicated column, "World Travel Watch," has appeared in newspapers in five countries and on WorldTravelWatch.com. As series editors of Travelers' Tales, they have worked on some eighty titles, winning many awards for excellence. Habegger regularly teaches the craft of travel writing at workshops and writers conferences, and he lives with his family on Telegraph Hill in San Francisco.

TRAVELERS' TALES

THE POWER OF A GOOD STORY

New Releases

Women's Travel

A WOMAN'S EUROPE $17.95
True Stories
Edited by Marybeth Bond
An exhilarating collection of inspirational, adventurous, and entertaining stories by women exploring the romantic continent of Europe. From the bestselling author Marybeth Bond.

WOMEN IN THE WILD $17.95
True Stories of Adventure and Connection
Edited by Lucy McCauley
"A spiritual, moving, and totally female book to take you around the world and back."
— *Mademoiselle*

A MOTHER'S WORLD $14.95
Journeys of the Heart
Edited by Marybeth Bond & Pamela Michael
"These stories remind us that motherhood is one of the great unifying forces in the world"
— *San Francisco Examiner*

A WOMAN'S WORLD $18.95
True Stories of Life on the Road
Edited by Marybeth Bond
Introduction by Dervla Murphy

— ★ ★ ★ —
Lowell Thomas Award
—Best Travel Book

A WOMAN'S PASSION $17.95
FOR TRAVEL
More True Stories from
A Woman's World
Edited by Marybeth Bond & Pamela Michael
"A diverse and gripping series of stories!"
— Arlene Blum, author of
Annapurna: A Woman's Place

Food

ADVENTURES IN WINE $17.95
True Stories of Vineyards and Vintages around the World
Edited by Thom Elkjer
Humanity, community, and brotherhood comprise the marvelous virtues of the wine world. This collection toasts the warmth and wonders of this large extended family in stories by travelers who are wine novices and experts alike.

HER FORK IN $16.95
THE ROAD
Women Celebrate Food and Travel
Edited by Lisa Bach
A savory sampling of stories by the best writers in and out of the food and travel fields.

FOOD $18.95
A Taste of the Road
Edited by Richard Sterling
Introduction by Margo True

— ★ ★ ★ —
Silver Medal Winner of the
Lowell Thomas Award
—Best Travel Book

THE ADVENTURE $17.95
OF FOOD
True Stories of Eating Everything
Edited by Richard Sterling
"Bound to whet appetites for more than food." — *Publishers Weekly*

THE FEARLESS DINER $7.95
Travel Tips and Wisdom for Eating around the World
By Richard Sterling
Combines practical advice on foodstuffs, habits, and etiquette, with hilarious accounts of others' eating adventures.

Travel Humor

SAND IN MY BRA AND OTHER MISADVENTURES $14.95
Funny Women Write from the Road
Edited by Jennifer L. Leo
"A collection of ridiculous and sublime travel experiences."
—San Francisco Chronicle

HYENAS LAUGHED AT ME AND NOW I KNOW WHY $14.95
The Best of Travel Humor and Misadventure
Edited by Sean O'Reilly, Larry Habegger, and James O'Reilly
Hilarious, outrageous and reluctant voyagers indulge us with the best misadventures around the world.

LAST TROUT IN VENICE $14.95
The Far-Flung Escapades of an Accidental Adventurer
By Doug Lansky
"Traveling with Doug Lansky might result in a considerably shortened life expectancy…but what a way to go."
—Tony Wheeler, Lonely Planet Publications

NOT SO FUNNY WHEN IT HAPPENED $12.95
The Best of Travel Humor and Misadventure
Edited by Tim Cahill
Laugh with Bill Bryson, Dave Barry, Anne Lamott, Adair Lara, and many more.

THERE'S NO TOILET PAPER…ON THE ROAD LESS TRAVELED $12.95
The Best of Travel Humor and Misadventure
Edited by Doug Lansky

—★ ★ ★ —

Humor Book of the Year
—Independent Publisher's Book Award

—★ ★ ★ —

ForeWord Gold Medal Winner—Humor Book of the Year

Travelers' Tales Classics

COAST TO COAST $16.95
A Journey Across 1950s America
By Jan Morris
After reporting on the first Everest ascent in 1953, Morris spent a year journeying across the United States. In brilliant prose, Morris records with exuberance and curiosity a time of innocence in the U.S.

TRADER HORN $16.95
A Young Man's Astounding Adventures in 19th Century Equatorial Africa
By Alfred Aloysius Horn
Here is the stuff of legends—thrills and danger, wild beasts, serpents, and savages. An unforgettable and vivid portrait of a vanished Africa.

THE ROYAL ROAD TO ROMANCE $14.95
By Richard Halliburton
"Laughing at hardships, dreaming of beauty, ardent for adventure, Halliburton has managed to sing into the pages of this glorious book his own exultant spirit of youth and freedom."
—Chicago Post

UNBEATEN TRACKS IN JAPAN $14.95
By Isabella L. Bird
Isabella Bird was one of the most adventurous women travelers of the 19th century with journeys to Tibet, Canada, Korea, Turkey, Hawaii, and Japan. A fascinating read.

THE RIVERS RAN EAST $16.95
By Leonard Clark
Clark is the original Indiana Jones, telling the breathtaking story of his search for the legendary El Dorado gold in the Amazon.

Spiritual Travel

THE SPIRITUAL GIFTS $16.95
OF TRAVEL
The Best of Travelers' Tales
Edited by James O'Reilly and Sean O'Reilly
Favorite stories of transformation on the road
that shows the myriad ways travel indelibly
alters our inner landscapes.

PILGRIMAGE $16.95
Adventures of the Spirit
Edited by Sean O'Reilly & James O'Reilly
Introduction by Phil Cousineau

ForeWord Silver Medal Winner
—Travel Book of the Year

THE ROAD WITHIN $18.95
True Stories of Transformation
and the Soul
Edited by Sean O'Reilly, James O'Reilly &
Tim O'Reilly

Independent Publisher's Book Award
—Best Travel Book

THE WAY OF $14.95
THE WANDERER
Discover Your True Self Through Travel
By David Yeadon
Experience transformation through travel
with this delightful, illustrated collection by
award-winning author David Yeadon.

A WOMAN'S PATH $16.95
Women's Best Spiritual Travel Writing
Edited by Lucy McCauley, Amy G. Carlson &
Jennifer Leo
"A sensitive exploration of women's lives that
have been unexpectedly and spiritually
touched by travel experiences.... Highly
recommended."
—Library Journal

THE ULTIMATE JOURNEY $17.95
Inspiring Stories of Living and Dying
James O'Reilly, Sean O'Reilly & Richard
Sterling
"A glorious collection of writings about the
ultimate adventure. A book to keep by one's
bedside—and close to one's heart."
—Philip Zaleski, editor,
The Best Spiritual Writing series

Special Interest

THE BEST $16.95
TRAVELERS' TALES 2004
True Stories from Around the World
Edited by James O'Reilly, Larry Habegger &
Sean O'Reilly
The launch of a new annual collection pre-
senting fresh, lively storytelling and com-
pelling narrative to make the reader laugh,
weep, and buy a plane ticket.

TESTOSTERONE PLANET $17.95
True Stories from a Man's World
Edited by Sean O'Reilly, Larry Habegger &
James O'Reilly
Thrills and laughter with some of today's best
writers: Sebastian Junger, Tim Cahill, Bill
Bryson, and Jon Krakauer.

THE GIFT OF TRAVEL $14.95
The Best of Travelers' Tales
Edited by Larry Habegger, James O'Reilly
& Sean O'Reilly
"Like gourmet chefs in a French market, the
editors of Travelers' Tales pick, sift, and prod
their way through the weighty shelves of con-
temporary travel writing, creaming off the
very best."
—William Dalrymple, author of *City of Djinns*

DANGER! $17.95
True Stories of Trouble and Survival
Edited by James O'Reilly, Larry Habegger &
Sean O'Reilly
"Exciting...for those who enjoy living on the
edge or prefer to read the survival stories of
others, this is a good pick."
—Library Journal

365 TRAVEL $14.95
A Daily Book of Journeys, Meditations, and Adventures
Edited by Lisa Bach
An illuminating collection of travel wisdom and adventures that reminds us all of the lessons we learn while on the road.

THE GIFT OF RIVERS $14.95
True Stories of Life on the Water
Edited by Pamela Michael
Introduction by Robert Hass
...a soulful compendium of wonderful stories that illuminate, educate, inspire, and delight."
—David Brower,
Chairman of Earth Island Institute

FAMILY TRAVEL $17.95
The Farther You Go, the Closer You Get
Edited by Laura Manske
"This is family travel at its finest."
—*Working Mother*

LOVE & ROMANCE $17.95
True Stories of Passion on the Road
Edited by Judith Babcock Wylie
"A wonderful book to read by a crackling fire." —*Romantic Traveling*

THE GIFT OF BIRDS $17.95
True Encounters with Avian Spirits
Edited by Larry Habegger & Amy G. Carlson
"These are all wonderful, entertaining stories offering a *bird's-eye view!* of our avian friends."
—*Booklist*

A DOG'S WORLD $12.95
True Stories of Man's Best Friend on the Road
Edited by Christine Hunsicker
Introduction by Maria Goodavage

Travel Advice

THE PENNY PINCHER'S PASSPORT TO LUXURY TRAVEL $14.95
(2ND EDITION)
The Art of Cultivating Preferred Customer Status
By Joel L. Widzer
Completely updated and revised, this 2nd edition of the popular guide to traveling like the rich and famous without being either describes, both philosophically and in practical terms, how to obtain luxurious travel benefits by building relationships with airlines and other travel companies.

SAFETY AND SECURITY $12.95
FOR WOMEN WHO TRAVEL
By Sheila Swan & Peter Laufer
"An engaging book, with plenty of first-person stories about strategies women have used while traveling to feel safe but still find their way into a culture."
—*Chicago Herald*

THE FEARLESS SHOPPER $14.95
How to Get the Best Deals on the Planet
By Kathy Borrus
"Anyone who reads *The Fearless Shopper* will come away a smarter, more responsible shopper and a more curious, culturally attuned traveler."
—Jo Mancuso, *The Shopologist*

SHITTING PRETTY $12.95
How to Stay Clean and Healthy While Traveling
By Dr. Jane Wilson-Howarth
A light-hearted book about a serious subject for millions of travelers—staying healthy on the road—written by international health expert, Dr. Jane Wilson-Howarth.

GUTSY WOMEN $12.95
More Travel Tips and Wisdom for the Road
By Marybeth Bond
Second Edition
Packed with funny, instructive, and inspiring advice for women heading out to see the world.

GUTSY MAMAS $7.95
Travel Tips and Wisdom for Mothers on the Road
By Marybeth Bond
A delightful guide for mothers traveling with their children—or without them!

Destination Titles

ALASKA $18.95
Edited by Bill Sherwonit, Andromeda Romano-Lax, & Ellen Bielawski

AMERICA $19.95
Edited by Fred Setterberg

AMERICAN SOUTHWEST $17.95
Edited by Sean O'Reilly & James O'Reilly

AUSTRALIA $17.95
Edited by Larry Habegger

BRAZIL $17.95
Edited by Annette Haddad & Scott Doggett
Introduction by Alex Shoumatoff

CENTRAL AMERICA $17.95
Edited by Larry Habegger & Natanya Pearlman

CHINA $18.95
Edited by James O'Reilly, Larry Habegger & Sean O'Reilly

CUBA $17.95
Edited by Tom Miller

FRANCE $18.95
Edited by James O'Reilly, Larry Habegger & Sean O'Reilly

GRAND CANYON $17.95
Edited by Sean O'Reilly, James O'Reilly & Larry Habegger

GREECE $18.95
Edited by Larry Habegger, Sean O'Reilly & Brian Alexander

HAWAI'I $17.95
Edited by Rick & Marcie Carroll

HONG KONG $17.95
Edited by James O'Reilly, Larry Habegger & Sean O'Reilly

INDIA $18.95
Edited by James O'Reilly & Larry Habegger

IRELAND $18.95
Edited by James O'Reilly, Larry Habegger & Sean O'Reilly

ITALY $18.95
Edited by Anne Calcagno
Introduction by Jan Morris

JAPAN $17.95
Edited by Donald W. George & Amy G. Carlson

MEXICO $17.95
Edited by James O'Reilly & Larry Habegger

NEPAL $17.95
Edited by Rajendra S. Khadka

PARIS $18.95
Edited by James O'Reilly, Larry Habegger & Sean O'Reilly

PROVENCE $16.95
Edited by James O'Reilly & Tara Austen Weaver

SAN FRANCISCO $18.95
Edited by James O'Reilly, Larry Habegger & Sean O'Reilly

SPAIN $19.95
Edited by Lucy McCauley

THAILAND $18.95
Edited by James O'Reilly & Larry Habegger

TIBET $18.95
Edited by James O'Reilly & Larry Habegger

TURKEY $18.95
Edited by James Villers Jr.

TUSCANY $16.95
Edited by James O'Reilly & Tara Austen Weaver
Introduction by Anne Calcagno

Footsteps Series

THE FIRE NEVER DIES $14.95
**One Man's Raucous Romp Down the Road of Food,
Passion, and Adventure**
By Richard Sterling
"Sterling's writing is like spitfire, foursquare and jazzy with
crackle...."   *—Kirkus Reviews*

ONE YEAR OFF $14.95
**Leaving It All Behind for a Round-the-World Journey
with Our Children**
By David Elliot Cohen
A once-in-a-lifetime adventure generously shared, from the
author/editor of *America 24/7* and *A Day in the Life of Africa*

THE WAY OF THE WANDERER $14.95
Discover Your True Self Through Travel
By David Yeadon
Experience transformation through travel with this delightful,
illustrated collection by award-winning author David Yeadon.

TAKE ME WITH YOU $24.00
A Round-the-World Journey to Invite a Stranger Home
By Brad Newsham
"Newsham is an ideal guide. His journey, at heart, is into
humanity."   *—Pico Iyer, author of The Global Soul*

KITE STRINGS OF THE SOUTHERN CROSS $14.95
A Woman's Travel Odyssey   *ForeWord Silver Medal Winner*
By Laurie Gough   *— Travel Book of the Year*
Short-listed for the prestigious Thomas Cook Award, this is an
exquisite rendering of a young woman's search for meaning.   — ★ ★ ★ —

THE SWORD OF HEAVEN $24.00
A Five Continent Odyssey to Save the World
By Mikkel Aaland
"Few books capture the soul of the road like The *Sword of
Heaven,* a sharp-edged, beautifully rendered memoir that will
inspire anyone."
          —Phil Cousineau, author of The Art of Pilgrimage

STORM $24.00
A Motorcycle Journey of Love, Endurance,   *ForeWord Gold Medal Winner*
and Transformation   *— Travel Book of the Year*
By Allen Noren
"Beautiful, tumultuous, deeply engaging and very satisfying.
Anyone who looks for truth in travel will find it here."   — ★ ★ ★ —
            —Ted Simon, author of Jupiter's Travels